The Chinese of Macau

A Decade after the Handover

Jean A. Berlie
韓 林

THE CHINESE OF MACAU A DECADE AFTER THE HANDOVER is an important contribution to the study of identity, a fundamental topic in the twenty-first as in the latter part of the twentieth century. Identity in Macau is studied not only from a local Chinese perspective but also from a Macanese viewpoint.

Society, culture and religion among the Chinese of Macau – and in particular the roles played by various Macau social, cultural and religious associations – are each studied in the context of economic circumstances.

Based on two years of laborious fieldwork, initially assisted by Macau University students and others, *The Chinese of Macau* benefits from and re-actualizes Jean Berlie's previous research, published by Oxford University Press, Oxford/New York, as *Macau 2000*. Coinciding with Macau's change in status to become a Special Administrative Region of the People's Republic of China, and providing a snapshot of Macau Society at this significant point in Macau's history, *Macau 2000*, was received with great interest.

The joint study of society and economy is a key point of both these complementary studies. Indeed, in Berlie's view, the current world economic crisis will be solved only when economists understand the interplay between these factors.

Geoffrey C. Gunn, Professor of International Relations at Nagasaki University, has contributed a foreword and Tong Io Cheng, Professor at the Faculty of Law, University of Macau and Deputy of the Legislative Assembly of Macau, has contributed a chapter to Berlie's new book, *The Chinese of Macau.*

JEAN A. BERLIE is a researcher, since 1991 based at the Centre of Asian Studies (CAS) (now re-named Centre for Humanities and Social Science (incorporating the Centre for Asian Studies)), University of Hong Kong. In August 2012 he joined the Centre for Greater China Studies at the Hong Kong Institute of Education as an Honorary Research Fellow. He is a member of the board of *Tai Culture,* Berlin (http://www.seacom.de/taicul/tc.html). Since 1990, he has been conducting research in cooperation with the Institute of Southeast Asian Studies, Jinan University, Guangzhou, and separately, also with the Academy of Social Science at Yunnan. Berlie's main research focus is threefold: China; Macau (funded by the Cultural Institute of Macau between 1995 and 2000 and the Macau Foundation in 2011); and Southeast Asia.

His books include, among others, *The Burmanization of Myanmar's Muslims* (2008), *East Timor Politics and Elections* (2007), *Islam in China* (2004) and *Macao 2000* (Editor) (Oxford/New York: Oxford University Press, 1999).

GEOFFREY C. GUNN (author of the Foreword) is a graduate of Melbourne University. From 1994 he has been Professor of International Relations at Nagasaki University. He is the author of numerous books and studies, including, *History Without Borders: The Making of an Asian World Region (1500-1800),* University of Hong Kong Press, 2011, *First Globalization: The Eurasian Exchange (1500-1800),* Rowman and Littelefield, 2003, and *Encountering Macau: The Rise of a Portuguese City-State on the Periphery of China, 1557-1999,* Westview Press, 1996.

TONG IO CHENG (author of Chapter Two) is a Professor at the Faculty of Law of the University of Macau. His numerous books include among others *Macau Contract Law – International Encyclopaedia of Law,* Kluwer Online, 2009 (*English Monograph*), *A Study on The Basic Theories of Civil Law and Macau Civil Law,* Malaga (Spain): SYS University Press, 2088, and *O Regime Jurídico do Contrato-Promessa,* Faculdade de Direito da Universidade de Macau, 2004 (*Chinese Monograph*). He has the rare chance of being able to teach law, as well as having the capacity to make law as a Deputy of the Legislative Assembly of Macau SAR.

The Chinese of Macau

A Decade after the Handover

Jean A. Berlie

韓 林

Proverse Hong Kong

The Chinese of Macau a Decade after the Handover
by Jean A. Berlie
2nd pbk edition published in Hong Kong by Proverse Hong Kong,
January 2016.
Copyright © Proverse Hong Kong, January 2016.
ISBN: 978-988-8228-32-4
Printed by CreateSpace.

1st pub. in pbk in Hong Kong by Proverse Hong Kong, November 2012.
Copyright © Proverse Hong Kong, November 2012.
ISBN 978-988-8167-37-1
Printed book(s) distribution (Hong Kong and worldwide):
The Chinese University Press of Hong Kong,
The Chinese University of Hong Kong, Shatin, New Territories, Hong Kong SAR.
Email: cup-bus@cuhk.edu.hk Website: www.chineseupress.com
Tel: [INT+852] 3943-9800; Fax: [INT+852] 2603-7355
Distribution (United Kingdom): Christine Penney, Stratford-upon-Avon, Warwickshire
CV37 6DN, England. Email: <chrisp@proversepublishing.com>
Distribution and other enquiries: Proverse Hong Kong, P.O. Box 259,
Tung Chung Post Office, Tung Chung, Lantau Island, NT, Hong Kong SAR, China.
E-mail: proverse@netvigator.com. Website: www.proversepublishing.com

1st pbk ed.
Proverse Hong Kong
          British Library Cataloguing in Publication Data
Berlie, J. A. (Jean A.),
  The Chinese of Macau a decade after the handover.
  1. Chinese--China--Macau (Special Administrative
  Region)--Ethnic identity. 2. Ethnicity--China--Macau
  (Special Administrative Region) 3. Chinese--China--Macau
  (Special Administrative Region)--Social life and customs.
  4. Macau (China : Special Administrative Region)--Social
  conditions--21st century.
  I. Title
  305.8'951'05126-dc23

  ISBN-13: 9789888167371

ACKNOWLEDGEMENTS

First of all, I wish to express my heartfelt gratitude to the President of the Macau Foundation, Dr Wu Zhiliang, who generously invited me at the end of 2010 and in 2011 to start this new research and fieldwork on the spot, in Macau. I am most grateful to the President of the International Institute of Macau, Dr Jorge Alberto Hagedorn Rangel, for his financial support. I would like to express my sincere gratitude to Dr Pansy Ho for her strong support for this book. Many thanks also to the Associação de Estudos de Legislação e Jurisprudência de Macau.

I would like also to express my gratitude to all the Chinese of Macau who have answered my questions. Some of them, such as the Lei family, have been my efficient informants for a period of more than fifteen years.

I am deeply indebted to the following prestigious personalities of Macau who agreed to be interviewed by me, Dr Pansy Ho, Ms Ho Teng Iat, Deputy Chan Mei Yi, ex-Deputy David Chow and Executive Councilor Leong Heng Teng.

My deepest appreciation goes to all the students who helped me administer the questionnaires and particularly to Professor Eva Hung, who kindly asked her students at the University of Macau to assist me. Dr Paul Pun and Dr Lei Cheong Lap were key actors in designing the questionnaires and they also contributed largely to the success of this research.

I would like to thank Shirley Heong Soi Lan, the executive secretary of the Tung Sin Tong Charity Association for her kind assistance. Without the kind support of the Vice-President of this association, Dr Peter Lam Kam Seng, I would not have been able to communicate efficiently within the Tung Sin Tong Charity Association. I thank also the Kiang Wu

Association (*Jiang Hu Cishanhui* in Putonghua) for its support of my research, and in particular Ms Ung Pui Kun (Wu Pei Juan) and her assistant, Ms Lam; also the Director of the Nursing College, Van Iat Kio; Ms Lau Van Iong, who is responsible for the Museum of Kiang Wu; Ms AQi Wei and the head of the director's office, Dr Winnie Che Sio Ieng.

My heartiest thanks to Dr Geoffrey Gunn for contributing a foreword and to Professor Tong Io Cheng for contributing a chapter to this book. I am most grateful also to Dr John Thorne for reading the typescript and for his advice about English grammar.

Lastly, I thank Echo Lo Pou Leng for her valuable contribution and also Professor Lam Fat Iam and Chan who helped me significantly.

Translations into English

In all cases, unless otherwise stated, translations into English from other languages are those of the author, Dr Jean A. Berlie.

Chinese characters

The Chinese characters used in this book are the simplified (not traditional) characters.

CONTENTS

ILLUSTRATIONS

**EARLY RESPONSES TO
"THE CHINESE OF MACAU
A DECADE AFTER THE HANDOVER"**

'The history and sociology of Macau has been neglected by researchers, but not by the intrepid Dr Jean Berlie who has already written *Macao 2000*. The parts of China that remained outside the PRC such as Hong Kong until 1997 and 1999 for Macau – Taiwan remains independent – have become important points of comparison with the mainland concerning the cultural evolution of each of these entities. Dr Berlie's study of Chinese society in Macau provides an important contribution to this ongoing discussion. Hopefully it will encourage other researchers to delve more deeply into other aspects of society and culture among the Chinese of Macau.'
—Grant Evans, Professor Emeritus of Anthropology, University of Hong Kong.

'Jean Berlie's book is an indispensable one for our deeper and comprehensive understanding of the evolution of identity in Macau. It is a must-read work for all those who wish to explore the topic of identity in Macau not only from the local Chinese perspective but also from the Portuguese and Macanese standpoints.'
—Sonny Lo, Professor and Head of the Department of Social Sciences, Hong Kong Institute of Education.

FOREWORD

Geoffrey C. Gunn

Postmodernist understandings of identity in Macau have reached a new sophistication. As this book reveals, many assumptions and established verities as to how Macau people perceive themselves need to be rethought in the light both of new research and the fast-changing environment since the retrocession of Macau to China in December 1999. This is not only a matter of putting Orientalism behind but also of challenging binary notions of history and identity in a space where 'alterities' and 'hybridities' continue to resonate. As underscored by this book, the study of Macau identity carries legal valances, just as Macau's Basic Law underpins Macau's legal status as a Special Administrative Region of China (SAR). Unquestionably, interpretations of the Basic Law are at the heart of many social and political issues in Macau today, however controversial they may be. But, as this essay recalls, there have always been legal and political anomalies in Macau, a Chinese territory which has experienced almost 500 years of Portuguese administration.

We cannot ignore that national – and even ethnic – identity is often a construction, contrived by scholars or by policy makers. Ever since Antonio Gramsci, we have a better understanding of the ways in which ideology manufactures consensus especially through the influence of religious institutions such as churches and temples and especially through the influence of educational establishments. Modern states command 'panopolies of resources' to win allegiances, to foster and reproduce cultural verities and social norms, and to forge civic identities. Along with the advent of the nation-state, arising from the European-centred Westphalia system of 1628, sovereignty and territory have become primordial to the

11

definition of the modern nation. Subjects – not quite yet, citizens – enjoyed protection, but also faced responsibilities. Loyalty to crown or country became a test of patriotism often tested in war, especially as the European nations were not equally powerful. Late medieval Europeans also shared a complex division of loyalties between crown and church, and so they arrived off the coast of China as both venture merchants and missionaries of both a new religion and a new 'way of life'. Even prior to the emergence of the European-centred system of 'competing but equal' sovereign states, long bureaucratic continuity under the central kingdom linked with the spread of a common (written) language, forged an unconscious identity that later came to be glossed as Chinese. When East met West in Macau in the sixteenth century, such a collision of identities – one, late-medieval, post-Renaissance Christian, the other, high Ming Confucian along with a ruck of folk beliefs such as enshrined in the A-Ma (Mazu) temple – must have been stark (at least until new hybrid forms of associations developed, which of course continue until this day).

Today, even museums – especially museums – are sites where identity is forged, through selective representation. New understandings of heritage can also help to forge historical lineages and allegiances, just as the reading, writing and teaching of history lead to new interpretations and revisions. Macau today does not stand outside of these understandings. Not only does identity formation operate at various levels; it shifts over time. As discussed below, there have been several major moments in Macau's half-millennium of recorded history, the most recent and wrenching being the social, political and environmental changes emerging after the historic 1999 reversion of Macau to Chinese sovereignty.

Interested in social aggregations and communities, I have been struck by the social and physical makeover of Macau during the thirty-year period in which I have been visiting there. For the significant numbers of Macau people whose lives straddle the colonial and post-colonial periods – a majority of adult Macau residents – memories, associations, loyalties and values (and the boundaries of these) have undoubtedly undergone significant shifts. This brief Foreword seeks to explain the conditioning and contextualising factors behind these apparent value shifts. It is also more ambitious. Where memory fades, some creative historical reconstruction is required. Moving beyond the 'presentist' orientation of the book, I also seek to set the scene by retracing its anthropological and historical roots. Taking a *longue durée* approach, I identify and discuss a handful of key turning-points and junctures, occurring over the past half-millennium, which I believe have had a considerable impact upon identities, loyalties and the imagination of Macau-ness. I will also be concerned to identify the rise of civil society in Macau from its embryonic beginnings down to the present.

The investigation of Macau identity is not only an academic exercise; it could be used by policy-makers as a valuable resource. The education and social welfare departments come particularly to mind. Additionally, the massive migration and demographic changes that have taken place mean that the investigator needs to interrogate an increasingly complex cohort of individuals and there can always be error. (For example, I was included in the 2011 Macau census by virtue of having been in residence in Macau during the short census period, thus adding one Ph.D. to the talent pool of Taipa Village. Undoubtedly this distorted the village profile which still has a mostly local population, including resettled fishermen and others offered low-cost housing in the late 1990s. No doubt it also distorted the generalized profile as well.) Statistics obviously disguise more complex assertions of identity or – in the words of one famed social thinker, Benedict Anderson – 'imagined communities'. This Foreword, then, proposes to identify the major historical events or epochs in Macau's long history which have been formative of community identities, albeit allowing that identity formation is always contested and fluid.

The Foundations

From such origins as are touched upon in the main text, there cannot have been any early identity in Macau beyond that of primitive community. Obviously, however, following the arrival of Hakka communities, creating permanent settlements – as symbolically marked by the foundation of the A-Ma temple – the Macau Peninsula became intricately connected with a wider Chinese world. The Peninsula not only became integrated with sea-borne Hokkien trading networks, but with a local Cantonese-speaking region, in turn a distant but integral part of the Ming Chinese world. It was to this outpost that Portuguese traders first connected in the 1550s (they may have been preceded by Arabs and/or Muslim traders). Beginning in 1557, the tiny peninsula became their permanent settlement, evidently with the express agreement of the harbourmaster of the Xiangshan district, then overseeing Macau and other local ports. Over time – over a considerable time in fact – there began a mutual 'othering' between, on the one hand, the Catholic Iberians (distinguished by what were, to the Chinese, their utterly unfamiliar-language, religion and mores) and, on the other hand, the Cantonese-speaking subjects of the Ming emperor.

The Intramuras System

Such distinctions were confirmed in the newly minted city-state on the periphery of China by the implementation of the *intramuras* system. Following the first seaborne Dutch attacks on the city in 1601-03, the first defensive walls were built. From 1606 to 1626 with the construction of the bastions of the Monte fortress, an almost completely – if not completely – walled city was built, in spite of the disapproval and frustrating activities of the Chinese authorities. The major Dutch attack of 24 June 1622 prompted a further wave of defensive constructions.

As implied by the Portugualised term, according to a long tested practice implemented by the Iberians, literally from Ceuta in North Africa to Manila in the Philippines, so in Macau the Portuguese looked to their defenses behind walls. As the walls and forts (*fortalezas*) were constructed, so those within the walls came under the strict control and protection of the Portuguese Crown, represented locally by the Governor and Senators, and spiritually by the church. It is not hard to imagine that this compartmentalised Portugualised-Catholicised community stood apart from those outside the walls (who were, in the Macau context, the Chinese community). This would have been true, whether they were boat people or settled agricultural people, whether they belonged to the new bazaar quarter, or indeed, to the mandarin or official class. (This last comprised the Chinese customs service, which had a permanent post on the Macau Peninsula from 1688, moving to the Praia Grande in 1732.) While Christian Indians, Japanese, Malays and members of other ethnic groups, along with slaves of mostly African origin, did enter this charmed circle, very few local Chinese met the basic tests required to do so. The major exception were members of the Christian Macanese society, which evolved over a long period of time. Nevertheless, the *intramuras* system did not preclude daytime movement through the city, for commerce was its lifeblood and all major daily services were provided by the swelling numbers of Chinese, especially those congregating in the bazaar district of the Inner Harbour. Macau was not Manila as under the Spanish with its prejudices and pogroms. Simply put, without flexibility, the two sides could not have worked together.

The major exception to this East-West compartmentalisation of society and institutions, as already indicated, was a local creolised group which evolved over time, the Macanese. Strictly speaking, these were Macau-born Eurasians resulting from Portuguese-Chinese liaisons. In the early centuries of development, the mothers of those who fell into this group could also be – and were – Goanese, Malaccan and even Japanese. Bilingual and bicultural, the Macanese earned their place in society as translators and cultural brokers. Yet – as Portuguese-speaking Catholics – their identity was also Portuguese. Interestingly, the cultural conservatism of Portugal was more than matched in the Macanese community. Period photographs of Macanese women dressed in *dao* express an ideal of Catholic seclusion, unknown even in the Chinese society of the time, which itself had strict practices regarding the protection of women.

We can summarize that, under the *intramuras* system (c.1557-1844), the three major elements of Macau society came into place. With the Catholic Macanese leaning towards a Portuguese identity, both the Portuguese and Chinese components of Macau society existed in largely compartmentalised worlds, separated by language, custom, religion and – though this was frequently contested – by legal regime. As suggested, each of these elements supported a strict sense of identity, although not a completely unchanging one. On the Portuguese side, the 1640 revolt ending the 60 year period of dual monarchy in Portugal and Spain under the Spanish Hapsburgs, was celebrated in the streets of Macau with elaborate *festas*. The Inquisition did not touch Macau directly as it did Portuguese India (Goa); nevertheless the injunction to religious orthodoxy must have sent ripples through Portuguese Macau as well. Close students of Macau history acknowledge that, by the 1820s, metropolitan political events also impacted upon local personalities and cliques. No doubt the advent of printed newspapers in Macau facilitated this sense of identity with the metropole and with European political issues. The rise of England and the relative marginalisation of Portugal within the new global system cannot have been lost upon the elite and the miniscule civil society emerging in Macau.

As concerns China and the Chinese of Macau there can have been no other identification than with the ruling dynasty of the time, whether it was Ming or Qing. (Even so, the Ming-Qing transition may have led, in complex ways, to some sense of conflicted loyalties, as it certainly did on the Fujian coast.) In addition to the Chinese customs house, from 1688 firmly implanted within the walled city, in 1725 the Chinese authorities opened the so-called Mandarin's House at Wangxia on the Macau side of the Macau-China border-gate area. Even as the mandarin ramped up his interference in Macau's administration, so at the same time he asserted legal jurisdiction over Chinese criminals. Some decades after this, beginning in 1783, the Portuguese crown sought to strengthen Portuguese sovereignty by reinforcing the garrison, strengthening the Portuguese customs house and other measures. Not surprisingly, this led to a long period of contestation between the Portuguese and Chinese. In spite of this, however, the Chinese continued to recognise the authority of the Portuguese-led Macau Senate.

Colonial Boundaries/Unequal Treaties

The 1840s marked another turning point in relations between Portugal and China, incontestably challenging the age-old *modus vivendi* between the major communities and, for the first time, marking out the Chinese of Macau as – however ambiguously – colonial subjects of Portugal. The allusion here is not only to events surrounding the foundation of Hong Kong. (Under Chinese pressure, the Portuguese obliged the British to depart Macau in August 1839.) It relates also to new assertions on the part of Portugal to confirm her sovereignty – her colonial possession – over the territory. But, although fiercely contested by Portugal, China still insisted upon her mandarinal jurisdiction, including long-standing customs privileges.

Admittedly the ways in which Portugal defined its colonial empire (which spanned Africa and Asia) underwent many changes over time. Events that influenced this included the end of the old order in Portugal, caused by the anti-monarchic and anti-clerical coup d'état of 5 October 1910, which ushered in the First Portuguese Republic. Also influential was the advent of the authoritarian pro-Roman Catholic Salazarist *Estado Novo* (1933-74) (which itself emerged out of the military coup against the First Republic). This further redefined the legal status of Portugal's 'overseas possessions' in line with racial hierarchies and assimilationist assumptions. But the facts are eloquent. On the cusp of the reversion of sovereignty in December 1999, Portugal granted citizenship in the form of passports to Macau residents, an offer taken up by thousands. Even so, as developed in the text, the mere possession of a passport does not guarantee an identity change although it certainly offers that possibility.

Viewed retrospectively, one of the most provocative events in modern Macau history was the refusal of Portuguese Governor J. Ferreira do Amaral to pay the *foro do chão*, or ground rent, a practice dating back to the foundation of Macau, which signaled irrevocable Chinese ownership of the territory. It is an action that has to be viewed also against the backdrop of Qing China's fate at the hands of the West, notably in the context of the Opium Wars and the following imposition on China of unequal treaties including the assertion of extraterritorial rights. Amaral destroyed two Chinese customs houses, re-established Portuguese tax authority, occupied lands between the city walls and the Macau-China gate, fortified Taipa Island and in other ways also asserted Portuguese ownership over the territory. Amaral was murdered by assassins on 22 August 1847.

Emboldened by the short punitive raid mounted by Col. Vicente Nicolau Mesquita on 22 August 1849 on a Chinese military post (Baishaling), Lisbon negotiated the Treaty of Tianjin (signed 13 August 1862), confirming Portugal as de facto sovereign power in Macau, albeit not gaining titular sovereignty as she sought. This led to the signing of the Treaty of Amity and Commerce by Portugal and China in Beijing on 1 December 1887 (ratified 28 August 1888), which appears to have settled the question of sovereignty. Although the Qing never ratified these agreements, and although the Chinese Imperial Maritime Customs service still maintained a massive presence in Macau, the point is that Portugal, following and similar to Britain and France and other European powers, received on paper an iteration of its colonial rights in Macau. Taken literally, metropolitan Portugal was now empowered to impose colony or overseas possession status upon Macau and its people. Although such a writ was never legally sanctioned by China, de facto that is what the situation was in Macau down until at least the end of the Salazar dictatorship, when the ownership question was seriously revisited. But between these two points, other wrenching events also took place between Macau and China, Macau and Portugal, similarly touching Macau people's sense of belonging and identity.

As is well known, the Amaral equestrian statue – seen by some as symbolising the former colonial relationship – did not survive the twilight of colonial rule but was discretely removed prior to shipping to Portugal. For, in the context of the aroused sense of Chinese identity, which took place around the time of Macau's handover to China, Governor Amaral had become a 'colonial other'; a veritable *bête noire* of modern Macau historiography. Subsequently, the site of the statue has been converted into both an above surface bus terminal and an underground car park, depriving Macau of a physical *largo* (and European space) of impressive proportions. All is not lost however, at least for the memory of this personality, as Macau's new (2011) modernised bus system announces and digitally displays in three languages the approach of the 'Praca Ferreira Amaral' bus stop, a surviving toponym on the map, written bilingually. That is as it should be. Historical events cannot be completely papered over, even if they are contested. In this narrative, the Amaral event and its sequels bookended the old order and ushered in a determinately reinvigorated colonial order, especially with respect to the legal regime.

Manuel de Castro Sampaio's *Os Chins de Macau*

Again it is largely a supposition but, paradoxically, it seems that – out of this sense of Chineseness – a strong sense of local Macau identity, also, began to crystallize from this epoch, at least among the business elite. Such an identity is in fact prefigured in the classic study by Manuel de Castro Sampaio, *Os Chins de Macau* (1867). Besides describing habitation, customs, religious practices, festivals, etc. – thus offering an invaluable benchmark on Chinese of Macau society – Sampaio's study also highlights the rise of *hão* (*hong*) or business associations in Macau. As he explains, it was a rare individual who belonged to none of these associations. *'O espirito de associação existe entre eles em supremo grau; e por isso, salvas rarissimas exceções, não comerceiam senão por meio de associação.'* ('The spirit of partnership exists between them to the highest degree, and so, with rare exceptions, they do not trade except through associations.') Of the forty major associations he identifies, mostly headquartered in the Inner Harbour, many had established agencies in China, Vietnam, Singapore, Malaysia, Thailand, etc. Writing during the Opium Wars and the age of unequal treaties, Sampaio also describes the judicial process imposed upon Chinese in Macau under the Negocios Sinicos da Cidade de Macau. The roots of these laws went back to 1583, but important codification was achieved, dated 22 November 1866. As Sampaio explains, the Chinese of Macau lived under the protection of the Portuguese flag.

The Chinese Revolution(s)

The importance of Macau to the Chinese revolution(s) is well understood in Macau, as evidenced by the Sun Yat-sen Memorial House on Avenue Sidonio Pais, and the publication of a number of books and the hosting of seminars and celebratory occasions at the time of the anniversary in 2011 of the Xinhai revolution. However, the impact of the 1911 revolution and the establishment of the Republic of China upon the population of Macau is more difficult to research, and indeed, is understudied. We know that Sun's appointment as provisional president of the new Chinese republic was marked by a flag-raising ceremony at the Leal Senado. Unquestionably, the end of the Qing dynasty (the Qing emperor abdicated on 12 February 1912) came as a relief to the Chinese of Macau as it did to overseas Chinese in general, including in Macau's sister 'colony' East Timor, where Chinese young people in the capital Dili celebrated the advent of the new Chinese republic.

Undoubtedly, along with the republican age came a new pride, not only in Macau's role in the revolution (as saluted by Sun Yat-sen himself in his famous letter to Governor José Carlos da Maia (1914-16), but in the prospects of a new modernising China based upon the 'three principles' of nationalism, democracy, and socialism. The psychological reactions of Chinese of Macau to the demise of the Qing Empire is not an issue which I wish to dwell on here, but undoubtedly these were more profound than the cutting of queues. There is no question also that the new medium of the typographic press, well represented in Macau by the early 1900s, broadcast and amplified this sense of participation in the continuing revolutionary struggles. As literacy levels rose in Macau, especially among the mercantile classes, so the audience expanded for the reformist literature coming out of the New Culture Movement with its embrace of modern ideas at the expense of Confucianism. This was no mere academic question, especially as Guangzhou itself emerged as the cradle of the Chinese revolution from the 1920s to the 1930s. As a busy port with constant traffic between Hong Kong and Guangzhou, and overland through Zhongzhan, Macau and her people took their place in a far larger 'imagined community' than that offered by even the veneer of the Portuguese overseas empire.

Wartime Communities

How Macau identities gelled at the time of Japan's invasion of China is an understudied question; but we can assume that all communities shared a sense of beleaguerment, deprivation, and isolation arising out of the armed Japanese encirclement of the territory and threats imposed upon the population. Although not directly occupied by Japan, as Hong Kong was, one feature of wartime Macau was its demographic expansion owing to a large refugee influx. According to the 1940 census (*Colónia Portuguesa de Macau*), Macau hosted a population of 340,260 inhabitants, of which 4,322 were Portuguese. But, after the Japanese invasion and occupation of China, the population of Macau doubled to reach 600,000. It should also be remarked that, from this period up until the early 1950s, some forty per cent of the population of Macau may have been maritime (down from fifty per cent in 1927) – in other words living on boats – consistent with the fact that the fishing industry was one of the props of the local economy. While a heterogeneous group of people made Macau a temporary home, Cantonese speakers from neighbouring Guangdong and Hong Kong were undoubtedly the largest component. Some of these may have been supporters of Wang Jing Wei, others may have been underground members of the West River communist guerrillas, but all were Chinese. Paradoxically, it was Macau's colonial status and wartime neutrality that spared it direct occupation by Japanese militarist-imperialists, anxious not completely to break relations with Salazar. In the tempest of war, calling Macau home – and having an identity document to prove it – was obviously an asset, even for the most humble people. Possibly the esteem in which Portugal was held in Macau increased under Portuguese Governor and Commander-in-Chief, Navy Commander Gabriel Mauricio Teixeira, in step with his making the territory into a kind of haven or refuge under the very noses of the Japanese.

The Postwar Pact with China

Early postwar Macau survived the political transition on the Mainland from Kuomintang to communist rule. As Moisés Silva Fernandes explains, beginning from February 1949 (eight months before the Chinese Communist Party took power) up to 19 December 1999 reversion of Macau to Chinese sovereignty, Chinese foreign policy towards Macau aimed at 'sustaining the status quo'. In other words, it sought to secure the maintenance of the Portuguese administration and to reinforce the intermediary role of Macau's Chinese business elite. Salazar's refusal to establish diplomatic relations with China at Beijing's invitation in 1950-51 and again in 1954-55 did not alter this situation.

But with its relatively porous borders, Macau again became a place of refuge for many Chinese, whether political or economic refugees. This is important, as the number and percentage of China–born residents in Macau began to swell – a postwar trend that has continued to the present when at least sixty per cent of Macau residents fall into this category. As new Macau residents, the newly arrived immigrants competed for scarce social resources including accommodation and schooling for their children, at the same time as they entered the work force. Again, the demographic suggests a major reconfiguration of identity. Today the children of these postwar immigrants have reached maturity, having grown up under late colonial Portuguese rule and taken part in the far more lively Macau civil society that then existed, with its many groups and commercial associations (albeit not yet mature political parties). Ineluctably Chinese by birth, language, and kin or clan association, their socialisation as Macau residents equally distinguished them from distant kin in Mainland China.

The 1-2-3 Incident of December 1966

Still, there was a pull of political loyalties between this 'privileged' Chinese of Macau identity and the powerful political magnetism of Chinese patriotism, as mediated by China or more accurately by the Cultural Revolution group. Notwithstanding the uses of Macau to China, the colony was also a colonial anachronism. A metropolitan minority, buttressed by local collaborators, ruled over a voiceless majority. Civil society was choked, civil liberties were strictly constrained, press censorship was the norm and political change was not countenanced. Although there were differences of nuance under Portuguese colonial law, only the Portuguese-speaking-Catholic component of society met the criteria of assimilated to Portuguese identity. In this situation, few who were not Macanese met the social criteria and only a minority of Chinese graduated through the Portuguese language stream education system. Even by the criteria of colonialism, Portugal failed in Macau to socialise a Portuguese identity, contrary to what it certainly did in many other colonial situations in Africa and Asia.

All these contradictions came into focus with the 1-2-3 Incident of December 1966 – essentially a spillover of the Cultural Revolution into Macau – which resulted in the de facto abdication of Portuguese authority in Macau. Overzealous Portuguese police responses to the construction of a pro-China school in Taipa soon morphed into a groundswell of mass protest and violence directed at symbols of Portuguese authority, to which the Portuguese authorities responded by inflicting casualties upon demonstrators. Certain targets were well chosen by the protestors, but the violence also damaged cultural assets. Eventually the foreign affairs line in Beijing prevailed and Cultural Revolution actions wound down in Macau. But at the same time, China reasserted the status quo ante by reversing Portugal's sovereign claims and reasserting China's ownership of Macau. China's clear statement of paramountcy had the consequence of making Portugal nothing more than an administrative custodian of the territory. In my view – contrary to the assertion made by Stanley Ho in the present book[1] – Macau's identity *was* deeply touched by this event. Behind the Cultural Revolution group's maneuvering stood a groundswell of China patriotism and indignation at old style colonialism and injustices historically imposed upon China. There were not too many defenders of Portugal on the streets at that time. It was decidedly not politic to go against the flow. Even Macau identity appeared to have collapsed into China identity, albeit not entirely. When I visited Macau for the first time in early 1972, the Maoist atmosphere on the street was palpable in slogans, in dress, in bookshops, and even in the cafeteria-style eateries that dotted the streets. The latter lingered into the 1980s. One stood adjacent to a cinema in the northern Inner Harbour. Another backed onto the Portuguese school and the public soccer field, today built over by the Grand Lisboa casino complex. Canto-pop and the bright coloured hues of present-day fashions had yet to make an appearance. A proletarian-centred view of the world was presented and celebrated, matching the vast majority of Macau residents, who belonged to the working classes. Many people still lived in temporary housing and poverty; decay even in physical surroundings was palpable. To provide viewing opportunities to those who had none of their own, black and white Chinese public television was strategically placed at the Centre of the only traffic island in Coloane village. Another was placed at the Chinese library pavilion in the São Francisco Garden. In both cases, public viewing events were well attended. And in general, a two-way traffic of people passed the Portas do Cerco (the border gate at Gongbei erected in 1849 in the wake of the Amaral affair), moving inbetween Macau and China. Revisiting Macau in 1982, I myself entered Zhongshan and China via the now-museumed 'heritage' border gate, finding a rustic scene of market gardens, duck farms, and paddy fields. 'So this is Macau's backyard', I reflected at the time. But I was also contrasting then rural Zhongshan with long-established urban Macau. The two were worlds apart. It was clear to me that Macau people inhabited a vastly different social space relative to their country cousins, in spite of their shared roots. Notwithstanding the proximity of China, local cultural practices and folk beliefs such as discussed in the text of this book, did not appear to be diminished in Macau, just as the territory retained its image and reputation as a bastion of traditional Chinese culture alongside Hong Kong, Malaysia and Taiwan.

The Twilight of Colonial Rule

Since my first visit to Macau (and there have been many more), there were two more years under the Salazar-Caetano dictatorship. Backed by NATO arms, Portugal faced down armed insurrections in Mozambique, Angola and especially Guinea Bissau. Essentially it was opposition to these wars by the military elite that led to the events of April 1974 in Lisbon which have been styled the 'Carnation Revolution'. Pledging elections in the colonies, the new metropolitan democratic government that emerged in the wake of the Carnation Revolution touched off events that would lead to declarations of independence (and civil strife) from Angola to East Timor. Because Macau was delisted from the United Nations committee on non self-governing territories at Beijing's request, Lisbon obviously could not countenance an alternative future for the territory outside of Chinese sovereignty. Still China was not eager immediately to resume sovereignty in Macau, presumably as the retrocession of the British colony of Hong Kong took priority. On the other hand, China did not demand a retreat of Portuguese administrative responsibility from the territory. In fact, the period of governance in Macau under 'democratic' generals, including the Governor Garcia Leandro (1974-79) and Governor Vasco Joaquim Rocha Vieira (1990-99) is surprisingly crucial to the shaping of Macau identity as we know it today.

Notably, this period coincided with economic reforms on the Mainland – such as those ushered in by Deng Xiaoping – and with a general buoyancy in the local Macau economy, accompanied by slowly rising incomes, increasing tourism numbers, and a more open Macau. No less important to the restructuring of Macau was bold new economic planning by Governor Rocha Vieira, involving the airport and other infrastructure projects, and the launching by China of the Zhuhai Special Economic Zone. The private University of East Asia was also launched during this period. Notably, as well during this 'democratic' period, the first political associations were launched in Macau and with local representation strengthened in a partially elected Legislative Council independent of the Governor, thus creating the nuclei of post-handover institutions in Macau today. Democratic reform in Macau may well have been ahead of Hong Kong during this period, although it did not progress. In the final Legislative Assembly elections under Portuguese rule – those of 22 September 1996 – business interests took four of the eight directly elected seats in the 23-member body, with pro-China groups increasing their share from three to four seats and pro-democracy groups reduced from two seats to one. In contrast to Hong Kong, where the post-handover Legislature was dissolved at Beijing's displeasure, Macau's elected body continued through the handover period.

Increasingly, Macau people were becoming stakeholders in what nevertheless continued to be a thoroughly colonial administration (as in Hong Kong, so in Macau the executive was appointed from outside and representation to a legislative body was highly restricted and not democratic). It was also a period in which Portugal, belatedly, began investing in Portuguese language, heritage, and other symbols of its near five hundred year old presence. Portuguese holidays, such as Camões Day (since 1977, known as Portugal Day), were still celebrated irrespective of local relevance. Again it is hard to evaluate how much of this Portuguese lore including displays of *saudade* or nostalgia was locally received. (In any case, the reception and assimilation of cultures is a complex issue.)

Whatever the case, in present-day Macau, legacies of Portugal's rule abound, certain of them now traded upon under the banner of cultural tourism. By far the most important of these, as recognised in the Basic Law of Macau, is the Portugal-derived legal system (itself based upon continental law) which guides local practices and conventions, sharply distinguishing Macau from mainland China and even with its counterpart in Hong Kong. For instance, it was not until 1993 that Hong Kong officially abolished capital punishment, whereas its prescription in Portugal and colonies goes back to the mid-nineteenth century. Visitors arriving from Hong Kong are bound to observe different bureaucratic and governmental practices in Macau such as handed down from Portugal. Neither can the legacy of the Catholic Church in Macau be ignored – either in the educational field or as a moral force – although to discuss this would require more space than is available here.

Certainly, the question can be debated but, it can be argued that a sense of Macau identity strengthened during this period, especially after the draft of the Basic Law was made public in 1991. Certainly, Chineseness may not have been any less relevant, as Macau legal specialist and lawmaker, Tong Io Cheng, discusses in this book. But when the Macau Basic Law came into force in December 1999, it prefigured another half century during which Macau's 'way of life' and rule of law (that is, Portuguese Law) is guaranteed. [2] Contrariwise, and a trend which continues today, it has to be said that the Macau middle class – like middle classes elsewhere in Asia, China included – has embraced consumerism and materialist values. Similarly, globalisation increasingly makes its mark, most notably through the expansion of the casino industry. As their level of education becomes even higher, perhaps in the future Macau residents can distinguish themselves by increasing awareness in the areas of consumer protection, environmentalism, heritage protection, humanism, and internationalism; possibly even borrowing from their own 500 odd years of recorded history as an east-west crucible of ideas and peoples.

Envoi
In many ways my synopsis has affirmed the crucial importance of Guangdong (including neighbouring Zhongshan) to the formation of modern Macau identity, a thesis finely developed and reiterated in the text of this book, which, in many ways, echoes the pioneering research on the Chinese of Macau undertaken by Manuel de Castro Sampaio almost 160 years ago. Remarkably few focused texts have appeared on the Chinese of Macau of parallel detail. An exception is the 30-year cycle of studies on Chinese of Macau popular culture by Portuguese investigator Ana Maria Amaro. More recently, in 2011, University of Macau academic Hao Zhidong has entered this field, inter alia positing a postcolonial 'Macauan' identity. But whereas Sampaio appears to have been a self-trained observer, working outside of modern sociological insights; the present author, professional ethno-sociologist, J.A. Berlie, brings to bear on this subject a range of sociological literatures, including his own cognate studies and investigations on Macau, Macau religiosity, and Chinese society, and also draws upon a range of contemporary English, Portuguese, and Chinese accounts and writings, including his own benchmark *Macao 2000* (1999), in which I was also privileged to write a foreword.

INTRODUCTION

Macau and the Chinese in Macau have a long history. In 1867, Manuel de Castro Sampaio wrote *Os Chins de Macau,* a pioneering work about this ethno-cultural group.

At present, Macau is a Special Administrative Region of China (MSAR). The group we call the 'Chinese of Macau' in 2012 is essentially linked to China, although it may also sometimes exhibit a cultural link with Portugal – not including any linguistic link – sometimes limited simply to a Portuguese passport rarely used to travel to Europe. A large proportion of the Macau population came from the People's Republic of China (PRC) during the last two decades, but Mainlanders started to become more numerous after the reforms of Deng Xiaoping in the 1980s.

This study is based on my first inquiries, made between 1995 and 2000 and on my more recent surveys in 2010, 2011 and 2012. My recent fieldwork in Macau included the administration of 225 questionnaires. The results produced many family genealogies,[3] showing that the mononuclear family of one child is a new tendency in the Macau SAR (*see Photograph 2*). The life stories received through these questionnaires inform the overview presented in Chapter One and are integrated into the text of this book as a whole.

Identity
Identity is a concept relating to 'the qualities and attitudes you have that make you feel you are different from other people'.[4] Do the Chinese of Macau possess a unique culture and a strong Cantonese identity that makes them feel different from other Chinese? The subjects of identity and way of life are developed in Chapter Two, which explains indirectly why identity is so important. (Way of

life is of course not exactly the same as identity.) Article 30 of the Basic Law of the MSAR of the People's Republic of China identifies and clearly documents the relationship between identity and human dignity.

Macau offers a 'picture of a Chinese-dominated society'. When this statement was made in 1999 it was in advance of the time, but it is certainly true today.[5] In 2011, is Mainland China the main cultural reference in Macau society? Ninety per cent of the MSAR's population is Chinese. However, Macau is an exemplary 'tolerant multicultural society'. Could this be the result of a shared sovereignty before the handover in 1999?

The main question is the identity of a particular group, the Chinese of Macau. Like everyone in the world, these Chinese people live, study, work, are susceptible to sickness, and die, but they also have a very specific identity. To be integrated among the Chinese of Macau, many years are necessary. – I do not refer here to the legal aspect of the number of years of residency in MSAR that are necessary to have a Macau ID card, but to the social and cultural dimensions of this question. [6]

We include among the Chinese of Macau Mainlanders and Overseas Chinese who have had their main residence in Macau: some of them naturally continue to look first to the Mainland and are primarily interested in the success of Greater China. Even if – like all Macau permanent residents – these Chinese accept from the Government of the Macau SAR a certain sum of money every year, as permanent residents,[7] this does not mean that they identify themselves with Macau. It is interesting to note that nineteen per cent of my interviewees declared themselves to be 'Chinese' without any identification with Macau.

Who are the Chinese of Macau?

Just before the Chinese New Year in 2012 the director of the daily newspaper *Hojemacau*, Carlos Morais, said that he felt that 'Macau has lost its identity'.[8] From a Portuguese viewpoint, I might agree, but what do the Chinese of

Macau think? These Chinese strongly defend, among other cultural traits, their Cantonese language. Who then are the Chinese of Macau? There are five main types of Chinese in Macau who could justifiably claim to be from Macau and who speak Cantonese:

The *Bendiren* ('Bundeijan' in Cantonese), from Guangdong Province, who are mainly Han Chinese born in Macau and speaking Cantonese.[9] The other categories are the Fukienese, mainly Hokkien; the Chaozhou (Teochew), the Hakkas ('Kejia' in Putonghua), and the Tanka fishermen. These fishermen migrated in mass to Zhuhai in 2000, although some of their families currently remain in Macau. The Hakkas constitute some two per cent of the population of the MSAR. Chapter Four deals with the Fishermen's Association (Yumin Huzhuhui).

In his *Macau History and Society*, Hao Zhidong emphasises national, political and economic identity.[10] I myself insist on social and cultural identity and on the paradigm of complexity more than diversity.[11] The Chinese of Macau constitute a group of people with complex biological, social and economic links. This is studied in particular in relation to the main important associations in the MSAR, in Chapter Four. A number of approaches are necessary to charactise these Chinese and the system includes feedback. I propose a general vision for a specific modern Chinese group. Language and family are, among other criteria, two main markers for understanding the identity of the Chinese of Macau. Identity has of course numerous meanings or constructions of meaning, depending on actors and situations. It is suggested, however, that a dramatic social change occurred after 20 December 1999, when the long expected return of Macau to China took place.

I have been compelled to ask basic questions and look for the facts about Macau's relationships with the rest of China, with the Hong Kong SAR and with Southeast Asia; its links with the Lusophone world and with the global world of the twenty-first century. I have considered carefully the surprising fact that, on average, the Chinese who cross the Zhuhai/Macau border every day are greater in number than those who cross the Shenzhen/Hong Kong border. The influence of the Mainland is great and undeniable. In late 2001, ex-President Jiang Zemin and later, President Hu, were the architects behind China's joining and becoming a powerful member of the World Trade Organization (WTO). In 2011, from the micro-viewpoint of Macau, under the leadership of President Hu Jintao, it is still useful to look at the macro-modernisation introduced by Deng Xiaoping in the 1980s and compare this with the new twenty-first century, looking at Mainland China and Macau. All is now linked to the concept of globalisation. We will see how this globalisation plays a role in the MSAR. Does this concept influence the identity of the Chinese of Macau? It is too early to answer this question in this Introduction.

I based this work mainly on 'classical' research, but research on identity requires a multi-disciplinary approach. My methodological checklist is the following: observing, listening, interviewing and questioning. Although this point of view could be discussed, I firmly believe that a 'Chinese-of-Macau', although difficult to define, does exist. I will also consider a link between identity, the place of origin, associations, and Professor Tong Io Cheng's legal and cultural concept of 'way of life', which is mentioned in the Macau Basic Law. Chapter One deals with Chinese identity and begins with an explanation of the relationship between the Macanese and the Chinese of Macau.

IDENTITY OF THE CHINESE OF MACAU

How can we demonstrate that the Chinese of Macau have their own identity? How can we define this particular Chinese group and its culture?

I start with the simple identity of the Macanese who are really from Macau as identified by Renelde da Silva and Alexandra Rangel. The Macanese were born in Macau but have not been considered Chinese by either the Portuguese or the Chinese, so it may seem strange to put them forward when studying the Chinese of Macau. The Macanese are the sons and daughters of many different cultures. Their identity is Portuguese and they have a mixed cultural origin. Their fluency in Portuguese is real and has nothing to do with recent statistics, which reveal that forty-one per cent of the civil servants of Macau have some knowledge of Portuguese.[12]

The account of Francisco da Roza in the 1950s explains the excellent cultural links between the Macanese and the Chinese.[13] During the post-1950 period, a large number of Chinese as well as Macanese were refugees in camps in Macau. 'The boredom of camp life was only relieved by the projection of films on Sundays evenings'.[14] Massive Chinese immigration during this period is confirmed by Paul Pun who has a deep knowledge of the evolution of social services in Macau.

For the Museum of Macau, 'identity and history' and 'Chinese and Macanese' are most important.[15] Many Macanese have Chinese blood, and all of them are called *Tusheng,* 'sons of the land', sons of Macau.

However, like it or not, it is clear that a new 'Macauan' identity is facing the challenge of merging the differences of Chinese, Portuguese and Macanese identities into one

'Macauan' identity.[16] I attended, from beginning to end, the last Macanese Encountering Event, on 28 November 2010 presided over by the Chief Executive, Fernando Chui Sai On, his predecessor as Chief Executive, Edmund Ho, General Rocha Vieira, and the Consul General of Portugal for Macau and Hong Kong, Manuel Cansado de Carvalho. In his speech, Fernando Chui Sai On recognised that 'the Macanese are an inseparable element of Macau'.

I met Chief Executive Fernando Chui Sai On face to face for the first time in December 2009, on the evening of the day of his election, and for the second time on 28 November 2010. He is now fluent in Putonghua (Mandarin), the national language of China. Without denying at all the importance of the Cantonese language in Macau, it is clear that this is a preliminary sign of the importance of the national language. Putonghua is becoming the new marker of identity and Chineseness among the Chinese of Macau. Sinicization, influenced by Putonghua, has not however dented the particular 'way of life' in Macau, and Cantonese remains the main language in the MSAR. A counter-example is given by CCTV 13, which broadcasts exclusively in Putonghua, combining its programmes with Macau Television and so implementing Sinicization. Some Chinese of Macau may not watch these programmes, but we are in the twenty-first century, Putonghua is more global than Cantonese, and this type of globalisation could be positive for the MSAR.

Ethnic relations in Macau have never been bad, thanks to both Confucian philosophy and Portuguese tolerance, as well as to the 'bamboo-identity' of the Macanese and also, over the centuries, the good will of the Chinese of Macau. The Macanese are as flexible and resilient as bamboo. The diplomacy of former Imperial provincial mandarins responsible for Xiangshan (now Zhongshan), and much later, from 1980 until today, the diplomatic cadres of Beijing – and of Guangdong Province – have also played a key role in maintaining good ethnic relations.

As a result of the 'Indic administration' system of Malacca mentioned by Geoff Wade in his *Southeast Asia in the Fifteenth Century* (2010), Macau was very early influenced by Southeast Asia. Macanese heterogeneity was originally a result of Goan[17] forebears, who represented a greater influx than any other Indians, or Malaccans, and only later included Chinese. (See below for the life story of Leão, a 'Portugalised' Chinese of Macau.) The late Ho Tin (贺田) (*see Photograph 9*), another Chinese of Macau of great culture and one of the rare grand entrepreneurs of the Sino-Portuguese territory, said: 'Ruguo meiyou Tusheng, jiu meiyou Aomen' ('The Macanese play a key role in defining Macau').[18]

Before the handover in 1999, some Macanese had become Chinese citizens. However, the book on cinema in Macau by the famous Macanese writer, the late Henrique de Senna Fernandes (1923-2010) – posthumously published and presented at the Macau encountering event in December 2010, already referred to – explains the distinctive hybrid culture of Macau, a bridge between East and West. Hao Zhidong himself quoted Fernandes' daughter, who stated rightly that, without the Macanese, 'Macau would lose its characteristics'.[19] The long history of Macau will hopefully provide support for local culture, which could be at risk in our global world.

For the Timorese deputy, Manuel Tilman, a former lawyer in Macau, identity is an essential cultural marker which was included in his programme as a presidential candidate for the elections in East Timor in March 2012. In this new country, the State Secretary for Culture, Virgilio Smith, thinks, like Hao, that national identity is a necessary component of culture.[20]

To show the importance of the Chinese of Macau in contemporary history, I mention Roque (Rocky) Chui, a fluent Portuguese speaker who, together with Dr Ho Yin, negotiated with Mainland China at the beginning of the Cultural Revolution in 1967, during a very difficult period in the history of China and Macau. The representative of the Governor of Macau, Carlos d'Assumpção, returned from Beijing without succeeding in reaching an agreement with the PRC. Later, Ho Yin and Roque Chui calmly managed to convey exactly the right message of peace and respect that was necessary, to restart good relations between the giant, China, and Macau. This shows the importance of the 'Sino-Portuguese bilingual legal language in Macau society', as developed by Tong Io Cheng in the *Isaidat Law Review* (Chapter Two). The adaptation to both cultures – Chinese and European – over a long period of time is part of the identity of the Chinese of Macau, even if many of them do not speak Portuguese.

Cantonese, Hokkien, Chaozhou (Teochew) and Others

Identity is a serious question and the Mainland is huge and omnipresent. Identities have national, political and cultural aspects. It is also true that the term 'identity', like 'religion', has no equivalent in Chinese. *Shenfen* (身份) is closer to 'social status', and *rentong* (认同) refers probably to the acceptance of an approved culture. The Chinese of Macau have multiple origins and are consequently complex, but finally they are 'themselves in relation to others', as are we all.[21]

Macau is a multicultural melting pot, with a long history, a meeting point of Chinese, Europeans, Indians, Southeast Asians and others, so Chinese of Macau are different from other Chinese. They managed to resist 450 years of Portuguese acculturation without any 'clash' and without changing the bases of their 'Chineseness'.

Wang Gungwu writes about Greater China;[22] I simply examine Macau as a microcosm of China.

In the sixteenth and seventeenth centuries, it was difficult for Chinese to enter Macau's walled city, and in the beginning it was not possible for them to stay *'intramuras'* overnight. However, Macau did attract

Chinese merchants, interpreters and labourers. Some Chinese, in particular refugees and orphans, were converted to Christianity over the centuries due to famines or other calamities on the Mainland. The Chinese Bazaar, at the Centre of the walled city, was a commercial gathering place which gave to the territory an ancient name *Oumungaai,* 'the Market of Macau' (澳门街). The Chinese villages within Portuguese Macau territory included Wangxia or Mongha, Longtian, Shalitou or Patane and Barra or Mazu Temple district among others.[23] Shalitou probably took its name from the old maritime pier where sand pear fruits might have been unloaded.[24] Patane probably refers to Patani in South Thailand, a port of call for sailing ships coming to Macau from Europe and the Middle East, but this etymology is uncertain.

The definition of the concept 'identity' in Chinese is difficult. Between the three following definitions of 'identity', we chose the third one which is the closest Chinese term:[25]

*Tongyixing (*同一性*)*, which more or less refers to 'identity and unity', is usually used to define 'Chineseness' more than 'identity'.

*Xiangtong (*相同*)* mean 'identical', not 'identity'.

Shenfen is the best translation, but it is not perfect. It refers to 'social status', and appears on the government-issued ID card, or *shenfenzheng (*身份证*),* which includes data about official residence and status, as well as official ethnic ('nationality') identity.

Identity is complex in Macau. In 2010, in *Juridikum,* Tong mentioned during the Qing Dynasty a case of exception for the 'Chinese residents who turned into Christians' to whom Portuguese Law was applied. At present, the Chinese Law is applied to the Portuguese who have a Chinese passport.

Language is an essential marker of identity. Chinese of Macau want to keep their mother tongue, Cantonese. The point is not that language is essential, but it means that we must ask questions about Cantonese and other languages in Macau. Putonghua is becoming more and more significant. Chinese characters are the reference under the legal, neutral and unsettled, phraseology of 'Chinese language' (Basic Law, Article 9). Both Portuguese and Chinese are official languages. However, except during non-Chinese official ceremonies and, for example, to get a job or a university degree, Portuguese is not really promoted in the MSAR.

On 28 February 2011, when the new Immigration Centre opened on Taipa Island, the signage outside gave priority to Chinese characters. The staff were polite, but foreigners had to read the characters 外国人 to understand *waiguoren* (meaning 'foreigners') and join the correct queue. Few foreigners were present that day, mostly some Filipinas without knowledge of written Chinese. However, the façade of the building respects the Basic Law in relation to Portuguese; the new building has the Portuguese word 'imigracão' (immigration) side by side with its Chinese equivalent.

The law of Macau is in Portuguese. Portuguese has consequently its own linguistic power. The Chinese translation of the law of the MSAR is not so reliable and Basic Law is the key law in Chinese and in Portuguese. The Basic Law is a reliable legal basis in the MSAR. So the Executive Board of the Consultative Council for the Basic Law, headed by the former Chief Executive, is an essential body of the MSAR.

Can we say: 'We do not dwell in a country, we dwell inside a language? – That is our homeland![26] Putonghua is not yet the dominant language in Macau, but Cantonese currently has less influence than in 2000. However, Cantonese remains very useful for many groups; for Cantonese speakers born in Macau, for many other Chinese who speak Cantonese, for a certain number of Macanese, and for the few Indonesians and Filipinos, who constantly speak Cantonese in Macau. Cantonese residents in the MSAR are very proud of their mother tongue.

Research on identity requires a multi-disciplinary approach involving social sciences, including geography, linguistics and the study of religion. For example, Catholicism is a *sine qua non* identity marker of the Macanese minority, or *Tusheng*. Currently, a duality exists within the post-1999 structure of Macanese identity, but rarely are the Macanese equally interested in both Portuguese and Chinese cultures.

The Macanese are often defined as 'flexible' in society. The Chinese are dominant and the Macanese perfectly adapted to the Portuguese culture at first, but at present in the MSAR they follow Chinese traditions more than before. Following the handover in 2000, Macanese and Chinese inter-marriages have become more frequent. However, for the late first Macanese wife of Dr Stanley Ho, Clementina Leitão, it was a courageous decision in 1942 to marry a Chinese gentleman rather than a Portuguese. Dr Stanley Ho it seems was not inclined to marry a Portuguese lady; he never studied Portuguese, liking the English language.

Different Chinese Components of Chinese of Macau Identity[27]

1. *Gwongdungjan* (Cantonese people): the majority of these are 'Bundeijan' (Cantonese for 'from Macau').[28]
2. *Fukginjan* (Cantonese for 'Fukienese people') including Hokkien or Hokhlo people, a key Fukienese group,
3. The Chaozhou or *Ciuzaujan* (Cantonese) linguistically related to the Hokkiens,
4. The Hakkas,
5. The Tanka fishermen or *Tengaajan* (Cantonese),
6. Other Chinese: Shanghainese or *Soenghoijan* (Cantonese), Hunanese and Chinese from other provinces,

7. The Overseas Chinese (from Indonesia, Myanmar-Burma, Thailand, Vietnam, and elsewhere).

Before the handover, in December 1999, the population of Macau, as reported in official statistics, was 'adjusted' partly because Mainlanders from Guangdong and other provinces, who had a main residence in Macau as well as on the Mainland, could not be registered in the Census reports of both the Mainland and Macau. My own estimate of the population of Macau in 1999, based on intensive research at that time, was 490,000.[29] The official population of Macau was 513,000 in 2006, 538,000 in 2007, 542,000 in 2009 and 552,000 at the end of 2011.[30]

In 1999 half the legal immigrants to Macau came from Guangdong Province (2,408 of a total of 4,984). In 2007 and 2009 these percentages increased to 75 per cent and 66 per cent respectively (1,514 out of 2,221 and 2,099 out of 3,121).[31]

In 1999, 2,206 legal immigrants came from Fujian (forty-five per cent of the total); in 2007, 223 (ten per cent of the total) and in 2009, 339 (eleven per cent of the total of legal migrants). This confirms the importance of the Fukienese in the MSAR.

Other provinces and regions are less important in relation to migration to Macau. From Hunan, 108 migrants came to Macau in 1999 (two per cent), 101 in 2007 (five per cent) and 117 in 2009 (three per cent).

From Guangxi, sixty-eight came in 1999, seventy-seven in 2007 and 131 in 2009 (four per cent). From Shanghai, thirty-seven immigrants entered Macau in 1999 and twenty-five in 2009 (less than one per cent).

In Table One, I use the results of my survey of 225 interviewees and their households. The following points should be noted. Each of the 225 respondents reported that they had lived in Macau for more than twenty years. Shanghainese and Chinese of provinces other than

Guangdong and Fujian are not intensively studied in Table One, as the necessary data is presently lacking.

Wong Hon Keong (Huang Hanqiang) at the University of Macau has forecast that the population of Macau will reach one million before 2021, because of increasing economic development and the new, closer relationship of Hengqin Island with the MSAR. Chinese of Macau answering my questionnaire in 2011 constitute a large majority; however, the percentage of Cantonese in Macau will probably decrease in the future, as Chinese from all provinces want to be part of the dynamic new MSAR. It follows that the Chinese of Macau are a 'social barometer' of current and future social change in the MSAR.

The origin of the visitors who come on 'the individual visit scheme' can give us an idea of the identity of the Chinese of Macau. The provinces most represented among such visitors are: Guangdong, Fujian, Zhejiang and Hunan. Shanghai and Beijing are also important in this context. From Guangdong in particular, more than four million entered Macau under this scheme from July 2010 to the end of June 2011 (4,103,174 individuals, compared to more than seven million visitors in all from Guangdong province). – It is not surprising that many of the visitors travelling on the overcrowded local buses of Macau speak Cantonese. – The Fukienese, who entered the Macau SAR on the individual visit scheme during the same period (July 2010 to the end of June 2011), were less numerous: 114,314 as compared with 755,153, who came as visitors in a group of Fukinese.[32] Among other visitors entering on the individual visit scheme on a one-year basis during the same period were 320,000 Shanghainese, 189,000 from Beijing, 177,000 from Zhejiang and many fewer from Tianjin, Chongqing and Hunan.

The most remarkable figures are those for the province of Guangdong, which show that the Cantonese identity of Macau is for the moment secured by the high number of Cantonese entering the MSAR. In second place come the Fukienese.

The Chinese of Macau – Mainly from Guangdong Province

The Chinese of Macau are of a complex ethno-cultural composition, but the Cantonese of Guangdong Province are the most important.

We do not have answers as to their place of origin from all 225 respondents, as only 137 interviewees gave their place of origin. The following analysis, therefore, is based on a sample of 137 respondents only. According to Table One, 55 per cent of the respondents have come from Zhongshan, Shunde and Panyu, all in Guangdong Province; this is higher than the forty-seven per cent found in my previous research in 1999. However, in the case of those Chinese of Macau whose ancestors came from Taishan, Foshan and Guangzhou, the percentage (thirteen per cent), as shown in Table One, is slightly lower than the estimated fourteen per cent in 1999 mentioned in my book, *Macao 2000*. In 2011, the percentage of those from Xinhui, Jiangmen, Nanhai, Toumen and Heshan is, however, higher than in 1999. The fact that ninety-two per cent (55+13+24) of respondents who answered this question are Cantonese is very important. Fukienese and others shown in Table One are part of the complex reality of the MSAR.

In my view, twenty years of residence in the territory of Macau – more recently, the MSAR – is really a minimum for a person to possess a 'Macau' identity.

Referring now to Tables 2 and 3: Among those who responded to my second questionnaire, administered to a representative of one hundred selected households,[33] the majority of respondents below the age of thirty who stated that they are 'Chinese of Macau', were the most numerous, at twenty-three per cent; while six declared themselves simply 'Chinese', and nineteen responded: 'Macau'. Of those respondents between thirty-one and fifty-nine years old, thirteen (thirteen individuals or thirteen per cent of a hundred respondents answering for their household) answered this identity question: 'Macau' (thirteen per cent);

thirteen responded, 'Chinese of Macau'; and only seven considered themselves more 'Chinese' than any other identity. Of those aged sixty and above, ten per cent (ten individuals) answered 'Chinese of Macau'. So we can say with certainty, that our data shows that the largest minority of our respondents (46 per cent) considered themselves 'Chinese of Macau' (23+13+10).

Those within the 'largest minority' of our respondents (as just discussed) identified themselves as 'Chinese of Macau' or whatever, and explained, according to Han patriarchal tradition, their father's ancestral origin; but, when we drew their genealogies, they also gave their mother's origin. Not all respondents did this, because many students made an *individual* and not a complete interview. (That is, they solicited answers from the family representative in relation to him or herself only and not relating to the whole family.) In administering my own questionnaires, I did my best to be accurate, but was unable to ensure the same level of accuracy for all respondents.

Among the total of 225 respondents, which includes many well educated young people, we found that exactly half had reached tertiary educational level. However, in the case of the one hundred selected households, only thirty-seven (37% of the total) were university graduates or otherwise had achieved university level. Indeed, the MSAR Government Statistics for 2006 show that only eleven per cent of the population has a university degree. This is in spite of the fact that, over the years, the number of university graduates in the MSAR has been increasing.

Some young people – as described in the previous paragraph and as studied elsewhere during this research – prefer to say that their identity is that of 'Macau', but some – such as Chan Tak Seng, Vice-President of the Alliance of the People – think that the elections in 2013 or 2014 will show a shift toward Mainland China.[34] Many of these young people have a Portuguese passport, but they do not speak Portuguese: nevertheless the identity 'Macau' suits their egos and corresponds to a certain ambiguity in their identity.

Because they are Chinese culturally, or influenced by their Chineseness, they do not want to advertise their Portuguese citizenship. So they generally prefer to travel to Singapore and Thailand rather than to Europe. If they have family in the United States, as my neighbour does, they may prefer to go on holidays to America.

Young people are the future of MSAR and some entrepreneurs – such as Dr Pansy Catalina Ho Chiu King – have understood the importance of believing in young people, and the dynamism that this can create. Pansy favours the recruitment of young 'employees' and 'cadres'; she wants to project herself into the future.

The number of young people who hold a Portuguese passport is large, and consequently many of them answered 'Macau' instead of giving any other response. Remembering that those below thirty years of age are over-represented among the 225 interviewees, we find that, out of the total of 225 interviewees (as reported in Table One), 48 per cent responded, 'Macau' (compared with 38 per cent as shown in Table Two, where the ages of respondents are more balanced, showing results for young people aged thirty years or below, middle-aged above 31 and up to 59 and older people aged sixty years or above). Of the 225 interviewees, 32 per cent responded, 'Chinese of Macau' (instead of 46 per cent as in Table Two) and 20 per cent responded simply, 'Chinese' (instead of 19 per cent in Table Two).

Note that 38+46+19=103. This total is greater than 100 per cent because, as already mentioned, three respondents gave two answers instead of one; for example, both 'Macau' and 'Chinese of Macau', instead of simply 'Macau'. This is how household Number 39 responded (*see Table Two*). The others, who gave two answers instead of one, are Number 20 and Number 111. Strangely, two of the interviewees among these three cases were not born in

Macau; but they also gave the Macau identity. I have not checked to see whether they have a Portuguese passport.

The majority of the Chinese who responded to my questionnaires were born in Macau; but others have come from Hong Kong, Guangdong Province, Southeast Asia, Europe and (even further afield) from South America. One Macau association – the *Guiqiao Zhonghui* – is composed of Overseas Chinese from more than twenty different countries. Of the respondents to my questionnaire, twelve per cent had family links in Southeast Asia and forty-one per cent had a brother, sister or other relative in Hong Kong.

Where I lived previously in Macau, most of the staff were Hokkien, equally fluent in Cantonese and Minnan and it is the same for other residents who are originally Fukienese. However, the majority of the Chinese in Macau are Cantonese. Not surprisingly, therefore, the main language in the MSAR is Cantonese; but Puntonghua is becoming more important.

Round about the year 2,000, a Nepali businessman in Macau, speaking about the main international language of communication, said: 'To become international, Macau must follow Hong Kong and speak English.' In 2008, Andrew Moody of the Macau University noted that 'Macau English should be recognised' as a language of education, media and commerce.

These statements should be of particular interest to the Secretary for Economy and Finance and to those working in tourist agencies, rather than to grassroots people (the majority of MSAR permanent residents), who continue to speak Cantonese. The increasing importance of Putonghua is, however, a key factor in the transformation of the MSAR. If we consider the long history of the Romanisation of Vietnamese in the 1920s, perhaps we can say that the current increasing importance of Putonghua in the MSAR has some analogies with the implementation of written Vietnamese *quoc ngu*, which has been described as an essential 'component of national identity'?[35]

However, we have to look constantly at the point of view of the Chinese of Macau. Monica is an ethnic Chinese woman, born and raised in Macau, where she has a prestigious job. She believes that 'Chineseness' represents something very ordinary: 'We just live the way we live, have our families and our little traditions or ways of doing things... with our history and customs'.[36]

In fact, history and culture strengthen Cantonese identity, the dominant identity in the MSAR.

Importance of the Cantonese Residents in the MSAR
There is an evident acculturation of Cantonese in Macau, that is linguistically and socially taking place, not through English as in Singapore and Hong Kong, but more through Putonghua. I discovered an increasing lack of knowledge of many kinship terms in Cantonese among informants, born in Macau, who are very fluent in their mother tongue. The new media orientation toward Putonghua in Guangzhou beginning in 2010 has evidently influenced the MSAR. However, thanks to their literature and the rich Cantonese opera ('yueju jyut kek' in Cantonese) (粤剧) we continue to believe in the resilience of the Cantonese language, at least up to the integration of Macau into Guangdong Province, scheduled for 2049. Cantonese opera is a key cultural marker of Cantonese culture. The importance of Cantonese, the beauty of the costumes and the majesty of the performances all play a part in the attraction that Cantonese opera holds for the Chinese of Macau. On Guia Hill, one of the favourite music programmes the daily strollers listen to on their portable radios is Cantonese opera.

Cantonese resilience is part of an essential mapping among the 'totality of Chinese ethnicities in all their subtleties'.[37] It is interesting to note an initiative of the Education and Youth Affairs Bureau (DSEJ), which organised a six-month course in Cantonese language for non-Cantonese residents. The course began on 19 February

2011, constituting an incentive tool for the promotion of Cantonese, the basis of Macau identity.

Hokkien from Fujian Province – the Second Largest Group of the Chinese of Macau

It is evident that Chinese of Macau from the Province of Fujian represent an important part of the population of the MSAR – some twenty per cent of a population of 552,000 permanent residents in December 2011. Table One shows that eight per cent were originally from Fujian Province. All of them could speak Cantonese. During the 1950s, in Taiwan, the Hokkien language became less important. However, nowadays, the Hokkien and their dialect, *Minnanhua* (閩南话), have a huge cultural impact, in particular in the MSAR. *Minnanhua* is also known as Hokhlo (福佬), which is said to have originated from Heluo (河洛語), spoken in Henan Province　(河南省). – The main goddess of Macau, Mazu, is primarily a Hokkien deity. – The dynamism of the Hokkien community and of *Minnanhua* speakers was demonstrated at the 'Singing Competition at the Forum', in February 2011. The Forum was packed and the audience enthusiastic. The majority of the 'Singing Masters' (judges) for the Singing Competition – four out of five – were from Taiwan. Deputy Chan Meng Kam, president of the Fukienese Association, and Leong Heng Teng, an Executive Council Member of the Macau SAR Government, were present at the Forum for this cultural event.

The Hokkien population most probably migrated from Henan, Middle China, to Fujian. In the Chinese term *Heluo* (河洛), *He* (河) refers to the River Huang He (黃河) and *Luo* (洛) refers to the Luoshui (洛水), a branch of the Huang He, the great river of Northern China.

To develop the economy and/or for political reasons, China is trying to reinforce the link among Hokkien speakers from Fujian, Macau and Taiwan. In my survey,[38] sixteen per cent of respondents said they spoke their own language, Hokkien, *Oklo oe* ('*Minnanhua*' in Putonghua).

'Hokkiens' belong to an essential 'ethno-linguistic' group.[39] There are some forty million Hokkien speakers in the world. Among the Hokkien speakers in Macau, those speaking the Xiamen and Putian dialects are dominant. The Hokkien constitute the second most important group in the MSAR, after the dominant Cantonese.

Following my enquiry among other Hokkien associated with the Fujian Association – located near the Macau Zhuhai border – I found that all are proud to use their mother tongue, but – elsewhere in town – the majority of them use Cantonese and prefer to use this language as a cultural marker. However, the Cantonese of both the MSAR and the HKSAR may detect the provincial origin of these non-Cantonese. The success of the Hokkien entrepreneur and Deputy of the Legislative Assembly, Chan Meng Kam (Chen Ming Jin), has played a role in the development of the Hokkien community. The following example indicates another significant socio-linguistic attitude at the grassroots level.

In 1975, Mr Lim left Xiamen and entered Macau with his wife and oldest son. He did not graduate from secondary school. He understands Hokkien of course, but he has become Chinese of Macau. His main language of communication is Cantonese, which now characterises his identity. He never returned to Xiamen, except once for the funeral of his father. Sometimes he even denies a good knowledge of his mother tongue, *Xiamenhua,* a branch of *Minnanhua.*

His younger son took advantage of his Portuguese citizenship, as a Chinese born in Macau under the sovereignty of Portugal before 1999. Now he lives in London. Lim himself has no intention of going to London. He works 365 days of the year and seems to survive quite well his harassing twelve-hour-a-day job as a hotel night receptionist. He speaks rather respectfully of Mao Zedong when he refers to the 'policies' of different periods between

1958 and 1976, such as those of the Great Leap Forward and the Cultural Revolution. The fact that he does not want to return to the Mainland is somehow strange and does not match his politeness when he talks about Mao. He goes once a year to Hong Kong.

The identity of the Chinese of Macau is complex.

Another example of cultural identity is the fact that the typical Brazilian martial art, Capoeira, is well developed in the MSAR. Numerous young Chinese of Macau, as well as Portuguese speakers, come many times a week to be trained. The large diffusion of this Brazilian martial art is playing an important part in the construction of a very positive community spirit in the MSAR. Its complement, the dynamic and popular Afro-Brazilian music, also demonstrates that, at present as in the past, things are moving. Macau is keeping its own way 'way of life' as part of a globalisation which started four centuries ago, before the term 'globalisation' was coined. Consequently, identity is complex in the MSAR. The identity of the Chinese of Macau does exist. Georg Noack notes that, 'Globalisation... [and the] widespread availability of international media and consumer goods have led to rapid societal change during the last twenty years and... [lead to] conflicts between desires to catch up with a perceived global modernity and fears of losing one's own identity, culture and values'.[40]

The Mainlanders who have become Chinese of Macau also subsequently begin to change their perception of 'global modernity'. The following seven life stories illustrate the constraints of globalisation and other phenomena relating to the fear of losing one's own identity.

Other Chinese Groups

The Chinese of Macau are not all from the Guangdong and Fujian provinces. All the following categories may, taken together, constitute 30 per cent of the MSAR population in 2011. This percentage will probably increase over the years.

These non-Cantonese and non-Fukienese Chinese of Macau may be the Chaozhou, linguistically related to the Hokkien, the Hakka, the Shanghainese, and the Hunanese, or from other provinces of China; they may also be Overseas Chinese, mainly from Southeast Asia. It should be mentioned that some Chinese permanent residents of the HKSAR may be permanent residents of the MSAR too. In general, they are initially from Hong Kong and they become permanent residents in Macau because they work in Macau or because their family has moved to Macau.

At present, the Chaozhou (Teochew) community is proportionally less important in Macau (four per cent of the Chinese community) than in Hong Kong (where some eight per cent of the whole Chinese population belongs to this group). They are not classified as Cantonese, even if they speak Cantonese fluently. The sea-oriented culture of the Chaozhou is a consequence of the lack of good roads in eastern Guangdong Province as late as the Qing Dynasty (1644-1911), and during the Republican Era. The Teochew have been sea-traders and travelers, and so are present in Southeast Asia, in particular in Thailand, and also in Macau.

The current president of the Macau Chaozhou Association is Hoi Sai Iun (Xu Shi Yuan). He is also President of the General Association of Trade, President of the Charitable Association Tung Sin Tong and Vice-President of the Kiang Wu Association and the Kiang Wu Hospital. He received the Grand Lotus decoration of the MSAR for his achievements and for his successful development of association life in Macau.

Seven Life Stories or Biographies

These short significant biographies are mainly based on my own interviews.[41] All my interviewees in this section of the book are Chinese of Macau, permanently resident in the MSAR, but only Mr Leão was actually born in Macau. These biographies will be used as and when necessary in this book.

João Baptista Manuel Leão (Liang)

Leão, born in Macau, has been the Chairman of the Consultative Committee of the Civic and Municipal Affairs Bureau since 2002, and he has been a Deputy in the Legislative Assembly of Macau from 1999 to 2002.[42] He is presently the President of the Executive Committee of the Association for Adult Education in the MSAR. His father and ancestors, as well as his wife, are from Xinhui, Guangdong.

Leão became a 'Portugalised' Catholic Chinese of Macau, thanks to his godfather, the late Alberto Antonio Angelo, former Head of the Social Welfare Department in Macau. His godfather indirectly contributed also in guiding the future Leão toward an administrative career, for which knowledge of the Portuguese language was a must before 1999. Leão, unlike the majority of Macanese, and even unlike some Chinese, has mastered Putonghua and written Chinese. As already implied, Leão is also fluent in Portuguese and can write Chinese, so the doors of the former Portuguese administration were open to him. In Hong Kong the medium of instruction was English, and Leão's attendance at the Hong Kong Polytechnic enabled him to read, speak and translate Chinese (Putonghua and Cantonese), as well as English, adding to his Portuguese language skills. Leão is thus quadri-lingual, a rare and very useful qualification in Macau, where, unfortunately, many Chinese of Macau still do not understand the importance of learning many languages.

Leão was first educated at the Colegio Dom Bosco in Macau. At the Hong Kong Polytechnic he graduated in Mechanical Engineering. We can say that he is a self-made man. He is able to teach courses in administration to other civil servants in both Portuguese and Chinese.

In 1971, Leão married Cecilia Chung. The couple have two daughters: Maria Vanessa, who has an M.A. in music from the Hong Kong Baptist University and Eugenia Florinda who has an M.A. in tourism from Surrey University, United Kingdom. On Saturday 18 and Sunday

19 December 2011, Maria Vanessa, Associate Professor of Music at Macau Polytechnic Institute, presented her choir *Dolce Voce* at Saint Dominic's Church and at the Military Club. In 2011 *Dolce Voce* was invited to participate in the International Choral Competition in Taiwan and also gave a concert in Canada.

Between 1974 and 1983, Leão was teaching mechanical drawing at Dom Bosco College. Always friendly and easy to contact, Leão is totally dedicated to promoting education, in particular adult education, which is very useful in Macau. Education is important for Mr Leão.

J. B. Leão is a member of more than a hundred associations in Macau, including the Xinhui Association and the Rotary Club of Macau Central. (*See Photograph 12.*) He is also a member of the Council of the City University of Macau. He is a standing member of the Executive Board of the Consultative Council for the Basic Law, which has about ninety members.[43]

Leão has many friends in Macau, Hong Kong, Europe and the United States of America. He likes to read, swim, sing in many languages, and travel. In 2010 he traveled with the Council for Youth Education of the MSAR to Estonia, Prague and Frankfurt. In October of the same year he went to Rome, Milan, Turin, Paris, and Lourdes. Leão's identity is clearly 'Chinese of Macau', but he likes to travel, as do many Macanese.

Leong Heng Teng

Leong Heng Teng was born in 1947 in Guangdong Province, the son of Liang Rong Gen. He married in Macau, as his son also did. Leong now has a grandson and a granddaughter Leong also has a daughter, who lives with her parents.

Leong's late mother came from Nanhai, Guangdong Province, and his father's family is from Shunde. Leong Heng Teng is a member of the association named the Shuntak Association ('Shunde Tongxianghui' in Cantonese). His father, Liang Rong Gen, is more than eighty years old and has four daughters and three sons living. Leong Heng Teng is the eldest son. All seven are married and all are resident in Macau. Another, older, daughter passed away at an early age. Liang Rong Gen has many great-grandchildren.

Leong Heng Teng completed his secondary school and college education at Hou Kong (Hao Jiang) School in Macau in 1965. He taught there as a primary school teacher for twenty years. At the age of fifty, he graduated from Jinan University on the Mainland. In 1960, Leong became interested in politics. He has been a member of 'Xinqiaofang' since 1980, and later became President of the closely related Kaifong, the Macau Union of Neighbourhood Associations ('Oumun Gaaifung Lyunhap Zungwui' in Cantonese). Leong Heng Teng is the founding President of another Kaifong, the Street Committee of Macau.[44]

Leong Heng Teng was an elected Deputy of the Legislative Assembly of Macau from 1991 to 1999. He is a dynamic community leader. In May 2008, he was a torch bearer at Macau for the Beijing Olympic Games, which began on 8 August 2008. Leong particularly appreciates tea parties ('cha gordo' in the patois of Macau), where he can meet both the elderly and young people of Macau, and listen to their problems. Sometimes he even sings at such functions to entertain them. 'Heping' (peace), is an essential element of politics for him.

Since 1999, Leong Heng Teng has been an influential Member of the Executive Council of the MSAR. During the first two weeks of March 2011, he went to Beijing with other key delegates from the MSAR Executive Council. (This is the most important period of the year for the China People's Congress.[45]) Leong is particularly concerned with the social problems of the MSAR and in particular with those of Qingzhou, the northwestern district of the Macau Peninsula. He wants to balance the economy and society; pure economic theories do not fit with what the people need.

He has proposed a reduction in the tax (currently totalling 300 million patacas), paid by those who possess their own flats, and who currently receive no assistance from the MSAR Government, unlike those who rent public (social) housing.[46]

In 2011, Leong Heng Teng was Vice-President of the Council of Creativity. On the morning of 20 December 2011, he demonstrated both his belief in education and his loyalty to the MSAR by taking one of his grandchildren with him to the Flag Ceremony in commemoration of the handover of Macau to China. Then on 23 December of the same year, as a member of the Executive Council of the MSAR, Leong went to Guangzhou to attend the Guangdong and Macau meeting of the Association of Industry and Commerce as the main representative of the MSAR.

Leong Heng Teng promotes modernity. The statistics of Macau show an average of 2.8 persons per household, with forty-five per cent of the population living in a four-person household. My recent survey found 3.6 persons per household, fewer than my 1999 finding of four persons per household.[47] Many newly-married modern Chinese of Macau prefer to have one child only, so as to be free to work, and also to take holidays. At the end of 2011, advertising in Chinese and in English appeared in MSAR buses supporting the policy of only one child. However, following Hong Kong fashion, many families have two children. This evolution shows a clear modernisation of MSAR society, influencing the binomial parameters, society and economy.

On 21 December 2011, just after the handover commemoration ceremony, as Spokesman and Member of the Executive Council of the MSAR, Leong Heng Teng was active in promoting legal assistance for the poorest Macau residents. Under this legal aid scheme, the payment of the fees for the lawyers involved would be decided by a public commission, and not by the courts, as at present. It is envisaged that this will accelerate the handling of the three hundred cases presented yearly, the majority involving Macau residents. This initiative is in conformity with the recent request made by President Hu Jintao and his successor Xi Jinping to MSAR Chief Executive Chui Sai On, to protect the people of Macau and their quality of life.

On December 23, in Guangzhou, Leong was the leading member of an important MSAR delegation to the 'Hengqin Island' meeting with cadres from the Province of Guangdong. The question of whether partly to 'merge' Hengqin and Macau or how far Guangdong Province would create new laws to administer Hengqin Island is far from being solved.

Ng Kuok Cheong

Ng Kuok Cheong is a Democratic Legislative Councillor. Speaking with Jill McGivering, as published in 1999, he said:

'I don't know when I was born (about 1957)... I might have been born in Macau... I always knew I was adopted...

'I would describe my childhood as one of hard work... I went to a Chinese school, only five per cent of people attended Portuguese schools in Macau then.

'I think there have been a series of major changes in Macau in my lifetime. The first was in December 1966 – [these events are] called um, dois, tres by the Portuguese – when the Chinese rebelled against the Portuguese governor – successfully... My sister was a small landlord, so she didn't support the rebellion...The anniversary of the founding of the Republic of China on 10 October 1911 is a key event...

'The second big change was Portugal's revolution in 1974. We didn't realise its importance at the time... The third change was the open door policy adopted by Deng Xiaoping in the late 1970s...

'In 1978, I went to Hong Kong to study at the Chinese University for four years. I liked economics and social sciences. I applied for every scholarship I could and worked as a tutor for local children to make ends meet... When I graduated, I wanted to stay in Hong Kong... I only have a Macau ID card... I was refused...

'When I came back to Macau, my priority was to get a job. I joined the Bank of China as a junior... In 1989, we formed the New Macau Association... and in 1992 I won, as one of the vice chairman of the association, one of the eight directly elected seats in the Legislative Assembly... All we can really do is call for reforms.'[48]

In 2010 and 2011, Deputy Ng is particularly concerned by the problem of Ilha Verde, Qingzhou.' (*See Chapter Three.*)

Gary Ngai
Gary Ngai, an overseas Chinese, who is the President of the Sino-Latin Foundation, had the chance to be well educated in Indonesia and in Beijing. He studied not only Bahasa Indonesia but also Dutch, English and Chinese. In Beijing he continued his tertiary education in Chinese and English. Later, in Macau, he also studied Portuguese. He was in Guangzhou during the Cultural Revolution and moved with his family to Macau in the 1970s and became the Vice-President of the Cultural Institute in the 1990s and remaining in that position until 1999. In 2000, he became the President of the Sino-Latin Foundation. In 2011, during interviews for my book, he said as follows:

'I consider that the Father of the Chinese Republic, Sun Yat-sen (1866-1925), a Hakka of Xiangshan, Zhongshan, was important for Macau because he used the enclave during his revolutionary activities.

'Founded in 1921, the Communist Party has a main political slogan, nationalism, to preserve the independence of China. Hong Kong and Macau are a sensitive question. To maintain an open Hong Kong and Macau was a very wise policy of the Communist Party. The Sino-Portuguese relationship was always pacific. I was a member of the

Youth Organisation. This is why I knew Mao Zedong personally and met him many times with other young people in Beijing. Mao made mistakes, this is why Deng Xiaoping praised seventy per cent of Mao's achievements and dispraised (*sic*) thirty per cent'.

Macau is not Hong Kong. During the negotiations between China and Portugal, the identity of Macau was recognised. The identity of Macau has to be fought for. It is the only way for Macau to survive, to continue to develop its own characteristics and maintain its differences from other Chinese cities. The Government in Beijing knows this, but some in Macau do not know it. Macau has a Latin identity.[49] Gary Ngai is quoted as saying that 'the MSAR is too 'hesitant', we have the money but there is a lack of decision and policy'.[50] Gary Ngai was very concerned about the nuclear disaster in Japan and in April 2011 organised a Forum on Clean Energies in Macau.

Stanley Ho

Dr Stanley Ho is very concerned about his longevity.

In an interview with Jill McGivering, published in 1999, Dr Ho said as follows:

'I came from Hong Kong to Macau as a refugee. Not to be taken prisoner, I left Hong Kong and – thanks to the relations of my first Macanese wife – I was extremely well treated in Macau. The tomb of this beloved wife is in Macau and the Government gave me a burial concession with a particularly good *fengshui*.

'I always wanted Macau and its people to be more prosperous. At the age of twenty-one, I earned one million dollars for the first time. The Japanese respected Portuguese neutrality and did not intervene in the administration of Macau. I exported products which were supposedly sent to East Timor, but in fact were sent to China.'

According to my own research, Stanley Ho, with the late tycoon of East Timor, San Taiho (Lay), was the owner of Hotel Makhota, the most prestigious hotel in Dili, East Timor. Later, Stanley Ho gave this hotel to the Orient Foundation and in 2002, just after Timorese Independence, it was transformed into the prestigious Hotel Timor.

Dr Ho also told Jill McGivering as follows:

'In 1962, STDM (Sociedade de Turismo e Diversões de Macau) won the gambling concession in Macau. It was very difficult to take the concession from its former owners. I went to Portugal five times or more, between January and March 1962, to win this privilege. There were people in Macau at the time who said that I was dreaming.'

'Ho Yin[51] also represented China in Macau. He controlled the very lucrative gold trade. I have to say that Ho Yin did a lot for Macau. After I won the concession we both became friends again. 'Pedro Lobo, a leader in Macau, sent many telegrams to Portugal to prevent me obtaining the gaming monopoly.

'Without Governor Silverio Marques, I could never have won the [gaming] concession. I still remember, at the Hotel Estoril, on the first of January 1962, five minutes after midnight and the opening of the casino, the Governor came. He pushed me into a corner and opened a telegram from the Overseas Ministry of Portugal, saying 'suspend immediately the operation of the casino'. The Governor, with a sudden gesture, tore the telegram into pieces, and said, 'Mr Stanley, I never received this telegram'. He was a great man, very courageous. I liked him very much.

'During the events of the Cultural Revolution, I remained confident. The events 1-2-3 of December 1966 in Taipa and the Macau Peninsula, linked to internal questions within the government of Mainland China, were merely a consequence of the Cultural Revolution, which lasted for ten years on the Mainland. The governor was confronted and required to sign a protocol accepting the entrance of more Chinese into the territory.

'It was not easy for the Governor and the Portuguese. Beijing was not willing to enter into confrontation with Macau and Hong Kong. Beijing wanted only to maintain the status quo. The Governor Nobre de Carvalho was very concerned. In a sort of diplomatic mission, the late Ho Yin and Roque Chui were key actors and went successfully to Beijing in 1967 to restore good relations among China, Portugal and Macau.

Beijing was not ready to take Macau. She needed time. China wanted to proceed cautiously. From Portugal came Governor Correia de Barros, a good friend of Ho Yin. This hostility toward Macau did not last. The protocol was signed. The events of 1-2-3 December 1966 and 1967 were very bad for STDM. We stopped operating for three weeks. For six months no tourists entered Macau. Everybody suffered a lot, but finally all went well. The Cultural Revolution did not play a key role relating to the ethos and identity of Macau.

'Came the 25th of April 1974, but the decolonisation of Macau could not be similar to that of the African colonies. The status of Macau was different. China asked Portugal to stay in Macau and was not ready to take over the enclave. In 1979, diplomatic relations were re-established. It was not until 1986 that the hand-over question was considered.

'My relationship with the Portuguese was always excellent, in particular with Governor Silverio Marques. I have always had excellent relations with the Government and with the Presidents and Prime Ministers of Portugal. Regarding STDM, I have to say that the enterprise gives employment to a large number of the active population and contributes to around sixty per cent of the annual budget of the Government. About the future, I am extremely confident. China has created for Macau and Hong Kong 'One Country Two Systems'. Macau will continue to be a capitalist society. Macau culture and identity will remain unchanged'.[52]

At the end of July, 2009, Stanley Ho had an accident in Macau and consequently underwent a surgical operation in Hong Kong. Many discussions have appeared in the media in Macau and Hong Kong about the transfer of Dr Ho's

Macau gaming empire, but it is a long process not yet solved. In early February 2011, Ms Pansy Ho, Dr Ho's very competent daughter, and Ambrose So, the CEO of the *Sociedade de Jogos de Macau* (SJM), Stanley Ho's main company, were doing their best to find a solution for the ownership and management of Dr Ho's economic empire. In March 2011, SJM Holdings announced a nearly fourfold increase in profits in 2010. Among his numerous decorations and outstanding merits, Stanley Ho was made a Chevalier of the French Legion of Honour in 2007. The resilience of Dr Ho is legendary. In November 2011, two years after his operation, the family of the tycoon celebrated his ninetieth birthday with joy.

Cheong and Sin Dohan

I have chosen to conclude this group of life stories with those of two ordinary men; former bus-driver, Cheong, and a former fisherman, Sin Dohan.

Cheong

Former bus-driver, Cheong goes every day to the Patane or Shalitou sports-ground. When I returned to Macau at the end of 2011, after an absence of six months, I found that not much had changed among this group of Chinese of Macau. There were some changes, however. Cheong, a seventy-eight year old informant, has, for the last fifty years, sung every day, facing the sea, near the gas station on Sul do Patane Street (*Shalitou Nanjie*) and the Macau Water Company. But the last time I saw him, he did not sing any more. The recent death of his wife on 4 April 2011 had damaged both his health and his legendary belief in his possible longevity. He no longer spoke of his physique. In early 2011, he used to point to his navel and his throat, and say, 'From there comes the vital force.' He did not walk to the Lou Lim Iok Garden any more. He had an electric wheelchair. His knees hurt, he said. In October 2012 I tried to see him again and was not able to find him.

I hope he is still in good health; he never gave me his telephone number.

This story illuminates day-to-day life in Macau which has sad aspects as well as happy ones.

Sin Dohan

Interviewed in 1999, as reported by Jill McGivering, former fisherman Sin Dohan said:

'I was born in 1934, on a boat off Taipa Island... Our family boat was a small fishing junk without a motor. I'm the very first generation to leave fishing and go to live on land, but I worked on a boat for decades before that.

'Three generations lived together in the same boat – my two grandparents, my parents, me, and my brothers. We lived at sea, in the boat, all the time. When the weather was good, we'd be out fishing. If a typhoon blew up, we'd take refuge in a typhoon shelter, where the racecourse is now...

'I never went to school. I can't read or write. The only thing I can read is my own name...

'During the Japanese occupation of China, we couldn't go out fishing far from shore...

'In 1949, life got better. In 1951, we joined the fishing association in Mainland China. I got a license from the Chinese authorities to fish around the coast of Guangdong.

'We mostly fished for Macau sole and yellow croaker. (We hung them up and then salted and stored them in the boat, and took them back to the wholesalers a few days later.) The best years were in the late 1960s to the mid-1970s. There were plenty of fish then...

'My father gave me a boat when I got married... When my father died, I inherited another boat from him, and I passed it on to one of my sons. I have four sons – they are all married now...

'From the 1960s onwards, we started to install motors in our boats... The Macau Government didn't help us financially... In 1978 I was able to buy a motorised boat for about MOP 200,000, a lot of money (USD 26,000)...

'There are far fewer people fishing nowadays... I sold my boat in 1990 and we came to live on land... I came ashore. Every day I go along to the fishermen's association here in Macau and help out there...

'Fishing is a hard life... China's reforms allowed both Hong Kong and Macau fishermen to quit fishing and move ashore...

'We bought our first flat in 1983, and another one in 1988, when I was still fishing....'[53]

As we see, Sin Dohan was impressed by the importance of China, and looked forward to the return of Macau to Chinese sovereignty: 'Most fishermen were delighted about this return to the motherland... The handover takes place on 20 December and I'm counting every day'.

Stories of the lives of ordinary working persons, like Sin Dohan and Cheong, are crucial to an understanding of the identity of a Chinese of Macau. Also essential for understanding Macau identity is the Basic Law. One aspect of the Basic Law, the 'way of life', is discussed in the following chapter.[54]

CHAPTER TWO

THE BASIC LAW
AND THE CHINESE OF MACAU

Tong Io Cheng

The name Macau was created in the sixteenth century.[55] Its Cantonese name was *Oumoongai* (澳门街) and is not used any more. The same location might previously have been the dwelling place of much earlier Chinese settlers, but there is no record of any such settlers in the history of 'Macau'.[56] As soon as the name Macau became known, the population increased, and once coincidental phenomena suddenly seemed intentional.

The Preface and Chapter One of the present study shown clearly that initially there was no genetic or cultural difference between the Chinese of Macau and Chinese on the Mainland. Today, of course, there are indeed some cultural differences, as the Chinese and Portuguese Governments have influenced the cultures of people in Macau differently. This statement applies to all sorts of Chinese, whether their origin is Cantonese, Hokkien or Shanghainese. They might be called, not merely 'cousins', but 'brothers and sisters' of one family. Yet, they are siblings who did not grow up together. Emile Durkheim developed the concept of 'solidarity'. However, solidarity is exclusive by nature, because we always group with a fixed number of people, while excluding others.[57]

It is Macau's history in particular which makes its 'way of life'. A community living in a named location has its own history which differs from that of other communities. Is it true that each community must have a particular way of life? Is there a paradigmatic way of life, so that we might group things together? When it comes to details, each way of life is of course different.

65

The Macau Way of Life: an Essential Element of the Basic Law

According to Xiao Weiyun, the expression 'way of life' refers to 'the means and mode of living. It includes the habits, customs, mores and preferences in entertainment. In order to maintain the capitalist system already existing in Macau, its proper way of life shall be maintained'.[58]

We can directly trace the formation of Macau to its demographic composition, from which the 'way of life' has arisen. Chinese from different parts of China, Africans, Indians, Malays, Portuguese along with other Europeans and other peoples and nationalities have come to play a part in the Macau way of life.

How to define Macau? It has its architecture (a southern European style of buildings, with squares and fountains), its religion (Catholic, and worship at different temples), its language (Chinese, represented by Cantonese and Fukienese dialects, Portuguese and English). Its local micro-economy should be considered, and also its social and legal institutions.[59]

As far as institutional construction is concerned, it may not be easy to turn details into rules. That is to say, the way of life, at the cultural level, is not reducible to a determinate legal concept. Nevertheless it is the way of life at the legal institutional level which protects a particular culture.

The Basic Law is the Guarantor of the Macau Way of Life

The Basic Law is the essential legislative text of the MSAR recognised by China and Portugal. To the surprise of many lawyers, the expression 'way of life' appears in the provisions of the Basic Law, which reads as follows:

'The socialist system and policies shall not be practiced in the Macau Special Administrative Region (MSAR), and the previous capitalist system and way of life shall remain unchanged for 50 years'.

The question that remains unanswered is: what is the way of life that is being protected by the Basic Law?

Doubtless, the protection of this constitutional provision is based on the logic of a sharp contrast in the distinction made between the 'socialist system' and the 'capitalist system'. Yet protecting the capitalist system is not equivalent to protecting the 'way of life'. In fact, the wording of the Basic Law provision demonstrates clearly that 'capitalist system' and 'way of life' are different matters.

In principle there is no doubt about whether the Basic Law protects the Macau way of life. However, you only need a bodyguard when you feel there is physical risk or as a counter-risk guarantor against intruders or the like. Others are not intruders until you say they are. Our guarantor is not the sort of 'protector' we used to see in Hong Kong triad films collecting 'protection' fees. In Macau, and also in Hong Kong, obviously, the Basic Law does not collect fees, nor does the Central Government.

Since the Basic Law is the guarantor of our way of life, we need to stick to the Basic Law. The Basic Law exists for us to recite, to assert. This is how it manifests its authority as a guarantor. Even in worst case scenarios, lawyers do not 'explain' the Basic Law; they only comment on whether certain acts correspond to the Basic Law. This is how we respect our guarantor.

A closer look will be taken at what we have done in the past, but it can be stated at the outset that the nature of the Macau Basic Law is unique.[60] Compared to the *Basic Law of the Hong Kong Special Administrative Region of the People's Republic of China*, firstly, Chapter IV, Section 7 (Articles 101 and 102 included), is peculiar to the Macau Basic Law. Unlike Portugal, the PRC doesn't recognise dual nationality. To solve the nationality problem of the Chief Executive, principal officials, members of the

Executive Council and of the Legislative Council, judges and procurators in Macau, Article 101 provides that these people must 'uphold the Basic Law of the Macau Special Administrative Region of the People's Republic of China, devote themselves to their duties and are [*sic*] honest in performing official duties, swear allegiance to the Macau Special Administrative Region and take an oath to this effect in accordance with law'. There is no similar provision in Hong Kong Basic Law.

Secondly, the provision, as defined in Article 7 of the Macau Basic Law, rules that land and natural resources within Macau are, 'State property, except for the private land recognised as such according to the laws in force before the establishment of the MSAR'; Hong Kong Basic Law does not provide for this exception.

There are also differences for privately held land and natural resources in Macau and in Hong Kong. This is because land and natural resources have always been state property in Hong Kong. Macau SAR Basic Law (Article 7) also recognises this fact of 'state property'. But the exception in this article is 'except for the private land recognised as such according to the laws in force before the establishment of the MSAR'. Some land belongs to the Roman Catholic Church, and some land was granted to local landlords by the Chinese Qing Empire and was recognised by the Portuguese Government as being under private ownership.

Thirdly, clauses about economic policies in the Hong Kong and Macau Basic Laws are divergent, mainly because of different geographical and economic conditions. Since 1962, the tourism industry and gambling have been essential to the economy in Macau. Gaming has a long history in Macau and is also a crucial pillar of the local economy. Gambling is also a useful factor in the HK economy but limited to horse racing.

Gambling, a very important part of the way of life in Macau, is manifested in the Basic Law.[61] Article 118 authorises gambling as follows. 'The Macao Special

Administrative Region shall, on its own make policies on tourism and recreation in the light of its overall interests'. It is legalised in Macau by government special permission, but this is not so in HK, where legalised gambling is very restricted. Also, the Basic Law provides that the Macau SAR shall, 'practice an independent taxation system' (article 106), and 'the taxation system for franchised businesses shall be otherwise prescribed by law' (article 107). This clause provides for the possibility that the legislature can make laws on gambling according to the Basic Law and it is an important factor in confirming the legality of gambling in Macau. Macau has never been an international financial Centre like Hong Kong. The Hong Kong Basic Law provides that the Government of the Hong Kong SAR shall 'provide an appropriate economic and legal environment for the maintenance of the status of Hong Kong as an international financial centre'.

Fourthly, there is also a difference in the clause about the Office of the Chief Executive. Hong Kong Basic Law provides that 'the Chief Executive of the Hong Kong Special Administrative Region shall be a Chinese citizen of not less than 40 years of age who is a permanent resident of the Region with no right of abode in any foreign country and has ordinarily resided in Hong Kong for a continuous period of not less than 20 years'. There is no similar provision in Macau Basic Law. This is attributed to the special historic background of Portugal-Macau relations. More than 100,000 Macau residents hold Portuguese passports; which means they have Portuguese nationality and the right to be permanent residents of Portugal. If not having the 'right of abode in any foreign country' was put as a precondition, more than a quarter of Macau residents would be deprived of the right to be elected. In every sense, the constitutional guarantee of, 'One Country Two Systems', given in the Macau Basic Law, as concretised by the preservation of original legislations, and the term 'Chinese language' – both concepts are part of the Basic Law – constitute the most important foundations for the formation of a unique legal culture. (Chinese means Putonghua and Cantonese in the MSAR and HKSAR.) It is also the greatest challenge for the Macau legal community in terms of its profession

Guarantees for the Chinese of Macau; Tough Conditions to get Residency

Those living in Macau are mainly Chinese, but there are many other groups. The Chinese in Macau speak Chinese (Cantonese and Putonghua) – albeit using the robotic pronunciation in both languages created after the 'new China' was built and appearing mostly in the CCTV News broadcast – Putonghua (the 'Deng accent'), or the 'local Chinese' accent (as the mode of speech of the Chinese of Macau is called). Irrespective of this, the Chinese of Macau certainly meet the criteria set forth by the 1980s' Hong Kong pop song, 'I am Chinese' (*Wo Shi Zhongguo Ren*). Chineseness is a cultural reality and an important concept studied in this book. Chinese people in Macau represent more than 90 per cent of Macau's population.

No one would challenge the view that Macau society is primarily made up of Chinese. It is quite evident. But it is still legitimate to raise some questions; for example: How can a Mainlander become a resident of Macau? He is of course Chinese. This question could be asked from both a synchronic perspective and a diachronic perspective. First, how did the Chinese currently living in Macau become residents of Macau?

Well, if a Chinese was born in Guangdong or Fujian fifty years ago or earlier, it is pretty easy for him/her to become Chinese of Macau. Many Chinese residents came to Macau just by chance. Otherwise, thanks to the reforms and the open door policy in the 1980s, if you had a relative who lived in Macau, then a letter from him was enough to bring the whole family to Macau to be reunited. It is not surprising that most of the relatively new Chinese residents of Macau are from Guangdong or Fujian Provinces.

As the population increased, it triggered a chain effect, sending property prices sky-rocketing, causing insufficiencies in social facilities, surpluses in the labour market, etc. These problems were solved only in the late 1980s.

Nowadays, Mainlanders can still become integrated into the Macau population by applying to reunite their families. The purpose is to create harmony within families by permitting parents and children to be reunited in Macau instead of remaining on different sides of the border. In fact, the number of families applying to be reunited in this way is far fewer than it was a few decades ago.

Up until the 2000s, some Mainlanders, if they already had a foreign residence in another country, could get Macau residency through investing over one million patacas in real estate. This is no longer possible. More recently, it has become less easy for a Mainlander to become a Chinese resident of Macau.

Why Do Mainlanders Want to Become Macau Residents?

In the 1970s and 1980s, Mainlanders wanted to become Chinese of Macau residents because the economic difference was great. People did not come to Macau because they had dreams about Macau in particular; simply, they wanted a place with a better living environment. Macau as such was not the attraction. Nowadays, however, the difference in living environment between the Mainland and Macau is not particularly great; nevertheless many Mainlanders (and others) would like to come to Macau, and are even willing to pay to come. From this, it appears that there are additional reasons.

Is it because Macau is a welfare city? – Traditional textbooks on immigration tell us that a welfare city is by nature exclusive and protective. It is said that a welfare state or a welfare city (if the city has boundaries comparable to those of a state) works well only when the dividing line between insiders and outsiders is clear. Since it is the insiders who contribute to the welfare, they should also be the beneficiaries of the welfare.[62] The existing members of such a community would certainly not like to share with new members what they already enjoy. If they did so, each of them would get a smaller share.

Good social welfare may be a point of attraction for people from Mainland China to come to Macau, but this is not the only attraction. Some would like to come because of the difference in the political systems; others may find the Macau economy attractive and would like to come and do business there.

The point is, Mainlanders are allowed to come to live in Macau as residents.

Why are Mainlanders not Free to Become Macau Residents?

As we have seen, the status of Macau is special because it is guaranteed in the Macau Basic Law. For some, such a guarantee is ideologically valuable; for many others, such a guarantee has no implication. For example, at the Olympic Games or Asian games, and in many organisations, Macau has its own delegation, distinguished from that of Mainland China. What does this mean? If an athlete wants to join the national team of China, he has to compete with the whole nation. If you want to join the Macau team, you compete with only half a million people. The same applies to education. Macau is open to the world and Mainland students have a high level of education; these students eagerly want to go to Macau or Hong Kong to join a university there.

The reason behind not allowing Mainlanders to reside in Macau is based on the assumption that many of them would come if they were allowed to do so. I believe this assumption to be true, as, at least at present, there is still a difference in income levels for the working classes as between the Mainland and Macau. If these income differences were to disappear, this assumption would be invalid. Such a day might not be far away.

If many Mainlanders wanted to come to Macau, Macau policy-makers would need to face the question of fairness, since the capacity of Macau is limited. The safest way to legislate for this would be to follow the history and tradition of Macau society. Only those who have a historic link with Macau society would be allowed to enter or stay as residents.

The Conditions for Chinese and Others to get Macau Residency are Tougher

I think we have made it quite clear that 'Chinese of Macau' is not a new nationality or citizenship. The Chinese of Macau are Chinese. The Macau Basic Law deliberately avoids using the concept of citizenship, for several reasons. First of all, Macau is not a sovereign state. Secondly, there are people of different nationalities living permanently in Macau; and, to respect the *status quo*, it would make no sense to exclude from this society those who are already members. Thirdly, as we have mentioned, not all Chinese are entitled to become residents of Macau.

However, the concept of residency adopted by the Macau Basic Law does perform one task which is traditionally inherent in the concept of citizenship: it distinguishes members from non-members of a certain community.

In the Roman Empire in ancient times and during the Middles Ages in Europe, being a recognised member of a society meant a great deal. Citizenship was sometimes the precondition for a person to be treated as a person under law ('*ius connubii, ius commercium*' defined the exclusive rights of Roman citizens), or at least it distinguished one class from another. For an originally non-member to become a member, he/she had to demonstrate his/her contribution to the society, for example by serving in the army or in the government, or by vowing subjection and loyalty to a master.[63] Nowadays, membership in a community does not confer as many privileges as it used to do, and correspondingly the price of membership is much lower, but we still distinguish members from non-members of a society.

Among those who are residents, the Macau Basic Law further distinguishes between permanent residents and non-permanent residents. For the attribution of permanent residency, the Macau Basic Law identifies three groups of people, namely: Chinese, Portuguese and 'others'. For each of these, the provisions of the Macau Basic Law mainly perform a filtering effect. Thus not all Chinese are entitled to Macau permanent residency, but only the following: 'Chinese citizens born in Macau before or after the establishment of the Macau Special Administrative Region and their children of Chinese nationality born outside Macau; Chinese citizens who have ordinarily resided in Macau for a continuous period of not less than seven years before or after the establishment of the Macau Special Administrative Region and their children of Chinese nationality born outside Macau after they have become permanent residents.'

In the above provision, the Macau Basic Law has adopted family ties, place of birth, and date and duration of prior Macau residency, as the criteria by which to determine the status of whether or not a Chinese citizen is or may become a 'permanent resident' of Macau. This rule is stricter than the one adopted in the Hong Kong Basic Law. However, the Portuguese are better protected in the MSAR than the British are in the HKSAR. It is believed that the drafters learned from what proved to be the 'defects' of the Hong Kong formula, and deliberately fine-tuned the Macau one accordingly. Similarly, not all Portuguese are entitled to Macau residency. Those who are so entitled are defined as follows: 'The Portuguese who were born in Macau and have taken Macau as their place of permanent residence before or after the establishment of the Macau Special Administrative Region; the Portuguese who have ordinarily resided in Macau for a continuous period of not less than seven years and have taken Macau as their place of permanent residence before or after the

establishment of the Macau Special Administrative Region
... shall have the right of abode in the MSAR and shall be
qualified to obtain permanent identity cards.' (Basic Law.
Article 24 (4-6))

To become 'permanent residents', persons who have
ordinarily resided in Macau for a continuous period of not
less than seven years'.

The conditions for Chinese and Portuguese to obtain
Macau residency are different from those for other persons.
In the case of those who are not Chinese or Portuguese, it
is possible only for those who have ordinarily resided in
Macau for a continuous period of not less than seven years
and have taken Macau as their place of permanent
residence before or after the establishment of the Macau
Special Administrative Region; persons under 18 years of
age born in Macau of those residents listed in the above
category before or after the establishment of the Macau
Special Administrative Region. The above mentioned
residents shall have the right of abode in the Macau
Special Administrative Region and shall be qualified to
obtain permanent identity cards. The non-permanent
residents of the Macau Special Administrative Region shall
be persons who are qualified to obtain Macau identity
cards in accordance with the laws of the Region but have
no right of abode.

Language and the Spirit of Macau's Legal System

Language

In principle, language is spontaneous. 'Way of Life' is
more elaborated. It means manner, life style and course of
conduct. *Sunna* is for example the way of life prescribed as
normative for Muslims. Obliging people to speak, in daily
life, a language that they do not know is painful for them.
Two thousand years ago, it is true, the Qin Dynasty
standardised the written language of its spacious empire.
But it did not unify the spoken language. Most probably
this achievement is and will remain unique. Many Western

linguists may have doubts, and may consider some Chinese 'dialects' to be different languages. Different languages may converge slowly; their structures and contents may change as time goes by. I believe in the power of Cantonese despite its changes over the time.

Another problem is that of an official language. The selection of an official language is a manifestation of power and policy. Of course, it is first linked to the habits of the people, but it may also be a consequence of a special political orientation. The case of the use of English as the main official language in Singapore is a good example.

The use of a language as an official language is inevitably linked to the sensitive question of the protection of certain ethnic groups, such as minorities or groups in weak political situations. In the modern world, for codified systems or constitutional documents, the critical moment is the entrenchment of a constitution.

Once a language is adopted by the Macau Basic Law as an official language, it immediately possesses the dignity of a 'constitutional good' or value protected by this constitutional document. For protection to be effective, a government needs to take adequate measures, and even promote them. On the individual level, it is certainly more complex to explain this psychological and legal process.

As far as Macau is concerned, the Basic Law provides, in Article 9, that: 'In addition to the Chinese language, Portuguese may also be used as an official language by the executive, legislative and judiciary authorities of the Macau Special Administrative Region.'

Not long after the Macau Basic Law was enacted, questions were raised in legal discussions as to whether the Portuguese or Chinese version should prevail if and when the two versions of a provision were found to diverge. The answer given by the authorities is clear: Chinese prevails. Xiao Weiyun explained it this way: 'The law of a certain country [China] provided clearly that the local organs of its Special Administrative Region can use a language of another country; this is already very flexible'... [64] Elsewhere, he stated: This 'stipulation demonstrated explicitly that both the Chinese language and Portuguese language can be used and have official status, on the other hand, the Chinese language occupy the principal place (sic) '.[65]

A very in-depth analysis with serious and sound argument was made by K.H. Kuan, who points out that doubts should be dealt with according to the rules of legal interpretation.[66]

The two opinions above do not necessarily contradict one another, but apply to representations of different stages of legal interpretation. Problems of semantics exist, not only in legal language, but in all types of language. The objective of legal interpretation is to clarify the meanings of certain legal norms through an approximately conventional process of reasoning. Therefore, whether a legal norm is written in one language or another, or in both, there is always the necessity to go through a process of legal interpretation. Any lawyer denying this process is directly denying his/her own professionalism and thus, the meaning of his own professional existence.

The problem, however, is that, for a bilingual system, since the 'construction' of one language is rarely comparable to that of another, we can never rule out the possibility that, after exhausting all the means of interpretation, a legal norm expressed in two different languages may render different meanings, both sensible. In this case, one must prevail over the other.

Of course, after going through the whole process of interpretation, if the doubt is not solved, then it must be a very special one. In fact, such doubts have never arisen throughout the short legal history of the MSAR. Many so-called conflicts can easily be solved within the process of interpretation itself. Therefore, we may even conclude that the tentative question of whether the Chinese or Portuguese version of the law should prevail is purely hypothetical, and make sense only at the theoretical level.

The true problem attached to the discourse of an official language is another: the existence of two official languages, namely Chinese and Portuguese. As most of the Portuguese authors involved in creating the Portuguese version of the Basic Law like to put it, the problem is that of bilingualism itself. The only question remaining is just how to maintain or promote bilingualism.

As generally understood, maintaining a bilingual legal and administrative system is not easy. As the President of the Macau Lawyers' Association has accurately pointed out, maintaining such a system is not free of charge. It really costs a lot'.[67]

However, we should never forget that *bilingualism is a solemn promise of the Macau Basic Law to its own residents.* If we go back to the above-cited Article 9, and even to the so-called most authoritative interpretation of this provision, we can easily notice that there is no doubt at all about whether bilingualism should be maintained.

Although many articles written in the Chinese language have cast doubt on the Portuguese legal culture, rarely any of them openly deny that bilingualism is guaranteed by the Basic Law. Much data is invoked to support the argument that Portuguese is not a common language in Macau. For example: more than 90 per cent of the Macau population is Chinese and most of the Chinese do not speak or read the Portuguese language. It is a proof that the Portuguese were clever to protect their language so well. However, the commercial world works with Chinese or English, and foreign investors favour the use of English.[68]

No matter how logical or illogical these and other arguments may be, they have no direct relation to bilingualism. The legitimate discourse confirms the importance of a constitutional document. Questioning a value guaranteed by such a document implies a proposal for the amendment of the Macau Basic Law, specifically to its Article 9.

Now, hypothetically, we may also discuss whether such a proposal for amendment prevails.

It is of course true that, at the time when Macau was under Portuguese administration, the only official language admitted was Portuguese. As a result, the majority of the population had to pay a high price for legal and public services. However, after the handover, all those who fulfil the requirements set forth in Article 24 of the Macau Basic Law are members of Macau society, whether they are of Portuguese, Chinese, or any other origin. At the moment of handover, a considerable number of residents used only Portuguese as their daily language. The elaboration of the Macau Basic Law is comparable to a constitutional entrenchment, and this means that we are able to treat residents of Portuguese origin well. By allowing Portuguese to continue as an official language after the handover, the Central Government demonstrated its determination to support and implement the One Country Two Systems policy. Of course, the selection of Portuguese as an official language was made having regard to the history and reality of Macau. It was more than a political decision. In my view, it was a brilliant decision. This is because the Portuguese language – in particular because it is the language of Brazil, maintains a high position among other key languages of the world such as English and Chinese.

Most important of all, although a bilingual society does bear a cost for its bilingualism, bilingualism does not prejudice different components within such a society. Admitting Portuguese as an official language has not suppressed in any way whatsoever the use of Chinese as an official language. Bilingualism im Macau in no way obliges a Chinese to use Portuguese in the public sector, but merely provides a chance for those who want to use Portuguese to do so. Nowadays, the population structure has not changed much, although the population has grown. We believe those who propose an amendment of the Basic Law should study the real significance of it more carefully.

The Spirit of Macau's Legal System

Around the 1980s, in linguistics, grammaticalisation created grammatical forms to legitimate a study. Language is part of a way of life, and law is the grammaticalisation of a core part of our discourse to create a legitimate discourse.

Being a discourse vested with the cloak of 'legitimacy', obviously the discourse itself has to follow certain rules of reasoning.

The Basic Law created the framework of a legal system, but it is not in itself the whole of the legal system – it is ordinary law that provides the details, and fills up the various institutions. In modern times the legislative power is a component part of the sovereignty of a country and it writes the texts, but it is the interests and the practice behind them that determine the meanings of those texts.

Ideologically, legal institutions have evolved very slowly, through accumulation. This is why some legal scholars claim that habits and customs are the real source of Law.

Nevertheless, for a transplanted legal system (such as Macau's), all these theories about the real source of law, as well as the legitimate process of law, seem not to apply. An imposed transplant of law into a community, which has little to do with the community from which the transplanted law emerged, is of course painful. It occurs only in extreme circumstances, such as the case when the sovereignty of a nation is violated, normally through the use of force, or through intimidation by the threat of armed force. Nevertheless, once a transplanted law has taken root in a society, its removal may be at least as painful as the implantation, since a transplanted law gradually becomes a habit as part of the life of the society into which it has been transplanted. The whole bureaucracy of government is organised according to this law. Businessmen carry on their business according to this law, drafting contracts, buying property and issuing cheques. Relations between employees and employers are also regulated by such a transplanted law.

Ordinary people are also involved: they register their marriages and property, as well as the birth of their children. Therefore, although a transplanted legal system is normally resisted at the beginning, after some time it becomes accepted. The Macau legal system before the handover was such an imposed transplant.[69]

When the drafters of the Basic Law were confronted with the contemporary situation, they made a decision which I consider correct. The Macau Basic Law, in Article 8, provides that:

> 'The laws, decrees, administrative regulations and other normative acts previously in force in Macau shall be maintained, except for any that contravenes this law, or subject to any amendment by the legislature or other relevant organs of the MSAR in accordance with legal procedures'. The reason for maintaining these normative acts is obviously to maintain the stability of the society'.[70]

Maintaining the legal text alone would not be sufficient to keep Macau society stable. A legal system is only stable when the application of law is stable, when people can form their expectations through the services of legal professionals. At this point, the transplant of law necessarily involves the transplant of a legal culture. 'For a jurisdiction built upon legal transplant, existing legal rules and legal theories should be preserved unless they are proven to be not suitable for the society or not corresponding to the common norms of the human society.'[71]

Nevertheless, the adverse effects of the transplantation of the legal system continue longer than people might expect, especially as the legal language is isolated from the ordinary Chinese population.

Therefore, more than one decade after the handover, Macau society is still constantly criticising the inherited system as falling behind social development, as it is not tailor-made and thus not best suited to the life of local society. Since 1999, the former Portuguese-drafted Law – particularly the Civil Code, Penal Code, Commercial Code, Code of Civil Procedure, Code of Criminal Procedure – has been transformed and admitted through proper legislative process, and thus has entered into the Law of Macau.

Over the past decade, Law in Portugal itself has been steadily developed. It is in the hands of the Macau people themselves to tailor Macau Law. We just need the will and the technique to do so. Of course, it is possible that, although in Macau we start from a position similar to that in Portugal, the results of our work may produce totally different results from those achieved there.

In Hong Kong, the language barrier was basically removed and the legal system gained a kind of conviction. The main reason is the complete and exact translation of the British Law of Hong Kong into Chinese. This is not the case in Macau.

Economy, society and welfare which were promoted by the Nobel Prize economist and sociologist, Gunnar Myrdal (1898-1987), already mentioned in this chapter, are also an important concern for all the people of the MSAR in particular when inflation is high, as in 2011.

CHAPTER THREE

SOCIETY AND ECONOMY

My methodology is constantly to check society against the yard-stick of the economy. David Yang – a specialist of civil society in Taiwan and the Mainland – considers the institutional context of Mainland China under the following headings: the state, the business elite and the working class.[72] As for the MSA, it could be considered under the following headings: local government, the gaming industry, the elite and the working class. The present book considers identity, local cultures and associations (Chapter Four). Macau is small and so it is probably easier to apply suggestions and make things better for society than in Hong Kong. Hong Kong continues to be an essential reference for Chinese of Macau and around 40 per cent of them have family link there.

Macau has almost no industry other than its thirty-four casinos. The elite are difficult to define, but the working class exists. All types of economic activities are present in Macau. Fishermen and farmer exist, although they are few. In 1986, two hundred peasant households were cultivating in total around ten hectares (150 *mu*), shared among them. Since 1999, very few of them have remained residents of the MSAR,[73] but in 2011 there is still an association of farmers and ex-farmers (the *Nongye Hequnshe*). This association is currently active in the northern district, where many of the remaining farming families are living. The president, She Shao Feng, with the assistance of a new board elected in 2010, wants to develop this association.[74] During my almost daily brisk climb to Guia (Songshan 松山), I often meet a farmer who produces vegetables for his own family, and take a look at his small plantation of banana trees. The person is not a real peasant-farmer, but to me he is. He has not joined the farmers' association, but was very interested to discuss its achievements.

In 1940 there were around 20,000 fishermen, but their number had decreased to 15,000 by 1984, and many of these moved with their boats to Zhuhai after the handover of Macau to China in December 1999. Others acquired a flat in Macau, and are no longer fishermen. Their children are better educated than those of previous generations. Consequently, their parents do not want their children to continue to be Tanka: – this term is much more than the name of a profession but an ethnonym which has become a disappearing identity. However, those who are still resident in Macau meet together regularly in their association (*Yumin Huzhuhui*).

In 2012, the condition of the Tanka fishermen became rather difficult despite assistance from the MSAR Government. There were fewer fish in the sea and the price of fuel became very expensive. Official registration records show 160 fishing boats, but in reality it seems that the number in the Interior Port decreased to 116. The year previously, 2011, twenty-eight fishermen asked for financial assistance from the Development Fund for Fishermen. This fund distributed MOP 29 million during the period 2007 and 2011.[75]

I have no power and the following remarks are just guidelines. Social harmony creates more opportunities for the whole world and for the people of a same nation living peacefully in mutual trust. It also seeks to establish a new century of peace, preventing wars and if possible poverty, to reach finally a sustainable balance of social groups and ethnicities. The aim is to avoid the 'disharmony of modern society' and the 'destruction of family' (UN Special Session on Childhood, 10 May 2002).[76]

In Macau, during the period from 1980 to 2000, 'mobility' and 'new society' have become sociological concepts applicable to Mainland Chinese with the right to be residents in the enclave.[77] Although the MSAR is small, in the twenty-first century it is evident that more Mainlanders will become permanent residents of Macau. The drastic economic change in Macau which took place between 2000 and 2010 has had a huge impact on Chinese of Macau. With the beginning of what is likely to be the long-term relative economic decline of Western countries, we may ask how Macau and its small society may contribute to help China to become more successful in a world that is becoming increasingly 'globalised'.[78] Like the increasing numbers of tourists, some Chinese of Macau may be fascinated by the number of casinos, the beauty and magnificence of some of them, and consequently may be lured to gamble. In 2012, the economy is given priority, but the particularly quiet society of the MSAR needs the attention of policy makers. The monopolistic economy cannot be ignored – it must be underpinned by social stability.

Social Harmony

The development of cultural affairs and social welfare are necessary but not sufficient conditions for social stability. Plato and other Greek philosophers are still important, but in the twenty-first century, the Chinese Government's stated philosophy is to promote the well-being of society and social 'harmony'. The following definition from the *Macmillan Dictionary* seems closer to what modern China wants to have: 'A situation in which people live and work well with each other'. Marcel Granet goes further and in particular in relation to the ancestor cult notes the necessary 'symbolic and moral value' of the rites of filial piety (孝 *xiao*) and an ancient and traditional 'correct harmony' (l'harmonie juste).[79]

One may ask if the giving of rewards may lead to social stability. Decorations are instruments awarded to persons of outstanding merit. To boost the elite, on 28 February 2011, Chief Executive Chui Sai On awarded the following official decorations:

To the former Chief Executive, Ho Hau Wah, Grand Lotus; to Io Hong Meng, Silver Lotus.

Medals of Merit were awarded to: Vong Hin Fai and Lai Ieng Kit, for the Professions; Wong Pan Seng, Lou Cheok Weng and J. Tang Kuan Meng, for Industry and Commerce; Ms Ho Sio Kam, Cheong Yung Sau, Man Kuan and T. Kwan Kit Mui, Education; Chan Wai Fai and Ms Lio Chi Heng, Culture, in particular, Sport: Lam Fai Hong, Ma Iao Hang and Mok Kuok Heng.

The Managing Director of the Casino Venetian, Antonio Ferreira, received the Grand Lotus.

In February 2012, Ms Ho Teng Iat (*see Chapter Four*) and Mr Wan Chun received the Silver Lotus. In total, thirty-eight persons received a decoration from Chief Executive Chui. The MSAR method of stabilising society has similarities to that of the new nation of East Timor, which was also under Portuguese rule for many centuries. Today, both the MSAR administration and the Government of East Timor favour social welfare associated with grants to the population. Although an ex-editor of the *Va Kio* newspaper thinks that this does not promote creativity and dynamism for the progress of society, all permanent residents of Macau received MOP 7,000 in 2011. Residents over sixty years of age had this sum paid into their bank accounts in January. In April 2009 the Chief Executive of Hong Kong, Donald Tsang, said 'Macau has Macau's way, while we have our way'; but in March 2011 Hong Kong's leaders copied the MSAR. Each HKSAR permanent resident was offered HKD 6,000. Macau's permanent residents will receive MOP 7,000 in 2012.

In January 2011, the question of disabled persons was raised. The four degrees of disability are, according to new administrative regulation 3/2011: mild, moderate, severe and profound.[80] The Social Welfare Bureau is considering giving such persons an annual subsidy of between MOP 6,000 to MOP 12,000. If this subsidy is approved, registration cards will be issued and re-checked each year. Applications to receive this subsidy were invited from 11 March 2011, but this question has not yet been completely resolved. The MSAR Government prefers to grant a new allowance of MOP 6,200, on certain conditions that are not yet well defined. Member of the Executive Council of the MSAR, Leong Heng Teng, used the term 'social reinsertion' concerning the question of invalidity. This probably means that he wants to help such persons to find a job.

I have no power and the following remarks are just guidelines. Social harmony creates more opportunities for the whole world and for the people of a same nation living peacefully in mutual trust. It also seeks to establish a new century of peace, preventing wars and if possible poverty, to reach finally a sustainable balance of social groups and ethnicities. The aim is to avoid the 'disharmony of modern society' and the 'destruction of family' (UN Special Session on Childhood, 10 May 2002).[81]

In Macau, during the period from 1980 to 2000, 'mobility' and 'new society' have become sociological concepts applicable to Mainland Chinese with the right to be residents in the enclave.[82] Although the MSAR is small, in the twenty-first century it is evident that more Mainlanders will become permanent residents of Macau. The drastic economic change in Macau which took place between 2000 and 2010 has had a huge impact on Macau Chinese. With the beginning of what is likely to be the long-term relative economic decline of Western countries, we may ask how Macau and its small society may contribute to help China to become more successful in a world that is becoming increasingly 'globalised'.[83] Like the increasing numbers of tourists, some Chinese of Macau may be fascinated by the number of casinos, the beauty and magnificence of some of them, and consequently may be lured to gamble. In 2012, the economy is given priority, but the particularly quiet society of the MSAR needs the attention of policy makers.

In December 2010, according to a report in the *Macau Daily News*, Macau ranked 130th in 'quality of life' worldwide among some two hundred countries. However, the Chinese of Macau and other Macau residents rarely mobilise against the MSAR Government. Related to this point, Xiong notes the 'immature civil society' of Mainland China. The MSAR is a civil society classified between the Mainland and HKSAR.[84] On 20 December 2010, at the Square Carlos da Maia (*Sanzhan Deng*) between 5pm and 7pm, many young female Indonesian domestic helpers, wearing red scarves, peacefully danced to prove that foreign workers are also helpful in the MSAR. Their goal, confirmed by a limited number of complaints in 2011, was to attract the attention of the Secretary for Economy and Finance, Francis Tam Pak Yuen (Tan Bo Yuan) who said: 'The government authorises the hiring of foreign workers. The interest of the local workers is also important. The dynamic growth of the economy cannot be forgotten.'[85]

Thus, although it is possible to increase the number of foreign workers, there is a concern about this.

In January 2011, Fanny Vong wrote in the *Macau Daily News Times* that local residents – meaning mainly the Chinese of Macau – should be prepared to work hard. However, she also wrote: 'Let the market work', and allow imported workers to return home when they are no longer required. Is this a way of saying 'make them' return to their country of origin? She advocated that employers should have a better strategy for attracting local staff. Near Horta e Costa – *Go-si-tak* in Cantonese – there is a Gurkha Agency that hires workers and security guards. We would have expected to see at least one Nepali in the agency, but all the staff are Chinese and Filipino. Briefly, others are taking advantage of these Nepalis.

America also wants to protect its citizens. Four thousand US citizens are currently living in the MSAR. The US Consul General for Hong Kong and Macau, Stephen Young, acknowledged a need for more transparent rules on the hiring of non-local labour during a press conference with Macau's media. The diplomat also advised that 'a flexible labour policy will be essential to diversify the economy'.[86] It is evident that economic diversification was a difficult goal to reach during the past Portuguese sovereignty, but it is currently more complicated with a 'monopolistic dominance' of the gaming industry.

Unqualified workers, at lower labour cost, constitute a particular example concerning employment. However, foreign imported employees with higher education may provide learning opportunities for local labour that sometimes cannot be provided by Macau residents.[87] With the opening of new casinos and new projects, there are still opportunities for outsiders to come to work in Macau. Local agencies are interested in recruiting outsiders because their labour can assure superior profits to those otherwise available from the recruitment of Chinese of Macau. This seems to be because the outsiders will accept lower wages. The MSAR Government, however, would like more transparency concerning the training of workers and their employment. The main problems for this are Macau's limited population and the difficulty of rapidly upgrading education. The key point is that Mainland China can play a crucial role, as there are still workers available from Mainland China. However, the period 2010-2011 was a turning point. Recently, Mainland workers have demanded increased salaries, and they now have more power. Recently events in Shenzhen show that the workers are stronger. This happens, in particular, when their boss is not a Mainlander.

To understand the question of the importation of workers, let us look at the 'visitors'. Since the handover, more Mainlanders are entering the MSAR each year. The Macau-Gongbei-Zhuhai border is a problem for the mobility necessary for mass tourism in China. In 1998, 300,000 visitors entered during the four days of the Chinese New Year.[88] On average, in 2010, twenty thousand more persons crossed this border daily than in 2009. The total for the year was six million higher than it was in 2009. In December 2010, the *Aomen Ribao* reported a record of more than 240,000 entries per day across the border on the busiest days. This clearly shows a considerable increase in mass tourism between 1998 and 2010. On the first of January 2011, 260,000 crossed the border between Gongbei-Zhuhai and Macau, a figure equivalent to half of the total population of the MSAR. During the first three days of January 2011, 780,000 crossed this border (*Gwanngaap* in Cantonese). This seems to be the highest number to date.[89]

For the ten first months of 2011, 23 million 'visitors' entered Macau.[90] In 2011, official statistics registered 28 million visitor-entries in one year. Fifty-eight per cent (58 per cent) – including 36 per cent individually – were from the Mainland, a total increase of 12 per cent over the previous year. Entries from Hong Kong represented 26 per cent, and from Taiwan, fewer than four per cent.[91] Some newspapers announced even higher numbers of entries.[92]

It is interesting to note that, during the Chinese New Year holiday of 2010, groups of people were mobilised to try to change the orientation of certain reforms. The police forbade a demonstration in the Avenue Horta e Costa (Go-si-tak), probably because it is densely populated. In the Chinese newspapers, such as *Aomen Ribao,* cartoons were published regarding the lack of people on that key artery, which usually carries a lot of traffic, as there was nobody there on that day.

Macau is not Hong Kong, and it is always difficult to mobilise demonstrators against the Government in Macau. However, this does not diminish the necessity of finding a relatively competent and well-trained labour force, and this is why the workers' association, 'Forca dos Operais', still has a certain popularity.

In the afternoon of 20 December 2010, on the anniversary of the handover, another lively mobilisation occurred at the Taipa Stadium. However, the 2010 mobilisation was much less ceremonial than that in 2009, when President Hu Jingtao attended. On 19 December

2011, I decided that the next day I would simply go to the Flag Ceremony at 8am. (*See Photograph 15.*) A few minutes after this ceremony, the Chief Executive, Chui Sai On, left his position at the centre of the high platform and went down to ground level to inspect the military police troops. The music team (including only one female musician) participated also in this annual event. I had the chance to see many high ranking officials and to salute MSAR Executive Council Member, Leong Heng Teng, as well as the Macau and Hong Kong General Consul of Portugal, Manuel Carvalho. However, the Chief Executive left by a secure exit, and I had no opportunity to see him close to.

To be creative is necessary and to make the handover anniversary a joyful occasion, a 'Latin Parade' took place in front of the main Public Library in Tap Seac Square. I myself went there at 5.30pm. The crowd was so big that I was unable to see any member of the Sino Latin Foundation, in particular its President, Gary Ngai (Wei Mei Chang), who had advised me to attend this important event.

Edilson Almeida and his Brazilian Samba team made one of the most popular presentations during this Latin Parade. The flame-swallowing demonstration by Master Eddy (as Edison Almeida is often called) was particularly spectacular. He trained hard in this art for three years in Sao Paulo and it took him more than a year to become really impressive and secure. As for his main art, music, however, it took him many more years before he was recognised as a master. He is mainly a musician, but his 'Capoeira' classes are famous in Macau, and in Guangzhou as well. The Brazilian star Cris and her partners, two other beauties, were present at this festival. This parade was more joyful than the commemoration of the handover in 2010 in the Taipa Stadium. Great numbers of the Chinese of Macau attended the event.

Brazil is essential to the opening-up of Macau and for its links with the Latin world. The Brazilian martial art,

Capoeira, is an intangible part of Brazilian cultural heritage. In Macau it is taught by the already-mentioned Edison Almeida (Master Eddy). Capoeira helps to create a positive community spirit and can also promote music (and, in this respect, is superior to the martial art, karate). It is also a vehicle for the Portuguese language, an official language in Macau, and a cultural mediator to improve the relationship of the MSAR with Brazil. Macau needs to improve popular links like this, to promote the value of its long historical past, and to be more connected to the global world.

Social stability also has to be considered. Macau cannot afford instability. Society and the economy need to be in harmony. A good hope at the beginning of the 2012 Lunar New Year is that creativity will be upgraded in the MSAR, as Dr Pansy Ho also wishes. Creativity is also on the agenda of the architect Thomas Daniell. This professor at São José University believes in innovative urban planning. His initiative will certainly transform the MSAR, make prouder the Chinese of Macau (who do not want to be expelled when new planning ideas emerge – as happened in the case of the northwestern district of the Macau Peninsula, Qingzhou-Ilha Verde), will attract more businessmen, and in particular promote culture in a challenging manner (a long-standing dream of the Portuguese). It is still a difficult cultural and economic task for the Chief Executive Fernando Chui, limited by land grants, space and other constraints.

Between 1962 and 1999, Macau's gaming industry was less prosperous. Most of the huge investment came in the 2000s. In 2011, the gaming industry became really prosperous despite a slight slowdown at the end of the year, but inflation continues to be a tough issue.

Inflation is now running at over ten per cent
To look at the day-by-day life of the Chinese of Macau is also important. This is why from a rather macro-economic point of view this paragraph is centred on unemployment

and inflation. The issues of harmony and employment were brought up during the ceremony of the anniversary of the handover, in December 2010. For this year (as well as for the first six months of 2011), the unemployment rate in the MSAR was 2.7 per cent, lower than most of the annual rates for the years 1994 through 2010. Observing this low rate – one of the lowest of Asia – is reassuring for society. In the first six months of 2011, the labour force participation rate was rather high – 71.6 per cent.[93] However, taking youth employment as a barometer of the evolution of society and economy, the younger Chinese generations are of crucial importance for the future of Chinese of Macau. The International Labour Organization (ILO) in Macau has noted a high unemployment rate among young people between the ages of twenty and thirty, who are twice more likely than others to be unemployed.[94] This highlights a deficiency of the MSAR administration, as young people are a key driving force of the economy, representing 35 per cent of the total number in employment in 2009.

Industrial production and services in Macau are also in a dramatic situation. The director of the Association for the Promotion of the Economy in Macau (APEM), Ieong Tou Hong, recently mentioned the risks involved in excessive dependence on a unique gaming industry.[95] However, in November 2011, during his 2012 policy address at the Legislative Assembly, the Secretary for Economy and Finance was optimistic concerning unemployment, which was stable at 2.6 per cent.[96] In May 2011, Macau's youth unemployment was 6.7 per cent, and Ms Ella Lei Cheng I of the Federation of Trade Unions urged the MSAR Government to strengthen, in particular, vocational training. On 14 September 2012, during his talk at the Hotel Sofitel, Deputy Coutinho mentioned clearly that he does not trust the too optimistic statistics concerning young people in particular. The MSAR needs more technical schools and universities. Macau also needs to upgrade tertiary education and develop the teaching of Western medicine. As for the latter, the Macau Polytechnic Institute has a Faculty of Medicine in Macau, but this is unique. The fact that the first President of the Chinese Republic, Sun Yat-sen (Zhongshan), after completing his medical training at the Hong Kong College of Medicine for Chinese, started his medical career in Kiang Wu, in Macau, can provide inspiration to young people.

The young people of Macau would also certainly benefit from further expansion of the services industry. They are young and flexible, but they should not be too demanding about salary when entering the job market. A degree from a university in Macau is not enough. Experience is very important, and work experience needs time to be acquired. In December 2011, during my second interview with Madam Ho Teng Iat, a very important leader, I was surprised at her optimism concerning youth employment in the MSAR.

To stabilise society, the smooth employment of young people is crucial. Wong Kuai Leng, head of the Youth Federation of Trade Unions, hopes that the MSAR Government will follow the Federation's proposal to launch 'Employment Training'; as a university degree in itself is often insufficient to apply successfully for a good job. Employment training could particularly help in the hospitality and gaming industries.

In the context of this question of employment, it is relevant to note that, while large families were numerous in Macau before the Cultural Revolution (1966-1974), in the MSAR, families with only two children are currently common, so there is hope to stabilise Macau society. However, in a dangerously inflationary world, young people and their employment continue to be a key point.

The question of economic diversification was briefly mentioned by Paulo Azevedo, publisher of *Macau Business*, on 18 January 2012, during a conference of the France-Macau Business Association. This journalist and editor proposed to develop the hospitality industry; but this is also a part of the gaming industry. [97]

Given the current period of world crisis, the wise warning, given by the Director of APEM, Ieong Tou Hong, about the risk involved in the fact that Macau has in effect a single industry – gaming – should be seriously considered. Gaming was prosperous in 2011, but the question of economic diversification remains a nightmare, as it was in the past for the last Portuguese Governor, General Rocha Vieira. This is probably the reason why the General wanted so much to develop the global lusophone network.

Diversification of Macau's economy remains a key question. So, in 2009 also, in Beijing, we may imagine that, Politburo members and General Rocha Vieira, when discussing the transfer of power to the new Chief Executive, Chui Sai On, also discussed this main socio-economic problem – diversification of the economy. General Rocha Vieira was strongly for economic diversification, and this is another less convincing reason why he had frequent meetings with the Governor of Hong Kong in Macau.

Poverty is another major cause of instability in society, and the MSAR Government helps the poorest permanent residents. At present, Macau residents receive a yearly sum for the education of their children and other essential areas of welfare for children.

Stabilising prices is a top priority in China, but may be more difficult in Macau, as it is so dependent upon the Mainland. To stabilise society, it is necessary to control inflation. This difficult question is linked to the dominant role of China, an economic giant sometimes shrunk by inflation. In 2010, the official inflation rate of 2.8 per cent seemed too optimistic.[98] In 2011, inflation was high. For example, I noticed that the price of the small Portuguese loaf of bread (*pão*) had increased by 20 per cent. On 5 January 2011 the price was MOP 2.50 in the Avenida do Ouvidor Arriaga (*Yalianfang Damalu*), a middle-class location. The more expensive (MOP 3.5) round loaf of bread lost both its shape and weight, and the price of this loaf of bread reached MOP 5.5 during the 2011 Chinese New Year. In December 2010 this shop produced perhaps the tastiest bread in the whole peninsula; so consumers were seduced and finally bought at this price. It was not the case in March 2011, when the wheat flour used was inferior compared to December 2010 and January 2011. In early 2012, the minimum price for this type of bread in the bakeries of Macau was MOP 3.8, but MOP 4 – or more – was common.

At the end of December 2010, the price of the major newspaper, the *Aomen Ribao* (ARB), increased by 33 per cent, from three to four patacas. By mid-February 2011, the same newspaper cost five patacas (MOP). At the new ARB head office, if you want to buy a newspaper from a previous day, the price is MOP 10 per copy. Demonstrably, in the MSAR, inflation does exist, and it hits the poorest first.

On 16 February 2011, under the front-page caption, 'January inflation figure beats forecast', the important Beijing-based English-language daily newspaper *China Daily*, also carried this story. Over the previous year, food prices had surged by 10.3 per cent across China, and prices in Macau had increased as well. Inflation in Macau in fact exceeds inflation on the Mainland. In early January 2011, some restaurants increased their prices by ten to twenty per cent. The prices of clothing, food and living expenses were also rocketing, and some residents felt depressed. In November 2010, the Statistics Department noted a 2.5 per cent increase in the consumer index over the month of October. Petrol prices at the pump increased strikingly.[99] This was similar to the situation in Hong Kong where, in February 2011, the *South China Morning Post* reported a current annual inflation rate close to 11 per cent.

Inflation is a *leitmotiv*. During the last quarter of 2010 consumer confidence was decreasing.[100] One day before Chinese New Year, 3 February 2011, the lowest price for ten good eggs increased by ten per cent, from MOP 10 to MOP 11. In the past, after this festive period, the price returned to its normal price, but this was not the case in 2011. Early in 2012, the price of hot tea aboard turbojets plying between Macau and Hong Kong increased similarly by thirty-three per cent.

The Macau Tourist Price Index (TPI) is an economic indicator which reflects the changes in the price of goods and services in Macau. More precisely, for the fourth quarter of 2011, the TPI, according to MSAR Government Statistics, increased by nineteen per cent year-on-year: Restaurant Services increased by nineteen per cent, Accommodation increased by 35 per cent and Miscellaneous Goods by 14 per cent. For the whole year of 2011, the TPI for Restaurant Services increased by 11 per cent, Accommodation increased by than 35 per cent, Miscellaneous Goods by 19 per cent, and Food by 12 per cent.[101]

This is why Leong Heng Teng (please see his biography in Chapter One) announced a 5.08 per cent increase in the salaries of civil servants in February 2011.[102] The President of the third Standing Committee of the Legislative Assembly, Cheong Chi Keong, announced that this pay rise would add an additional MOP 539 million to MSAR Government spending. The 2011 Budget Plan would need an increase of MOP 750 million to maintain a basic reserve of one and a half times the total estimated expenditures.[103]

Inflation is a problem of survival for the poorest. Hong Kong reported inflation of three per cent per month at the end of 2010, and sometimes the increase in food prices was even higher.[104] However, at the end of 2010 in Macau, both Portuguese and English newspapers timidly announced only 2.8 per cent inflation for the entire year.[105] However, a more than ten per cent yearly increase in food prices was expected. In 2011 this proved correct. It seems useful to mention that in early January 2012 the price for a pound of tangerines in Guangzhou (2.5 RMB – *Renminbi*) is five times cheaper that in Macau.

The economist Albano Martins forecast a timid 8.2 per cent inflation rate for 2011 in the MSAR – a great deal higher than previous food increases in 2010.[106] He spoke of the 'cumulative processes' involved in the price index and of 'imported' inflation, but without quoting sources. Based on my own field research, it seemed more realistic to predict inflation of more than 10 per cent in 2011, and this became a fact in January 2012. The statistics mentioned above demonstrate that my previsions about inflation for the year 2011, sent in March 2011 to the Macau Foundation, were close to the reality.

The MSAR Government has been wise to watch carefully the weakness of the world economic and financial system, and this raises the question of necessary economic reforms. More closely, in the MSAR the question of housing is fundamental for the Chinese of Macau and other permanent residents, so let us start with a particular case, the Qingzhou area.

Housing and city planning.
Case study, Ilha Verde (青洲 *Qingzhou*)
The question of housing in the northwestern suburb of Qingzhou was the key social question at the end of 2010. In Qingzhou many buildings were demolished. The small groceries there disappeared at that time, so it was difficult for Chinese of Macau to buy what are for them the most important eatable items; rice, bread and tea.

The following facts are more disturbing. In 2010 and 2011, some residents were alleged to have been attacked by workers who wanted to continue their demolition work in the northwestern Bairro (district) of Ilha Verde (Qingzhou). The residents evidently did not want to be relocated in inconvenient or faraway places by the MSAR Government and did not like to face the stress of being obliged to leave their homes suddenly. This did happen in Qingzhou. In early January 2011, it seemed that only five houses made of wood were still standing. On the fourth of that month, out of 1,400 wooden shacks, only three remained and it was no longer possible to use them as dwellings.[107] All the others were said to have been demolished.[108] Qingzhou residents are said to have been relocated by the MSAR Government, or to have been sufficiently well-off to have had access to other property. On the first day of Chinese New Year 2011, I went there with my assistant to check if this information was correct. We found that, in Qingzhou, more than five wooden houses remained. In fact, we photographed more than five such houses that day, on the hill above the Canal of Ducks (*Yayong he*), between Zhuhai and Ilha Verde.

Of course it is more difficult to build on this hill, but there are still pieces of land available in Qingzhou and one does not have to compete with MGM or the *Sociedade de Jogo de Macau* to purchase them. Cotai in Coloane is unique in Macau in that it is possible to build and give less trouble to existing residents. Interestingly, following an interview on Bloomberg TV in mid-July 2011, one of the directors of Casino Wynn confirmed that the competition was becoming more Chinese. It is a fact that the American-owned Sands Casino did experience, for a short time, difficulty in purchasing land in Coloane and the Cota area. This can be explained by a study of the importance of the Chinese concept *guanxi* (relationships) and the lack of knowledge of local culture in some Western companies. The former Casino Sands manager (who did have good contacts) was fired, so Sands was out of the competition in Cotai for a while and could not buy plots of land in this open area of Macau. All this means that the pressure to find land is high; this is equally true for the MSAR Government. Consequently also, for its development the University of Macau have to move to Hengqin Island in 2012 and 2013.

One of the reasons for the restructuring of Qinzhou is to find space. Early in 2011, the MSAR Government was preparing a Grand Plan to reassure the population of Qingzhou. Certainly, the creation of a nursery by the Women's General Association of Macau and the planned improvement of the Health Centre of Qingzhou are priorities. Two deputies of the Legislative Assembly, José Chui Sai Peng (Cui Shi Ping) and Ho (He Run Sheng) supported the MSAR Government plan, although it was not yet fully detailed.[109] Housing prices are too high, so the MSAR Government is working hard to try to find cheap land. The restructuring of Qingzhou is to the fore.

Early in January 2011, a taxi driver, Mr Ho, said in a conversation with the author that he approved the MSAR Government plan, which 'cleans the city and gives a better aspect to a remote part of Macau'. However, some shack-dwellers have claimed that the demolition of their homes was carried out without legal permission.

Deputy Ng Kuok Cheong stated that new projects were expected elsewhere in similar city areas. Macau pro-democrats wanted details about such projects in the north of the Peninsula and Barra district (Mazu). They were right to ask questions: in 2012 many residents and many of those applying to be residents in social housing are not happy to move into small appartments which closely face other buildings. They do not want to be moved without being asked what they want. Perhaps one hundred plots of land were taken back by the MSAR Government from the developers who wanted to be involved in Qingzhou and elsewhere. In particular, Deputy Ng wanted to increase political pressure to avoid further developments like that in Qingzhou.[110] Early in 2012, the MSAR Government announced that it will sell cheap property in Taipa.

Social housing is a big question in Macau. The older people who were relocated to Qingzhou over the last six months of 2010 were not satisfied.[111] Hua Rong and Shui Seng, who had been relocated to the northern part of Macau, to the Madam Robinson Building in Areia Preta (*Haksa Wan*), finally had the good fortune, to be relocated within Qingzhou. However, there was a fire on the twenty-fifth floor of their building and they were transferred to the fourteenth floor. It was equipped with a fire alarm and security protection. Yet they had further complaints: they found that there were no toilets on the fourteenth floor.

They believed that they were isolated in Qingzhou, which, according to them, lacked frequent buses going to places such as Sao Januario Hospital. They also complained about the current lack of green spaces, sports grounds and shops. They politely asked the MSAR Government to find solutions to their problems.

In March 2011, Chief Executive Chui Sai On announced in his Policy Address that all social housing households would be exempt from paying rent between January and March 2011. In addition, it was expected that 'most social housing residents would pay lower rent after that period'.[112] – Leong Keng Seng, Vice-President of the Social (Public) Housing Affairs Committee, announced either no increase in rent, or a reduction in rent, for 90 per cent of social housing residents.

However, the key question of building 19,000 social housing flats in the coming years is not fully solved. There are already some 24,000 "economic flats" in 2012, but this jump of an additional 19,000 units will be a burden for the MSAR Government. This is a constant subject of debate in the Legislative Assembly. Many elected deputies are linking their future re-election to this question of social housing.

The existing rent ceiling for a four-bedroom social housing unit is MOP 2,500 per month on Macau Peninsula and MOP 2,200 on Taipa Island, where – as in Coloane – land property is less expensive.

According to calculations presented in the *Macau Daily Times* in February 2011, if the income of a one-person household were to reach MOP 9,000 a month, the rent would jump from MOP 600 to MOP 1,254. However, if this person's income dropped to MOP 3,000 per month, he or she would pay only MOP 130, a sharp reduction. Whether renting or buying at a low price, access to social housing is limited to low-income applicants. If these persons overshoot the income limits for three consecutive years, or if the maximum salary ceilings for those benefiting from such social housing are more than double the upper limits for their renting categories, their housing contracts may be unilaterally terminated by the Housing Bureau. Macau Government Spokesman, Leong Heng Teng, who is also chairman of the Kaifong Association, thinks that the law concerning Social Housing – now in preparation – will allow people to buy flats more easily, but at the same time will make it tougher for them to sell their property. In 2011, speaking of pensions in his capacity as a Member of the MSAR Executive Council, Leong Heng Teng, stated that he thinks that public consultation is necessary, as does Sonny Lo.[113] In Qingzhou and elsewhere, the people were not previously consulted, but the MSAR Government seems to be more careful at present. Leong Heng Teng and directly elected Deputy José Coutinho are right to be very attentive to what the people think.

Influential deputies, such as the Hokkien leader, Deputy Chan Meng Kam, criticised the Government of the MSAR, and in particular the Housing Department, for their inactivity concerning Qingzhou. Law 6/93/M, passed before the handover, notes the obligation of the Housing Department to register and control wooden shacks or 'simple, roughly-made barracks' and states that, if necessary, the security forces may assist in this task. However, it seems that the Department sometimes ignores its duties. Since 8 December 2010, the brutal demolition of shacks by force has occurred, sometimes before the residents have moved out and even before the order for demolition has been issued.

How do the MSAR Government and the police forces evaluate their performance? By what right do they force persons to move out of their homes? In Hong Kong, there are strict laws concerning this type of expulsion. In Macau, for the coming project to reconstruct old suburbs, such as Qingzhou, it is necessary to have rules, but it seems that there are none. This type of appropriation by the MSAR Government of property for common use requires precise laws, including dates by which the inhabitants must depart.

Eventually, the Court of Justice may have to intervene, but this has not yet occurred.[114] Qingzhou is thus a key problem not yet fully solved. On 13 January 2011, Deputy Ng Kuok Cheong handed a petition, signed by many citizens, to the Legislative Assembly. The type of violence seen in Qingzhou in 2010 and 2011 was new in Macau, according to Deputy Ng. In fact, in February 2011, three pro-democratic deputies – Ng, Au Kam San and Paul Chan Wai Chi wanted to pursue this issue, which they had started to do actively a month before. On the other hand, it was evident that some deputies, such as Leonel Alves, had taken a softer position. Lawmakers Kwan Tsui Hang and Ho (He Run Sheng) agreed to a slow resolution of this question, while others asked for an acceleration in the construction of new social housing units. As of 2012, new rules are still necessary. A proposal for a public hearing for Qingzhou was rejected by the Legislative Assembly in February 2011 by nineteen deputies to seven.[115] The Macau Kaifong Association and Party ('Oumun Gaaifung Lyunhap Zungwui' in Cantonese), the General Union of Neighbourhood Associations, *Jiefang Lianhezhonghui*, and its president, Leong Heng Teng, wanted to protect the rights of the residents.

To cool society down, the head of the Urbanisation Department, Lao Iong (Liu Rong), presented the Grand Plan of the MSAR Government for Qingzhou. Historical monuments in Qingzhou Hill were to be preserved. Mr Lao announced clearly, in February 2011, that nine thousand housing units would be ready in 2011. However, he did not give a date, and did not mention the other additional ten thousand new units promised by the MSAR Government.[116] In fact, the first nine thousand units were still not completely available at the end of 2011.

Improvement of the environment and the creation of green spaces – the logic of the modern urbanisation plan for the new Macau which has so far been applied to Qingzhou – will certainly contribute to upgrading the international image of the MSAR However, in January

2011, it was difficult to imagine any quick resolution of this crucial and sensitive housing question.

On 7 December 2010, the debates and interventions of two deputies – Madam Kwan Tsui Hang, Vice-President of the General Association of Trade Unions (*Associação Geral dos Operários de Macau* – AGOM), and José Pereira Coutinho – significantly demonstrated a certain tension at the Legislative Assembly. Deputy Coutinho is President of the Macau Civil Servants Association ; on 30 December, he confirmed by telephone in a conversation with me the importance of the housing debate. On the MSAR Government side, the President of the Housing Institute, Tam Kuong Man, was trying to find solutions. Some twelve thousand families were on the waiting list for the proposed nineteen thousand housing units, and this cannot be ignored. Too many families had been waiting for years to get a flat.

Ng Kuok Cheong, an elected democrat, put up a sign on 7 December 2010, announcing that there were 754 days left to build over sixteen thousand units, but many deputies did not care about this particular deadline for the delivery of housing units to the public. However, the announcement that older social housing would be renovated did not satisfy the majority of lawmakers, and the Secretary for Transport and Public Works, Lau Si Io, said he was confident that the nineteen thousand units would be built on time.

Meanwhile, Member of the Executive Council of the MSAR, Leong Heng Teng stated that he wanted to balance the relation of economics to social welfare in his own way – this what I mean when I use the word 'society' – and he proposed to reduce the amount of three hundred million patacas in tax, which those who possess their own flats were paying in December 2010. These proprietors do not receive any assistance from the MSAR Government.[117]

Early in March 2011, the editor of the *Aomen Ribao* nostalgically presented to its readers an old photograph of the Hill of Villa Verde (Qingzhou), originally published in

1993 in the *Album Macau 3*.[118] A clean Qingzhou would certainly push Macau forward as a cultural city; and this is a dream of both the former Portuguese administration and the current MSAR Government. It would also attract more V.I.P. tourists. Macau needs more international shops, able to compete with those in Hong Kong and Shanghai.

City planning is essential. The Professor of Urban Planning at the University of Naples, Francesco Forte, notes the role that history and the use of relevant models should play in urban planning for Macau. Creativity has to be developed in the MSAR. Is it possible to do something concerning community aspirations?

MSAR Government efforts and efficient governance to anticipate the desired evolution of life in the MSAR is a necessity.[119] A creative effort is also necessary to improve Macau urban-planning. The case of Qingzhou, previously studied, is a case in point. To be creative, economy has to be constantly cross-checked with social issues, and the MSAR this is mainly dependent on up-grading education.

Education is a priority for the MSAR to become more global

We must take into consideration both the power and the weaknesses of globalisation, but certainly the MSAR has to think in terms of becoming more integrated with the global community when planning changes in the education system. The MSAR lacks geographical space, so the outside world is more important than it might be elsewhere.

Looking at the issue of globalisation, the English language has a long history in Macau. The year 1750 was an important turning point for the English language in Macau, when half of the eighteen ships that arrived in the Pearl River Delta were British. When their husbands travelled to the Mainland, English-speaking wives were compelled to stay in the Portuguese enclave.[120] As a result, Macau became a place where Chinese Pidgin-English was used. It was a safe spot for both legal and illegal merchandise. Most importantly, English was the communication bridge between Macau and British India. The former 'globalisation' of Macau under the Portuguese – linked as it was to Asia, Africa, Europe and South America – was motivated by silver currency, to pay for Chinese silk in particular.

Today, Chinese and Portuguese are the official languages of the MSAR. Nowadays Mainland China is involved in globalisation, and the MSAR needs to improve its 'globality' to succeed. On 16 December 2011, David Chow, former MSAR Legislative Council Member, Executive Director of the Landmark (a grand casino and magnificent building), confirmed the importance of globalisation and the necessary 'global' opening of the MSAR. In an attempt to diversify the economy of Macau, in February 2012, he went to America and Africa. As he mentioned in an interview, given in his capacity as Honorary Consul of Cape Verde, economic issues are important, and investing elsewhere is a key issue for the MSAR. For this, English is essential. The Chinese of Macau, who have links with the Hong Kong SAR, are directly affected by the current role of English in the MSAR. The Hou Kong (Haojiang) Secondary School, in the northern part of the Macau Peninsula, signed a protocol in 2010 to develop the study of English in a programme called 'English for the 21st Century', based in Beijing .[121] Without English, it is not easy for the young Chinese of Macau to find a job, particularly if they have no experience in a dynamic public or private enterprise.

Those oriented toward the study of law must study Portuguese. Portuguese keeps its supremacy in this field because the Portuguese Law in Macau has a long tradition. It is better written and more understandable in Portuguese than in its Chinese translation. The Basic Law, a constitutional document, is the only law of the MSAR that is perfectly clear in both Chinese and Portuguese. However, Hong Kong is more global, with its complete system of law in both English and Chinese.

The Chinese of Macau are changing jobs, and many today want to work in the casino industry. It is hoped that better instruction in English and a general concern about education from the top to the grassroots will allow them to acquire this language. Education and *guanxi* 关系 relationships are clear factors for success. The question is not to give students tuition to succeed, but to reform education.

Consequently, for the social stability of the MSAR, upgrading education is essential not only for the Chinese of Macau but also for all Chinese and permanent residents. Upgrading education will improve general knowledge in the MSAR, as well as improve the level of English. Hong Kong, in comparison, has been shaped by the British examination system. Upgrading education in Macau cannot be done in one year, but if it is carefully and systematically implemented, the students of the MSAR will better master not only Chinese but also English – and even Portuguese, in the case of the few students who are interested in it. Unfortunately, the Portuguese language is less popular in Macau than in many universities on the Mainland, as Portuguese-speaking Brazil attracts the Mainland more than the MSAR. It is interesting to note that the new dean of the Faculty of Law at the University of Macau, John Mo Shijian, has no Portuguese language proficiency. (He served as Dean at the China University of Political Science and Law, beginning in 2005, and previously served at Deakin University in Australia.) The president of the Macau Lawyers Association, Jorge Neto Valente, has pointed out that the Macau legal system is based on Portuguese legislation and Professor Mo has promised a curriculum reform of the Faculty of Law 'to attract more outstanding students with bilingual proficiency'.[122] We understood this to mean primarily Chinese and Portuguese, but Chinese and English bilingual proficiency is also important.

Generally, then, Macau society needs to be reformed through education. A former head of a famous secondary school of Macau thinks that the MSAR Government should intervene more actively in education, following the examples of Mainland China, Hong Kong and Taiwan. However, the government of the MSAR may be too diffident to do this; another reason may be that the legacy of the Portuguese has been a lack of management capacity in education. There are perhaps too many private schools. This does not mean that the level of well-known schools such as the Portuguese School, College Dom Bosco, São José School, and the Sacred Heart School, or of the numerous Chinese schools, is not satisfactory, but that a harmonisation and general upgrading of education would certainly help to develop Macau.

The University of Macau (formerly The University of East Asia) was founded in 1981, following the dynamic idea of Dr Stanley Ho. The *Sociedade de Jogos de Macau* (SJM) – the strongest asset of Dr Ho's family – continues to help the University of Macau. Ambrose So (Su Shu Hui), the chief executive officer of SJM, met the Friendship Association of the University of Macau in February 2011 to confirm continuity of support from Stanley Ho, emphasising that the development of education and a very entrepreneurial spirit are very useful in the MSAR.[123]

Social and Economic Prospects

Sociology and economics are rarely combined, except perhaps by anthropologists studying micro-societies, but both are relevant for the study of the Chinese of Macau. These Chinese are the key economic and social actors in the MSAR. The first part of this section will deal with the economy – that is, with the gaming industry. The second part will deal with a leading family of Macau. The social stresses involved must be studied.

Developer programmes and new ideas exist, but it is the MSAR Government that decides whether to implement these or not. However lawmakers do not follow a single leader and the important Macau associations also play a role. We must therefore say something about these actors. Certainly Dr Stanley Ho and his grand family are Chinese of Macau, and indeed key economic actors; but Macau is changing fast.

On Friday, 10 December 2010, the Consul General of Romania, Sorin Vasile, invited many personalities of Macau to a function. At this function, H.E. Consul Vasile said that Chief Executive Fernando Chui and ex-Chief Executive Edmund Ho 'have done a lot to boost the profile of Macau in terms of economy and tourism'.[124] In fact, in tribute to his contribution, Mr Edmund Ho Hau Wah was officially honoured on 28 December 2010 with the highest decoration of the MSAR, the Grand Lotus. The *Aomen Ribao* (ARB) very politely complimented the Honourable Recipient. On the following day, ARB also complimented Mr Ho for his support for the dynamic gaming industry.

A question comes to the mind. With thirty-four casinos in 2011, is it possible for the economy and society of the Macau SAR to be sustainable in a very troubled twenty-first century? Is it possible to diversify the economy? In 2010, with a substantial increase in visitor arrivals, the total receipts of the gaming sector reached MOP 190.67 billion.[125] Total MSAR Government expenditure for 2010 amounted to MOP 91.27 billion, up by 44 per cent year-on-year. Gross fixed capital formation for the gaming industry, however, shrank significantly by 63 per cent from 2009, to MOP 1.1 billion. Just before the 2011 Chinese New Year, the *Aomen Ribao* praised the Casino MGM, owned by Pansy Ho.

Dr Pansy Ho, a graduate of Santa Clara University in marketing and business, Chevalier of the French Mérite National, is the heiress of Dr Stanley Ho. Former MSAR Chief Executive Edmund Ho endorsed the *Sociedade de Jogos de Macau* (SJM), Stanley Ho's main company, not forgetting to say nice words to Dr Pansy Ho.[126] Obviously, the MSAR cannot risk problems with its main source of income.

However, before speaking of the economically dominant Ho family, we should point out that, at a time when the MSAR Government receives more revenue from the gaming industry, it is not certain that the citizens of Macau, and in particular the Chinese of Macau, benefit. The gaming sector of the economy has reached an unprecedented level. An increase in its income of 57.8 per cent over the year 2010 is on record. (During the first six months it was even higher – 67.5 per cent.)[127] In 2010, with a strong double digit increase, earnings of the Casino Wynn rose to HKD 18.4 billion. The Sands, another gaming operation, gained HKD 19.36 billion in income in 2010. The MGM gaming operation came third, with earnings of HKD 11.7 billion. SJM Holdings reached HKD 12.76 billion. Finally, Galaxy Entertainment's earnings went up to HKD 9.29 billion.

The report of gaming revenues released by the Gaming Inspection Bureau for January 2011 showed an increase of 33 per cent over gaming revenues in January 2010, to MOP 18.57 billion. For February 2011 it showed an increase of more than 40 per cent over February 2010, with revenues of MOP 19.8 billion for the month. SJM was well ahead of other gaming companies during January 2011 – with a market share of 31 per cent. In February 2011 it had 32 per cent of the market. Sands followed with 18 per cent.[128] Such reports seem to confirm the confidence of SJM's CEO, Ambrose So. A slight slowdown occurred at the end of 2011, but the year 2012 will be also another record year.

One aspect of the competition between gaming organisations is the 'battle' for the Cotai land lots numbers seven and eight, north of the Lotus Flower Bridge. This competition demonstrates the importance of *guanxi* or 'relationship' among the Chinese of Macau. So far, it seems that unawareness of the Chinese cultural tradition of *guanxi* has barred Sands from competition with other companies. This leaves three companies – MGM, SJM and Wynn – seemingly able to develop their facilities in this part of Macau, Cotai.

Wynn won a plot in Cotai for a long initial term, but surprisingly its concession will expire in 2022. This allotment of 51 acres (20.6 hectares) is located close to the Campus of the University of Science and Technology and was already fenced off in September 2011. Wynn has already agreed to pay MOP 1.55 billion for this plot. Secretary of Works and Transport (DSSOPT) Lau Si Io, and the Macanese Jaime Carion, Director of the Land, Public Works and Transport, are responsible for this crucial question of Cotai land.[129]

Economy and society are, or course, linked. Dr Stanley Ho was the *de facto* key entrepreneur in Macau for many years. Despite his Hong Kong origin he is a true Chinese of Macau. Without his 'Daoist' diet, and other good practices such as tennis and dancing training, Dr Ho (who was born on 25 November 1921) would never have reached his present age. However, in January 2011, the most striking news about Dr Ho, since his 'accident' at the end of July 2009, appeared in gigantic characters on *Aomen Ribao*'s front page: 'Gaming King resigns' (*Duwang yintui*).[130] However, Dr Ho's step down was, in fact, not quite a complete step down. STDM (*Sociedade de Turismo e Diversões de Macau*) – the monopoly founded in 1962 – is controlled by SJM with 56 per cent of the shares. Although Ambrose So is the CEO of SJM, in December the great magnate, in principle, gave control of SJM to his wife, Deputy Angela Leong On Kei, who refused to make any comment. SJM's controlling share of STDM – through another company, Lanceford – is in principle divided as follows: 50.7 per cent for Ho's third wife, Chan Un Chan, owner of the Action Winner Company; and 49.5 per cent for Ho's children Pansy, Daisy, Maisy, Josie and Lawrence, who, together, are owners of Ranillo Investments. Shuntak Holdings, part of the family financial empire and the iconic jewel of Stanley Ho, is co-owned by

Pansy, Daisy and Maisy Ho, and has globally increased its stake in the gaming conglomerate from 6.8 to 18.4 per cent.[131] Pansy Ho is the current Managing Director of Shuntak and MGM.

It is not surprising that a family dispute occurred about the division of Dr Ho's property, but a consensus among the numerous members of his family was finally reached. It seems that, despite a drop in the value of STDM shares on 24 January 2011, a deal was to prevail. Ambrose So commented optimistically that the basic structure of the entire operation had not been affected by these recent events.[132] However, to show optimism concerning ambiguous news, the *Sociedade de Jogos* announced a five per cent pay rise for its employees. The same day Ambrose So, CEO of the *Sociedade de Jogos*, was very clear in what he said: 'Nothing has changed' he said.[133] The MSAR Government also expressed optimism, and the Secretary for Economy and Finance, Tam Pak Yuen, claimed that he was not worried.

The family of Dr Ho is a grand family. Dr Ho's first wife, Clementina Leitão, was Macanese. She largely contributed to building the basis of the familial fortune during WWII, and also in 1962, when Governor Silverio Marques granted the gaming monopoly to Stanley Ho. Clementina Leitão passed away in Lisbon and was buried in 2004 in Macau, with MSAR Government honours. She had four children: Jane, the late Roberto, Angela and Deborah.

Dr Ho's very beautiful second wife is Luciana Lam King Ying. She is the mother of Pansy, Daisy, Maisy, Josie and Lawrence. The inspiration for the flower names of the two older daughters came from the experience of Pansy Ho who, at a young age, visited a garden near the northern border of Macau. The English names of Stanley Ho's children also demonstrate the importance of the English language in the family. The royal family of Thailand speaks French at home, but Dr Ho has always favoured English in his magnificent residences in Macau, Hong

Kong and Vancouver. Dr Ho's third wife is Ina Chan Un Chan (Chen Wan Zhen). Her children are Florinda, Laurinda and Orlando. Ms Ina Chan takes great care of the tycoon. The last wife, Deputy Angela Leong On Kei, has five children: Sabrina, Arnaldo, Mario, Yo Yau Kai and Alice.

When, on 1 February 2011, the news came that Dr Ho had been admitted to the Hong Kong Sanatorium and Hospital, the ARB[134] reported that this was for a routine medical check-up.[135] However, the frail appearance of Dr Ho at the Sanatorium at the end of January 2011 may have been the starting point of the family disunity. In 2011, on the eve of the Chinese New Year, some of SJM's shareholders started to be worried about their money. Dr Ho's lawyer, Gordon Oldham, had previously posted a video conversation between the tycoon and himself on *YouTube* on 31 January 2011.

Based on *New York Times* (19 March 2010), *South China Morning Post* sources and my interview with Dr. Pansy Ho in 2012, it seems that she is the only person in the family with the determination and strength of her father, whose health, at the time of writing, seems fragile. She is a Western-educated entrepreneur, a graduate in Marketing and Business, and is the chairwoman of the French Business Association of Macau. Dr Pansy Ho is not at all afraid to speak of business ethics. Influenced by her Catholic school education and from being tutored in French by a Catholic nun, she early developed serious Christian religious beliefs. She built the Macau Tower Convention Hall in 2002 and in 2006, MGM, the fifth biggest casino in Macau.

'When my father is wrong' she says, 'I must stand up to him, it's my duty'. The author checked these information during his personal interview with Dr. Pansy Ho. In the past, Pansy Ho often protected her younger sisters despite the tough decisions of her father. Dr Stanley Ho was a king, but it seems Pansy was not afraid. However, she also listened to Dr Stanley Ho when he advised her against re-marriage in the 2000s.

In February 2011, another signal was sent to the public and the shareholders of the Macau gaming empire when a video showed Dr Ho in a wheelchair on a jetfoil of his company plying between Hong Kong and Macau. This video was released because Dr Ho wanted to demonstrate that his health was in fact much better than expected. In the same video, Pansy Ho presented her best wishes from the headquarters of Shuntak at the Hong Kong Maritime Terminal to jetfoil travelers and the public, hinting that she might be the one to replace her father.

The relative prosperity of society in Macau is linked to the monopolistic casino industry, but this is risky for society. In 1985, the gross revenue from casino games was MOP 1.7 billion; from Greyhound racing, MOP 47 million. Trotting and Pelota Basca each brought in MOP 6 million; and Chinese lotteries, MOP 2 million.[136] In 1996, MOP 5 billion, representing 57 per cent of Macau revenue, was from gaming. The booming post-handover revenue has been impressive. In 2005 the annual gaming revenue was MOP 46 billion, and this soared to MOP 104 billion in 2008. In 2010, annual gaming revenues amounted to MOP 188 billion, nearly 80 per cent of the economy. In 2012, it represents 90 per cent of the MSAR's economy.

In Cremer's book, *Macau City of Commerce and Culture*, Antonio Duarte A. Pinho, former advisor to the Macau Secretary for Economic Affairs, expresses the following view of gaming in Macau: 'The casinos of Macau add significantly to the uniqueness of the territory (now Region). In a sense, gaming symbolises the symbiotic relationship of Chinese commerce and culture ... Chinese beliefs are ever present in gaming'. [137]

However, the continuous increase in gaming revenues may not be economically and sociologically sustainable during the present period of global economic instability. The Secretary for Economy and Finance, Francis Tam, has declared that 5,500 gaming tables should be the maximum until 2013. The statistics for 2010 mentioned only 4,791 tables and 14,050 slot machines.[138] In principle the Government of the MSAR wants to reduce the annual development of the gaming industry because recent crises may affect Macau and its economic stability.[139]

Dr Pansy Ho, who is optimistic and believes in economic cycles, has said 'Macau is sleazy'.[140] According to her, to balance the relationship between society and economy, Macau requires a fresh type of thinking and, in particular, needs to create a new spirit of creativity. A key issue for her is 'to be open-minded' – to have a global approach for investments to develop the whole Pearl River Delta. According to her, 'borders' have become 'less and less important' nowadays. In 2012, regional co-operation is well marked on the agenda of the Chief Executive Fernando Chui. Guangdong province and Macau are more integrated, but entrepreneurs have to 'project' themselves into the future and be creative because competition is becoming tougher and tougher.

Opportunities and the development of transport are linked. Before 2017, Susanna Wong Soi Man explained that 'there will be no change' in the location of the Outer Harbour Ferry Terminal.[141] However, work is necessary to keep the overcrowded terminal operating. The Shuntak group continues to be powerful, thanks to its jetfoils and its helicopter company. Its helicopters are among the safest in the world thanks to the excellent guidelines given by the company's former manager, Miyagawa San. Transferring the University of Macau to Hengqin Island is a first step towards uniting Guangdong and the MSAR more closely. However, the question of investments in Hengqin was not on the agenda of the Government of the MSAR in mid-December 2011. This is also part of the crucial question of mass transit to improve communication.

To modernise the MSAR, a light metro rail system of 21 kilometers, called the Light Rail Train or Light Rapid Transit (LRT) is planned. This will improve communication between the historical main Border Gate between Macau and Zhuhai and the Taipa Maritime Terminal, not far from the airport, across Sai Van Bridge. The normal LRT speed will be 30 km/h. The trip between Taipa and Nam Van is planned to be twenty minutes, and the construction is scheduled to start in 2012. The deputy director of the Transportation Infrastructure Office, André Sales Ritchie, has planned a possible LRT-Hengqin Island link to begin operation in 2015. An LRT connection to the future Guangzhou-Zhuhai Intercity Mass Rapid Transit is also planned.[142] Mitsubishi Heavy Industries won the contract, beating Siemens-China Civil Engineering and Bombardier-China Road. However, Deputy José Pereira Coutinho objected to the conditions under which this contract was awarded. When interviewed by the author in mid-January 2011, Lawmaker Coutinho spoke of 'lack of public services' and some problems of 'security' for the proposed Sai Van Bridge, but it seems that Mitsubishi defended itself successfully.

Macau is at the Centre of the Pearl River Delta and operates according to the principles of Corporate Governance. This is a major challenge for Greater China. Pansy Ho calls the ethics for private companies a 'guideline'. The MSAR has to demonstrate its capacity to engage in ethical development, a hard task when facing the numerous experienced cadres in Guangdong Province. Economists know that, for local Mainland private companies, it is difficult to demonstrate the reality of any consistent Corporate Governance, as, in Mainland China, private companies rely too much on the Boss (*Laoban* 老板).

On 18 December 2012, Paulo Azevedo at the France Macau Business Association gave a general overview concerning the economy and the challenges facing Chief Executive Fernando Chui. The MSAR can be proud of its economic record, but a better enforcement of existing legislation could be a solution to many problems. In particular, the lack of follow-up for the numerous projects always well advertised needs to be solved; in particular those relating to social housing, the telecom market, regional co-operation, Hengquin Island, the Light Rail Transit System, Cotai and Urban Planning. A close and scientifically managed follow-up could solve these challenges. The MSAR has huge monetary reserves and this is an excellent asset in a very troubled global world.

Medium-size enterprises are feeling the strain and cannot match the salaries of large hotels and casinos. Consequently the problem of economic diversification is hard to solve. Human resources continue to be a problem despite the very low unemployment rate of some 2.6 per cent. This human resources problem must be addressed.

The MSAR wants to maintain its legitimate reputation as a cultural destination. In 1996, eight million people visited Macau, twice the number in 1990. In 2010 the record number of persons who entered in Macau and returned to Gongbei (Zhuhai) or vice-versa in one year was close to 25 million. On 16 December 2010, in one day, this figure reached 168,000.[143] This increasing number of visitors has an impact on social change and traditions. With such a large flow of people, Macau's culture requires better protection, and this may in turn increase the MSAR's social stability. Macau's many important associations in particular contribute to social stability by improving and sustaining the best possible community spirit.

CHAPTER FOUR

ASSOCIATIONS IN MACAU

A study of the many associations in Macau is essential to understand the Chinese of Macau. David Yang argues that, on the Mainland, Chinese civic organisations remain closely linked to the state.[144] Similarly, it seems true that associations in the MSAR are linked with the Government of the MSAR, but also – through the Basic Law – indirectly dependant of the Central Government in Beijing. Formal associations are largely concerned to keep a good relationship with the MSAR Government and the state – the latter term regarding the Mainland often refers to institutions in Guangdong and Fujian Provinces.

Many of the associations referred to in this chapter mirror Chapter One, in terms of social and cultural identity and relationships with the Mainland. Forty-three per cent of the interviewees in my survey belonged to at least one association. In fact associations are the bases for the construction of identity, ensuring the preservation of the social structure, and they are involved in the maintenance of identities within the overall social structure.

Already in the nineteenth century, the Chinese of Macau were integrated into numerous associations. In Southeast Asia as well as in Australia, South America, and in Cuba, associations contributed to transform the plight of the 'coolie' into the success stories of many Chinese communities.

The first part of the present chapter deals with associations which have been researched on the spot between 1995 and 2011. These include, among others, Southeast-Asian associations and Rotary Clubs. Intensive fieldwork was conducted in parallel with the administration of my questionnaires – but during the period 2010-2011 I also gained an overview of these associations from the Chinese newspapers published in Macau. These references cannot be considered perfect, but at least they constitute a snapshot of Chinese society during this period, as well as the journalistic vision of the life of these associations. Not surprisingly, for those who know Macau, this newspaper study results in a disproportionate emphasis on the celebration of the Chinese New Year, a crucial annual rite of passage. There are many other aspects of social life not reported by the media. The second part of this chapter is based on interviews and research concerning women's associations and charitable associations.

Macau has a long recorded history and was a centre of nascent globalisation in the nineteenth century. The economic and geopolitical relations of Macau at that time included those with Asia, Europe, Africa, and South America (from which silver, the real currency of the Middle Empire, came).

Fok's historical 'Macau Formula' was recently discussed by him and the author.[145] 'The Macau formula offered a compromise between two seemingly incompatible interests. A dominant factor in Ming diplomacy was a pragmatic pro-trade attitude. The formula also reconciled two extreme positions based on politics and trade, which often separated the staunchly doctrinaire central officials and the more practically-minded provincial officials.'

This is the basis for the elaboration of the author's sociological formula. In fact, the handover to Chinese sovereignty in 1999 changed nothing concerning the tolerant Luso-Chinese Confucian alliance and so a sociological 'Macau Formula' prevails.

All the associations in the MSAR today are organised on two levels according to the proverbial 'Macau Formula'. The upper level has a president and vice-presidents who deal with the Government of Macau, and with Beijing if necessary. The lower level encompasses directors or members who are part of the board, and other members who do not belong to the board. The power of the upper level is different in Macau than it is on the Mainland, where the role of the Party is paramount. In the MSAR the upper board of an association may or may not have strong links with the Party.

Often, in the associations of Macau, the upper board has the power. Traditionally, the president or chairperson of the association rarely delegates his or her power to others.

Decisions may be discussed, but nobody can deny the long history of Macau which involves a particular type of relationship that prevailed from the sixteenth century to the recent past among the Chinese of Macau and the Portuguese. The 'Macau formula' reflects in a sentence the historical continuity of Macau and a certain lack of transparency. However, nowadays, associations have an inspectorate level more powerful than that which existed before the handover, which may allow more transparency and a rare possibility to learn more about the upper level of the associations, which have not yet been well studied by scholars.

Associations are the roots of social life, improve the well-being of the society of Macau, maintain a close relationship with the Mainland, and are essential in developing MSAR's complex economy. Almost every day a page of the *Aomen Ribao* is dedicated to Macau associations. Without speaking of secret societies and triads, there are all sorts of associations in the MSAR. There is an association for each profession. For example, there are 10,000 taxi licences, and the taxi drivers have their own syndicate, the Macau Taxi Drivers Association (*Aomen Deshe Lianyihui*). There are also two main tourist guide associations – one of them, the Guide Association (*Daoyou Xiehui*) is under the presidency of Ms Wu Wui Fong.[146]

One of my interviewees is a member of not fewer than a hundred associations!

Different kinds of associations link the MSAR both to the Mainland and to Southeast Asia – for example the Cambodian Overseas Chinese Friendship Association

(*Jianbuzhai Huaqiao Lianyihui*), which is headed by Chan (Chen He Biao). Around 12 per cent of the Chinese of Macau have family links with Southeast Asia. In early December 2010, representatives of the Tan clan in Macau ('Tam' in Cantonese) went to Malaysia and Singapore to visit their kin.

Another clan, the Yu, has a total of 6,000 resident members in Macau.[147] It was formerly called the *Yu Fengcai Tan* – founded on 13 January 1911 – and later became the *Yushi Zongqinhui* of today. In 2011 the president was Yu Hua Ci. On 2 November 2010, the Bureau of Overseas Affairs of Guangdong Province recognised this association. This reflects one of the theses of this book: Guangdong is of crucial importance for Macau identity.

Two other main links of Macau associations are with Hong Kong as demonstrated by the Chaozhou community, and with Southeast Asia. Overseas Chinese from all over the world are essential in the Returned Overseas Chinese Association. Many are from Southeast Asia, but their families came originally from Guangdong and Fujian provinces, and this provides a strong provincial basis for the association.

Leading Role of Associations and the Chinese Networking System

Chinese society works mainly through a network of relationships, or *guanxi*. The MSAR cannot function without this type of network. In their relations to the Mainland, associations are essential even if some of them are not very active. The associations linking Chinese of Macau with their places of origin are very important.

Social welfare is another reason for the existence of associations in the MSAR. From 2002 to the present, Deputy Chan Mei Yi, president of Sin Meng, has thought the Christmas Party to be very important for her association. It is a key event of the year, to which children from single-parent families are invited, so that they may meet other children and feel less lonely. In 2011, the Christmas Party was opened up more to other children too. The second most important event of the year for this association is the gathering of older people every Chinese New Year.[148]

Provinces and Identity: Guangdong, Fujian and the Chaozhou

For the Chinese of Macau, Guangdong (in particular Zhongshan – see photos 1 and 2 of families originally from Zhongshan) is the most significant reference to the Mainland. This is historical. Macau as a Portuguese territory was under the close attention of the Madarins in charge of the nearby Xiangshan district, this the former name of the District of Zhongshan (see Foreword and the beginning of Chapter One). Zhongshan, from where many Macau Chinese come, is a cultural marker for Chinese of Macau identity and, since the handover of Macau to China, the cadres of Zhongshan district have wisely promoted Zhongshan to Macau people, using all possible means of communication: media, television, newspapers, radio and even the web. In recent years Chinese of Macau have been buying property in Zhongshan, as well as in nearby Zhuhai. There is still space available that is quieter and less populated than in the MSAR. Many more continue to work in Macau while residing in this nearby part of Guangdong. The constant improvement of communication has been significant in recent years and will continue to accelerate the relationship between the MSAR and Guangdong Province.

Guangdong Province, the dominant place of origin of the Chinese of Macau

Macau has priority links with Guangdong Province. Guangdong is essential for the Chinese of Macau, so Cantonese associations are numerous in the MSAR. Among them, the associations of Enping, Heshan,

Jiangmen, Kaiping, Taishan, Wuyi, Xinhui and Zhongshan work in close co-operation.

Table One shows that 55 per cent of the respondents to my questionnaires come from Zhongshan, Shunde or Panyu, all in Guangdong Province. Among them, 39 interviewees come from Zhongshan. This suggests, at least numerically, the key role of Zhongshan. In fact, the dynamism of the Zhongshan Association in the MSAR is remarkable and shows the long historical continuity of friendly relations, from the sixteenth century to the present time, between *Xiangshan* (the ancient name of Zhongshan) and Macau. Many Chinese residents of Macau during the last four centuries have had their roots in Zhongshan. On 18 December 2010, the Zhongshan Overseas Association (ZOA) from Guangdong Province visited Macau. Sixty persons attended a conference at the Arc Hotel in Macau (*Kai Xuan Men*) to promote cultural co-operation with the Macau Zhongshan Association (*Zhongshan Tongxianghui*) under the chairmanship of Su Wei Qiang who came from Zhongshan.[149] President Su is particularly attentive to the question of harmonious development of the economy and the society of both the MSAR and Zhongshan.[150]

The Macau Zhongshan Association (*Aomen Zhongshan Tongxianghui*) is particularly active. The President of the association is Lo Wai Shi (Lu Wei Shuo). In February 2011, Lu organised the Association's New Year Party and he is particularly concerned to promote the cultural and economic links between Zhongshan and the MSAR.[151] All the associations of Macau consider the New Year meetings very seriously, as means to keep their members in touch and improve their living conditions when it is necessary. Social welfare development is often a key point, but the annual meeting of elderly people is a necessary but not sufficient condition for efficient welfare.

In 2011, to confirm the results of conferences and meetings in Macau, the Macau Zhongshan Association sent representatives to a meeting held at the Zhongshan Overseas Association in the City of Zhongshan. The Vice-President of the Macau Association, Hu Jia Yi, was the highest representative of the MSAR. This meeting mostly concerned the Youth Association, and the majority of the members of the Youth Association of Zhongshan were present. In addition to the Macau Association, the Hong Kong Zhongshan Association also sent delegates to the conference. Zhongshan is, and has long been, the region of Guangdong Province with the closest cultural links to Macau.[152] In February 2011, under the leadership of Huang Shu Shen, the Zhongshan Youth Association of Macau (*Zhongshan Qingxiehui*) organised a meeting to follow up the recent conferences in Zhongshan and Macau.[153]

In February 2011, the Shiqi Association (*Shiqi Tongxianghui*), under the leadership of its Director Hong Shan Shan, had its annual New Year celebration. These recurrent meetings are part of the social welfare role of these associations. Elders above sixty years old received 'lucky money' (*laisi*) and gifts.[154] The *Sanshui Tongxianghui* had a similar traditional gathering in March 2011.[155]

In December 2010, the key event for the Foshan Association (*Foshan Lianyihui*) was its participation in the charity march, *Baiwanhang,* organised by the *Aomen Ribao* Association (Macau Daily News Association).[156] This annual march mobilises every year between fifty thousand and a hundred thousand Chinese of Macau including the Chief Executive, Fernando Chui and ex-Chief Executive, Edmund Ho. Dr Stanley Ho and Dr Pansy Ho also often marched to support the 'Walk for Millions' or 'Baiwanhang' in the past. On Sunday morning, 11 December 2011 one tenth of the elite and the population again marched from the Statue of

Guanyin, in NAPE suburb, to Mazu Temple. This event is symbolically meaningful, but to start from the statue of a goddess and finish near the main temple of Macau has no religious significance.

The Nanhai Association (*Nanhai Tongxianghui*) also celebrated the Chinese New Year. The president, Feng Zhi Qiang, mentioned the key role of the Assistance Fund (*Yuanzhu Jijinhui*) in helping its most needy members.[157] To develop more links with the Mainland among members of Macau associations, visits are organised. In January 2011, thirty members of the Association of Compatriots of Nanhai (*Nanhai Tongxianghui*) visited Guangdong Province for three days, under the patronage of the Overseas Association of Xiqiao.[158] One day was spent in Xiqiao, and the following two days were spent in Enping and Kaiping. The group returned to the MSAR via Hengqin and Zhuhai. In the coming years Hengqin Island will almost become part of Macau when the transfer there of the University of Macau will be completed. This visit of a Macau association to Guangdong Province thus demonstrates the increasing relationship between the MSAR and the Mainland and the rapid integration of Macau with Guangdong.

The Friendship General Association of Huizhou (*Aomen Huizhou Tongxianglian Yihui*) is active and has good relations with the City of Huizhou. Its president is Fong Seng Wah (Fang Sheng Hua).

However, not all the associations linked to Guangdong are very active; many associations lack financial resources. For example, although the Enping Association had a meeting on 6 February 2011, its gatherings are rather rare.

There are many active student associations in the MSAR, which are linked with Guangdong Province. This is the case for Jinan University in Guangzhou, where many Chinese of Macau graduated – in particular medical doctors and dentists. On 6 March 2011, the Chief Executive Fernando Chui received the president of Jinan University. The Macau Student Association of this University, under the influence of its president, Ma You Heng, is very active. The Chief Executive praised the role of Jinan University in relation to the development of tertiary education in Macau.[159]

Fujian Province

More than 15 per cent of Chinese of Macau come from Fujian Province. It is not surprising therefore that every year Xiamen University and Quanzhou University receive students from Macau.

We have seen that to be Hokkien is an important identity in Macau. (*See Chapter One, 'Hokkien from Fujian Province'*). The Fujian Association has a President, Chan Meng Kam, a businessman and a Deputy of the Legislative Assembly and Director of Tung Sin Tong. Deputy Chan is a very active association president.

There are separate youth associations for young people with ancestry from Quanzhou, Jinjiang and Huian. The key Fujian Association of Macau is located at Iao Hon Street. On 14 December 2010, some of the members of the Fujian Youth Association celebrated in advance the 11th anniversary of the return of Macau to China.

On 27 January 2011, I went to the main Fujian Association (*Aomen Fujian Tongxiangzhonghui*) to attend its annual lunch for older people. (*See Photograph 7.*) From 10am to around 3pm many came and registered at the counters corresponding to their places of origin, and each received a lunch-box, a tangerine, and a brown glutinous rice New Year's cake (*niangao*). A cadre of the association was very proud to show his photo taken when he joined the People's Liberation Army (PLA) at the age of twenty-one. This is another indication of the integration of Macau with the Mainland.

In February 2011 the central Fujian Association met again, under the leadership of its president, Yan Yan Ling. Congratulations for this meeting were sent by China's Liaison Office in Macau, and the Vice Director of the office, Xu Ze, encouraged the Fujian association to continue its good work of the past year, 2010.[160]

The Chaozhou

Many Chaozhou left Guangdong Province for Southeast Asia in the past, but are not classified there as Cantonese. In Thailand and elsewhere they are called Teochew. Their association is powerful in the MSAR. Some of them are Overseas Chinese who left Guangdong Province for Cambodia and finally returned to Shantou and Macau. A retired father, who had just turned ninety, came from Shantou to Macau to meet his three restaurant-owner sons and his grandchildren for the Chinese New Year, 3 February 2011, and had the traditional dinner in family on the evening of this day.

During 2011, the Seventh Annual Conference of the Chaozhou Youth Association was scheduled to be held in the MSAR. Two cadres, Yao Iong Lei and Chow Sin (Zhou Xin), were responsible for this international event.[161] The Chaozhou in Macau and their local association link eastern Guangdong Province with Macau, and the MSAR with Beijing and the world. The Chaozhou community is particularly powerful in Southeast Asia, and even in Europe and America.

The Macau Chaozhou Association (*Aomen Chaozhou Tongxianghui*) has strong relationships with the most famous associations, such as the Teochew Associations of the United States of America. On 5 September 1993, President Hoi Sai Iun attended the International Teochew Convention organised in the USA, and in May

2004 he also attended the Hong Kong meeting of all Teochow associations worldwide.

For the 20th anniversary of the foundation of the Macau Chaozhou Association, the 13th Meeting of the Association's International Union (*Guoji Chaotuan Lianyininghui*) was held at the end of November 2005. Around 3,000 Chaozhou from ninety-six associations all over the world were present. The Chief Executive of Macau, Edmund Ho, gave a speech. The Teochew International Union had been set up with its permanent secretariat in Hong Kong the same year. The International Chaozhou Study Association was also created during this November 2005 event. A series of exhibitions and conferences were held during the period in Macau, including Chaozhou food, art and commercial conventions.

The powerful Macau Chaozhou Association operates according to the Chaozhou work ethics, and its secretaries are well trained. Following my second meeting in the association, on 17 February 2011, Chan (Chen Xin Tao) invited me to have more meetings.

The president of this association, Hoi Sai Iun, also President of the Tung Sin Tong and Vice-President of Kiang Wu, another charitable association of the MSAR, has received the Grand Lotus for his achievements and the successful development of these organisations, but he was unfortunately unavailable during my visit to the Chaozhou Association. Later in March 2011, he went to Beijing before and during the National People's Congress meetings with many MSAR's V.I.Ps. In March 2012, I met him shortly at the Tung Sin Tong Association.

Southeast Asia Continues to be Fundamental in the MSAR

The Chinese of Macau from Southeast Asia are numerous. The Secretary of the Returned Overseas Chinese

Association of Macau, Vong Iek Soi, explained clearly the past political tensions in Southeast Asia, which have been the main cause of the arrival of Overseas Chinese in Macau. They have come mainly from Burma, Cambodia and Indonesia.

In the late 1990s, the life president of this association, Lu Xuefeng, born in Java, explained the central importance of his association, when I first interviewed him with Professor Cao Yunhua from Jinan University. We discussed the evident necessity of welfare in Macau and the reality of the familial and sentimental link with Southeast Asia.

In 1971, President Lu came to Macau from Eastern Java with his wife, his son and three daughters. Hakkas, such as himself, are dominant in this part of Java, as well as in Timor. Almost every year he returns to his birthplace, Kalisat Jember, in Eastern Java, where his parents' tomb is located, to pay respects to his ancestors, who went there from Meizhou in Guangdong. He speaks Bahasa Indonesia (Indonesian), Cantonese and Putonghua fluently.

President Lu is a very active man. Although he is now eighty years old, he walks three kilometers every morning at a brisk pace. He likes to travel and is an ambassador of the Returned Overseas Chinese Association of Macau, as he can use English when necessary. He always promotes both Macau and his association, and he did so in Canada and Asia in 2010. In 2011 President Lu planned to go to Thailand to represent his association, but due to the floods in Bangkok, his travel was cancelled.

The Returned Overseas Chinese Association of Macau meets on Saturday afternoon, but lacks participation by young people in its activities. Young people are the future of the MSAR, but they are too concerned with finishing their studies and trying to get good jobs to attend association meetings often.

An example of a type of relationship between Indonesia and Macau is the following: in December 2010, fifteen members of the Women's Association of the Returned

Overseas Chinese went to Indonesia, to Jakarta in particular, led by Zhou Ni, a leader of the association.[162] The aim of the journey was cultural. – The women wanted to learn more about the Indonesian musical instrument called *angklung*. – They studied the elementary technique for playing this instrument. In the following months I was surprised by their interest in Indonesian music and culture. This declined in 2012. Nevertheless, singing continues to be a key activity in the association. Near the Returned Overseas Chinese Association office there is a shop owned by an overseas Chinese who was educated in Indonesia. The wife of the shop-owner is Indonesian and never studied Chinese, but in Macau she does her best to improve her knowledge of Cantonese, as do many Indonesian women in the MSAR. The shop sells Indonesian products directly imported from Jakarta and the shop assistants use Bahasa Indonesia, although Cantonese remains the key language of communication necessary for smooth socio-economic integration in the MSAR.

Other Associations
The idea to have a Rotary Club started in 1938, but it was established for the first time on 11 January 1947, by thirty-six founders, many of them from Hong Kong, according to J. B. Leão. Its international recognition came a few months later under Charter Number 6662. The main projects were centred on the Red Cross, the Tung Sin Tong and Kiang Wu Associations and the Salesian orphanage. In 1951, the District Governor of Macau attended the International Convention of Detroit, USA. Since the mid-sixties, the Rotary Club (*Fulunshe*), District 3450, has been very active in Macau. In fact, before the handover, Cantonese, English and Portuguese-speaking Rotary Clubs were active in Macau. However, although English and Portuguese were each used in particular clubs before 1999, at present the Cantonese language dominates. In 2012, one English-speaking club is still alive and this shows the importance given to English versus Portuguese in the MSAR. Few

Macanese have joined the Cantonese speaking Rotary Clubs since 2000, perhaps because they are not be able to write Chinese characters, although many of them are fluent Cantonese speakers.

The Rotary Club currently helps China in the field of education in particular and with relief funds in case of natural disasters, unfortunately common on the Mainland. In 2012, the past president of Macau Central Rotary Club is Hokkien. There are currently many sections of Rotary in Macau – Central, Guia, Hou Kong, Macau Islands and the English-speaking club.[163] On 30 December 2010, an annual general meeting of all the Rotary clubs of Macau was convened at the panoramic Rocks Hotel, near the Maritime Terminal, at the end of the scenic modern Fishermen's Wharf. One year later, on the evening of 28 December, the Rotary Club of Macau Central also had its most important meeting of the year at the same place.

Macau is sometimes more dependent on Hong Kong than was the case before the handover in 1999. In January 2011, the Rotary Club of the Macau Islands was inspected by Hong Kong Rotarians. Ho (He Shou Luan), a former president who attended this key meeting, had joined the International Rotary more than twenty years previously. Among the prominent ex-presidents and members who attended were Yeong (Yang Kai Jin), Kun Siu Wui (Kuan Xiao Hui), Lam (Lin Run Jing), Wong Vai Tin (Huang Wei Tian), Nelson Wong Vai Kit and others.[164]

In January 2011, before the Chinese New Year, the Rotary Club of Taipa decided to help the poor through the Macau Salvation Army (*Jiushi Jun*).[165] This traditional support for social welfare during this period of the year by this Rotary Club used the dynamic of another association, highly specialised in poverty, to help the poorer. In 2011 and 2012, the Rotary Club of Macau also developed its voluntary dental assistance for older people with two mobile units, with the support of the Macau Foundation, and a team of dentists of the association. The youngest of these Rotarian dentists is Kevin Lei, who graduated from Jinan University, Guangzhou..

On the eve of the 2011 Chinese New Year, the Fishermen's Association *(Yumin Huzhuhui)* met to receive New Year gifts from the MSAR Social Welfare Bureau *(Shegongju)*. During the New Year celebration more than 300 gifts were offered to single-parent families and older people at the office of the association, in the Inner Harbour. The Bureau expressed its support for the association and gave good wishes for good health and family happiness to all fishermen.[166]

Last but not least, many members of the Kaifong Association *(Jiefang Lianhezhonghui* or *Jiezhonghui)* were present at the Lian Fong temple association and attended the Chinese New Year Party for older neighbours at this Chinese temple and museum.

The Kaifong Association of Macau (Street Committee of Macau) is one of the main mobilising forces in the MSAR. It became really important after 1967 and has since become a key political 'party'. Probably no other association would have been able to mobilise more than 200 young people to form a 200-metre long dragon for the 2012 Chinese New Year.

Unlike Hong Kong, in the civil society of Macau the democrats have no power, but associations are part of the civil society. Before the last Chinese New Year, in mid-February 2011, this was clear, as a mobilisation by democrats opposing the expulsion of families and companies located in Qingzhou had lost its momentum.

During the last weekend of February 2011, the association of the suburb of Tidu Avenue *(Tike Fanghui)* – related to the Kaifong Association – near Almirante Lacerda Avenue, Ribeira do Patane, and Avenue Horta e Costa, organised a New Year Party and distributed *laisi* to its members. The administrator of the Kaifong Association, Yao Hong Ming, attended the tea party given by this suburb association.[167] The Union of Associations of

Residents (*Aomen Jiefonghui Lianhezhonghui*) is located in Patane or Shalitou, near the sports ground. Daily in the morning, ladies perform their own style of physical movements, inspired by *taijiquan,* in front of this association. This Shalitou Sports Ground mirrors the popularity of the Union of Associations of Residents.

The Carpenters' Association (*Shangjiahang Huiguan*), at Camilo Pessanha Street, was established in 1840, the first workers' association established in Macau. It is today the oldest association in Macau. Its headquarters is located in what was formerly a Chinese temple, although it has no religious significance at present.

On 12 February 2011, at a meeting of the Workers' Federation (*Gonglian),* Association President Ho (He Xue Qing), declared the question of the establishment of a minimum wage to be the priority for the Federation. Deputy Ms Kwan Tsui Hang (Guang Cui Xing) attended this crucial meeting. One of the prime concerns of the Federation of Trade Unions' workers and employees is salaries. Since the handover to China at the end of 1999, there has been an increase in salaries and wages in Macau. However, the gap between the rich and the poor has widened, and Association President Ho suggested that the MSAR Government might play a leading role concerning the minimum wage.[168] It is clear that increasing inflation concerns workers more and more. In Hong Kong, inflation has mobilised grassroots associations, as Hong Kong's civil society is much more powerful than that of the MSAR. On 14 February 2011, the *Macau Hoje* newspaper put forward the question of ethics and governance. Both are important, but the control of inflation requires a political consensus, difficult to meet, as owners of enterprises do not want to be alone in supporting the establishment of a minimum wage in Macau. This minimum wage would cut into profits during a rather difficult time for the entrepreneurs as well as for workers. Ethics and governance are important to give a good image to the gaming industry, the major employer in Macau. From the sixteenth century to the present time governance has not been constant in Macau. – Many ups and downs have been linked to calamities and international events, such as the 1929 crisis, which affected Macau in the 1930s more than it did in the economically isolated Portugal.

The question of a minimum wage should be resolved within the framework of individual and collective negotiations, which will certainly be tough. The Workers' Association, like many other associations in Macau, is very concerned to maintain a high spirit and to develop many activities to maintain social peace. As an example of their efforts, the Workers' Association opened a *qigong* class – a sort of Chinese yoga – at the Workers' Stadium in February 2011, in order to keep social peace in a time of demand for better wages. [169] As of September 2012, there are only four directly elected deputies in the MSAR in September. These four deputies and this Workers' Association - which has indirectly elected deputies – most of the time protect the rights of permanent residents.

On 30 January 2011, another association – the Workers' Self-Helping Association (*Gongren Zijiuhui*), which lacks official support – invited hundreds of elderly persons, including disabled among them, in wheel-chairs, as well as children, to receive rice at Iao Hon Square, a densely populated district with more than 140,000 people per square kilometer. All of them wanted to get a packet of rice and other gifts. Some older people fell to the ground, were near fainting and were screaming for help. Still others behaved badly and jumped the queue. After an interruption of the distribution, however, the rice was again offered to the persons present.[170] The Association's leader, Zhang Rong Fa, blamed a lack of police efficiency for the failure to maintain order among the crowd.

This particular disturbance of a peaceful meeting shows an evolution in Macau society. The police, oddly, did not act quickly in solving the problem. Why? Are the activities of the association considered politically incorrect? What is a 'recognised' association?

The *Aomen Queniu Lianyihui* (Macau Sparrow Friendship Association) is located near Lacerda Market on Horta e Costa Avenue (*Gositak* in Cantonese; an older name, *Ho-Ko*, was closer to the Portuguese name of the avenue). In fact the real objective of this association was, and continues to be, gaming. The association does not want to advertise its gaming activities. Also, the members of this association – in a street absolutely 'normal' – simply did not want 'strangers' to attend their meetings. Macau has a long history of such meetings. Macau was famous for cricket-fighting and related betting in the past. Before the handover of Macau to China, other 'ornithologists' met in a teahouse close to Lacerda Market. This teahouse is now closed.

There are multiple art associations in Macau interested in promoting art, for the elite of the MSAR like art, and such exhibitions contribute to the promotion of culture and counter-balance the gaming image of the MSAR. The Macau Foundation plays an important role in promoting art and exhibitions. A remarkable Chinese painting exhibition of Han Meilin's work was held in the afternoon of 23 January 2011.[171] Among the honourable guests were the director of *Aomen Ribao*, Lei Pang Chu, and Dr Carlos Marreiros, a Member of the Electoral Commission of the Chief Executive.

On 22 February 2011, at 6pm, under the dynamic impulsion of the president of the Macau Foundation, Dr Wu Zhiliang, another painting exhibition was launched at the cultural and gastronomic Military Club (*Lujun Julebu*). Jiang Yuan, an artist who exhibited his painting under the patronage of UNESCO, had collaborated with the Beijing City Artists Association (*Beijing Meishujiaxiehui*), and also Hangzhou and Chaoyang cities, to present this exhibition in Macau.

The Women's General Association of Macau

Women are very active in the MSAR and their associations also promote culture.

Elizabeth Sinn's thesis concerning 'power and charity' (2003) takes the example of the Tung Wah Hospital in Hong Kong; similar studies could equally well focus, in particular, on the Tung Sin Tong and Kiang Wu associations, and also the Women's General Association of Macau.

The Women's General Association of Macau (*Funu Lianhezonghui*) was founded in 1950 on the model of another association linked with Beijing, the Macau General Workers' Association (*Aomen Gonghuilianhe Zhonghui*). These associations have been modernised. In the 1950s women in China were encouraged to be good 'socialist family women', to encourage their husbands to work hard, and to educate their children in the proper way.[172] Macau at that time was very different, but this does not change the close relationship between Beijing and the Women's General Association of Macau. Women's 'participation is not solely about numbers and percentages; consciousness is far more important'.[173] A new law was promulgated in 1992 in Mainland China concerning women, and this has certainly influenced the philosophy of The Women's General Association of Macau concerning politics, economy, culture, marriage, divorce and the family.[174]

The Women's General Association of Macau currently has 20,000 members. Its headquarters is located on Rua do Campo (*Shuikengwei*). A *sine qua non* condition for membership is to be female. In 2011, the association suggested that people should not throw useful things away during the New Year festive period, and should engage in wise consumerism (in Cantonese *mo sai ye* 'don't waste').[175] The Association also suggested that the red envelopes for *laisi* (traditional money gifts during this period) might be re-used.

Previously, on the eleventh anniversary of the return of Macau to China, a children's competition was organised by the Women's General Association of Macau, to develop creativity and strengthen the link of young people to the Mainland.[176] The theme was 'Love the Country (*aiguo*) and Macau'. The idea was to change the 'local' mentality of young people. Such a declared theme can be considered an attempt to advance patriotism and/or nationalism. However, the project also involved the participation of a large number of children and parents to improve the environment and to make Macau cleaner.

On 3 February 2011, the first day of the Lunar New Year, the Women's General Association of Macau had its Sixtieth Anniversary dinner, hosted by its President, Ms Ho Teng Iat (He Ding Yi). Women and staff associated with its six kindergartens, the school of the Association and a particular section of the General Women's Assocuiation of Macau, named Young Women's Association a total of three hundred persons – attended.

The managing Vice-President, Ms Yeong Siu Man (Yang Xiu Wen), explained the numerous activities that the association had been engaged during 2010. She stated that, in 2011, the Association would continue to be a harmonious point for social gathering for women of all classes. Women would be promoted, their rights protected, and all services for them and their children would be organised. The aim of the Association was to continue current efforts to help one another, and to meet together. However, to do this, she felt the activities of the Association would have to be more numerous and better organised, and that members would have to continue to do these things well.[177] A toast was proposed. As often during this period of the year in the MSAR, a lucky draw was organised for prizes, and songs were sung.

The structure of this Association has similarities with that of the charitable association Tung Sin Tong. The president, Ms Ho Teng Iat, former Deputy to the Legislative Assembly (1999-2009), prefers to be called 'chairwoman'. She is also one of the thirty-eight Directors of the Tung Sin Tong. From 1978 to date, she has devoted the majority of her efforts to the Women's General Association of Macau which is the centre of her life. In February 2012, the Honourable Silver Lotus was awarded to her. The Tung Sin Tong Association also has ten vice-presidents on its Board: Wong Kit Ching (Huang Jie Qing), Wong Lei Chen (Huang Li Zhen), Lam Sin Mei (Lin Xi Mei), Lam Siu Iun (Lin Xiao Yun), Lao Kam Leng (Liu Jing Ling), Lo Tak Va (Lu De Hua, who is also a Director of the Tung Sin Tong, Ng Siu Chiung (Wu Xiu Qiong), Yeong Siu Leng (Yang Xiu Ling), Leong Siu Man (Yang Xiu Wen), and Alice Cheng Siu Meng (Zheng Xiu Ming, also a Director of the Tung Sin Tong, a member of the board of the Rotary Guia, and the owner of the daily newspaper *Van Kio*). In 2011, Ms Wong Man Yi (Huang Min Er) was in charge of administration andis also an advisor to the 'Chairwoman' Ms Ho Teng Iat; she is also an influential member of the Guangzhou Women's Association.

The power, in this Women's General Association of Macau is concentrated at the top. Its president seems to have an equivalent power in her association to that enjoyed by the president of the Tung Sin Tong in his. However, the Executive Secretary of each of the charitable associations Tung Sin Tong and Kiang Wu seems to have more autonomy than does the Executive Secretary of the Women's General Association of Macau. As mentioned, the main power in Macau lies in the 'higher Board', which includes the president and – in 2012 – ten vice-presidents in the case of the Women's General Association of Macau and six vice-presidents in the case of the Tung Sin Tong. Four Inspectors in this last Association seem to have gained in power. These inspectors control the finances and have access to all documents. Lei Hon Kei is the head of the Board of Supervisors of Tung Sin Tong.

The Women's General Association of Macau, with its large number of members, seems gigantic. Unlike, for example, the Tung Wah Hospital in Hong Kong which is regulated under the pragmatic British type of administration, but is also in close contact with Beijing, the Tung Sin Tong, founded in 1892 (see below), is 'Portugalised' in its structure, has its own administrative system, and does not follow special regulations. The Women's General Association of Macau has been related to the political structure prevailing in Mainland China since 1950. In 2011, this Association is, according to Association President Ho Teng Iat, 'structured and regulated' – meaning that it has a strict internal organisation.[178] In January 1950, another association, the General Student Association of Macau (*Aomen Xuesheng Lianhezhonghui*) has the same initial structure. [179]

The Women's General Association of Macau is rich and powerful. For the first time, early in 2011, it accepted the participation in their activities as associate members of members' husbands over fifty-five years of age. Since, from the beginning, membership has only been open to women, this is a modern and creative way to develop the Association.

Summary of the Author's Interview with The Women's General Association of Macau President

On 3 February 2011, I was able to interview Ms Ho Teng Iat, President of The Women's General Association of Macau,. Ms Ho (photo 11),[180] certainly inherited the entrepreneurial spirit of her father, the late Ho Tin (He Tian), in terms of work ethic and collaborative approach, with the goal of sustaining growth and improving welfare. Madam Ho is the managing director and CEO of her father's company. She is the elder sister of the Vice-president of the Legislative Assembly of Macau, Ho Iat Seng. The first modern electronic factory in Macau was established by Ho Tin and has been an industrial success, not only for the Ho family, but also for Macau. Ms Ho, who has family links with the prestigious capital of Zhejiang Province, Hangzhou, a key cultural city, in relationship with Macau and Zhongshan, rejects firmly the idea of creating a museum in her father's historic factory.

She prefers to devote herself to promoting women, and to act, rather than to look back. She does not regret having left the Legislative Assembly, where she sat during the first ten years of the MSAR.

The importance of 'teamwork' – the only English expression used by 'Chairwoman as she prefers to be called – Ho' in the interview – expresses the spirit of the Women's General Association of Macau. This model of administration contrasts with that of some other associations in Macau, where few staff are available, except on meeting days.

Ms Ho Teng Iat emphasises the fact that the Association is regulated internally, which is not so common in the MSAR. Neither the Portuguese administration nor the current regime tried to impose an internal organisation on such an association.

Concerning education, ex-Deputy Ho thinks that the Macau Government is equally fair to both sexes. Men and women are treated with equality in education, including tertiary education, where more women have access to tertiary education than before. Ms Ho considers that fifteen years of free education, as voted in 2007, is a great achievement for the Special Administrative Region.

Due to the importance of her current seat as a member of the Chinese People's Consultative Conference in Beijing, her membership in the National Women's Federation of China, her presidency of the Women's General Association of Macau and her directorial position at the Tung Sin Tong, Ms Ho does not want to concentrate her attention on other activities. She is fully occupied. However, she has also been appointed to the board of the Macau Foundation.

As an example of her concerns, the primary school and the six nurseries of the General Women's Association need to be managed carefully. The plan is to have more nurseries. To show the interest that exists for such facilities, it was planned to double the capacity of the nursery of Santa Casa de Misericordia and enroll 258 children in September 2011. Ms Ho Teng Iat recognises the importance of nurseries in the life of Macau's women. A new nursery was established in Qingzhou in 2011. This northwestern part of the Peninsula is to be completely transformed, despite a series of discussions at the Legislative Assembly (see the Chapter, 'Economy and Society'). Democrat deputies have often criticised the modernisation of Qingzhou.

Young people, in particular young people in single-parent families, as well as older people, also require the attention of Ms Ho. Women want to play a greater role in Macau, and Ms Ho says the Women's General Association of Macau is promoting unity (*tuanjie*) and development.

Before the handover in 1999, the wife of the Portuguese Governor of Macau was president of the other Macau Women's Association, the Mothers of Macau (*Muqinhui*). Ms Ho Teng Iat is currently an influential member of the board of the Mothers of Macau, which offered traditional Lucky Money (*laisi*) before the Chinese New Year in 2011 and 2012. This association is located near the Dom Bosco Middle School. The Macanese representative and treasurer of the *Muqinhui*, Ms Fei Man Wah, was present during this event.

The General Women's Association is particularly concerned about older people living alone, single-parent families and families in need. Ms Van Iat Kio (Yin Yi Qiao), director of Kiang Wu Nursing College, is also an important director of The General Women's Association.

The Red Cross

The Red Cross, part of the globalisation process, is mentioned here only in relation to some recent activities. The Macau main branch of the Red Cross recognised its outstanding volunteers in early February 2011, on Praia Grande. The president of the Branch, Mr. Eddie Wong Yue Kai (Huang Ru Jie) personally congratulated these volunteers, who had participated in the collection of money for Red Cross interventions in Haiti, Qinghai and

Southwest China. The Red Cross is trying to recruit more volunteers.[181] In December 2010, the Red Cross received MOP 40 million from the Macau Foundation and MOP 4 million from DFS Cotai Limitada.[182]

Tung Sin Tong and Kiang Wu

Tung Sin Tong and Kiang Wu are the main charitable associations in Macau. Kiang Wu was founded in 1871 and Tung Sin Tong in 1892.

In 1852 (before the great medical development which took place in Europe after about 1870), the cure and prevention of smallpox, typhus, typhoid, cholera and scarlet fever were just starting in Hong Kong and Macau. However, the preliminary studies of modern western medicine cannot be ignored, including the following. In 1862, Louis Pasteur made the first test of germ theory. In 1876, Robert Kock discovered the anthrax disease cycle. Between 1883 and 1897, Joseph Lister was the first to practice antiseptic surgery.

Power and charity are linked with Chinese traditions. Sponsoring charitable associations is common among rich Chinese entrepreneurs.

The two main charitable associations of Macau, Kiang Wu and Tung Sin Tong, assure the social stability of society, in particular for those who need sustained medical and social support. The International Red Cross has close links with Tung Sin Tong.

The Macao Daily Association is also very important. But because it is part media, part charity we will not discuss this association here.

Tung Sin Tong Charitable Society

This society is dedicated to the people of Macau. It was founded in 1892 by a group of influential Chinese leaders and businessmen. It manages an important clinic of Traditional Chinese Medicine (TCM), a Western Medicine Clinic, and pharmacies. In 2011, as with other

Associations in Macau, the Association structure includes two boards – the higher board includes the President, six vice-presidents – and the lower board is composed of four Inspectors and thirty-eight directors (2012).

In Chinese societies, both in the MSAR and on the Mainland, various associations exist. Among the various types of Chinese association in Macau, it is useful to analyze charity associations such as the Tung Sin Tong, to try to understand better the Chinese of Macau, who tend to rely on such institutions. This particular charitable association explains in itself some of the fundamental realities of the MSAR, its history, its society, and its powerful relationships. Such an analysis of this particular institution can provide an account of the efforts of the Chinese of Macau to hold to their own formula within the 500-year-old multi-ethnic society of Macau.

As mentioned, the management of the Tung Sin Tong is different from that of the Tung Wah Hospital in Hong Kong.[183] The Tung Wah Hospital was influenced by British administration under the Ordinance of 1870. In contrast, the system of management of the Tung Sin Tong illustrates both the advantages and inconveniences of the Portuguese model. However, since 1892 the Tung Sin Tong has worked, and it continues to work, to help the Chinese of Macau and other patients and poor people who are in need. Both organisations are responsive to the fact that, whether under the Anglo-Chinese system of Hong Kong or under the present system of Macau, the Chinese prefer to be governed according to Chinese Law and customs.

The Tung Sin Tong provides unique insights into the Macau system of organisation of medical services, which has survived many crises. Tung Sin Tong is a key association for understanding the Chinese of Macau and their achievements in medicine. In the early nineteenth century it was through Macau that 'Western vaccination' (*Yangdou* and later *Zhongdou*) was introduced to China.[184] Edward Jenner's inoculation against smallpox through inducing cowpox had been unknown previously in China. Wang Qingren (1768-1831) and Wu Yang in particular, were precursors concerning this domain in the history of medicine in China.

Tung Sin Tong is a key association for understanding the Chinese of Macau and their achievements.

During this period people were kidnapped or decoyed as 'coolies' and transited through Macau, where both immigrants and coolies underwent medical examination (which they often failed). Before the existence of the Kiang Wu Hospital and the Tung Sin Tong clinics there were no facilities to care for the poor, and no dispensaries for the Chinese in Macau. However, from the beginning of its foundation, the Tung Sin Tong has provided free burial and basic coffins for the poor.

Today the Chinese of Macau know the Tung Sin Tong clinics, its schools, its homes for the elderly, its youth centres, the nurseries it runs, and its annual fund-raising campaign. Today, as before, besides Western medicine, the Tung Sin Tong offers free Chinese medicine. The use of this traditional Chinese medicine is still strong in Yunnan, one of the major sources of herbs and plants in China. Macau is also a stronghold for Chinese medicine. The main activities of the Tung Sin Tong are the provision of free medical services, a free supply of medicines for those in need, financial and medical help for expectant mothers, food for the poor, and clothing and blankets in winter. Its three clinics are located in Camilo Pessanho, Toin San and Praca de Ponte e Horta.

Eight medical departments exist in the Tung Sin Tong, practicing both Chinese and Western medicine. They are: Internal Medicine, Ophthalmology, Dentistry, ENT (Ear, Nose and Throat), Otolaryngology, Head and Neck disorders, Acupuncture, and Chinese Orthopoedics. In recent years, a Surgery Department has been established.

The Tung Sin Tong Free School was established in 1924 to provide free schooling for poor children. The Tung Sin Tong Secondary School was established in 1991. In

2012, there are also kindergartens, as well as primary and secondary sections, and finally a senior high school to prepare for college examinations. The Free School also provides evening courses for adults in computer training, accounting, Putonghua and other subjects. The school assists outstanding students by giving scholarships and grants-in-aid including to attend university or to undertake other forms of further education. The Secondary School also provides musical training.[185]

The Tung Sin Tong assists and alleviates working families' burdens by helping to take care of their children. Since 1976 it has run four nurseries with a total capacity of 500 children, free of charge. These nursery services are provided in the highly populated northern, southern and central districts.

In 2010, the Tung Sin Tong spent MOP 60 million for social work and charity, and made the decision to build five new buildings for older people. During the winter of 2010-2011, the Annual Fund Raising Campaign of Tung Sin Tong collected MOP 250,000 from the Casino Galaxy (*Yinhe Yule*).[186] The Hong Kong and Shanghai Bank gave MOP 100, 000, and the Wynn Casino gave MOP 250,000.[187] In total, the Tung Sin Tong received MOP 10.36 million. Deputy Chui Sai Peng, in his capacity as a Vice-President of Tung Sin Tong, congratulated all the donors on behalf of the Tung Sin Tong Board of president, vice-presidents and directors. – Vice-President Chui Sai Peng is the son of former president of the Tung Sin Tong, the late Chui Tak Kei (Cui De Qi) who passed away in 2007 at the age of ninety-six. Chui Sai Peng is also a cousin of the present Chief Executive of Macau.

On 12 January 2011, the President of the Association, Hoi Sai Iun, Vice-President Mok Kuam Iek (Mo Jun Yi) and Director Ms Ho Teng Iat visited the home for the elderly in Huang Chao. They offered gifts and cash grants to thirty-five of the attending senior residents. The same day, Vice-President Chui and Director Elias Lam Iat Cho (Lin Ri Chu) visited the Saint Francisco Home for the

Elderly and donated gifts and presents of cash to sixty-eight residents. The president, assisted by Vice-President of the Association, Mok Kuan Iek and Ms Ho Teng Iat, also visited Guanghui and gave similar donations to fifty older people there.

Prior to the Chinese New Year period of 2011, the Tung Sin Tong Association worked hard to help the most forgotten citizens of Macau. In mid-January 2011, Vice-President of the Association Mok Kuan Iek (Mo Jun Yi), a member of the higher board, presented gifts to more than two thousand elderly persons in thirty-three institutions.[188] On 17 January 2011, the Tung Sin Tong donated rice, oil and money-gifts ('laisi' in Cantonese) to thousands of Chinese of Macau in need. That day, President Hoi Sai Iun (Xu Shi Yuan) and Director Mok (Mo Gui Bo, d. December 2011) donated five hundred gifts to older people of the Macau Peninsula, Taipa and Coloane. On 18 February 2011, Vice-President Chui Sai Cheong offered books in the name of the Tung Sin Tong to two hundred students of the Pui Ching (*Peizheng*) primary school.[189]

The Tung Sin Tong is a venerable institution giving 'face' and demonstrating the ethical culture of Macau. The six Vice-Presidents are Chui Sai Cheong, Lei Loi Tak, Chui Sai Peng, Antonio Wu Sun Him (Hu Shun Qian), Mok Kuan Iek (Mo Jun Yi), and Dr Lam Kam Seng.[190] The Executive Secretary, Shirley Heong Soi Lan, has had ten years of experience in the Association. She worked for three years in an intermediary job in a private company, and this was very useful for her career. Chinese Medicine constitutes Tung Sin Tong's golden asset but, among the Directors, the only one specialised in Chinese Medicine is Lam Iat Cho.

In 2011, the lower Board of Directors experienced some change. The General Inspector, Lei Hon Kei (Li Han Ji), was previously an ordinary director of this board, but at present he has three assistants. This reflects a legal change in the MSAR. Among these inspectors, another important Vice-President of this board is Ho Hau Tong. So, the power of the inspectorate board continues to grow, but it is difficult to know exactly why. Many new names appeared among the directors in 2011, and these present a modern, younger image of Tung Sin Tong.

Regarding gender inequality, six women, instead of the previous seven, are at present members of this lower Board of Directors. However, in 2012, the 'Chairwoman' of the Women's General Association of Macau, Ho Teng Iat, is a Director and will deservedly become Vice-President of Tung Sing Tong.

Yearly, some schools in Macau collect money to donate to the Tung Sin Tong. One of these is Pui Ching, a famous middle school, which prepares students to enter university. The foundation of Pui Ching School was inspired by American Chinese Baptists. Originally located in Canton, the school was transferred from Canton to Macau following the Japanese invasion of China before World War II. There is also a Pui Ching Middle School in Hong Kong founded in 1889. In 2011, to participate in the Tung Sin Tong annual campaign to raise funds for its charitable work, Pui Ching students collected MOP 24,190 and forwarded it to the charitable institution. However, the funds that Pui Ching students collect and give to the Aomen Ribao Charity Association are ten times more than to the Tung Sin Tong and this demonstrates the difference in importance and popularity of these two associations. The dominance of the *Aomen Ribao* (*Macao Daily Newspaper*) among Macau's media and the popularity of its charitable institution reflects the Mainland's influence in Macau.

The question of 'charity and power', discussed by Elizabeth Sinn, is relevant for the Tung Sin Tong. Macau Chief Executive Chui's uncle, Chui Tak Kei, was president of the Tung Sin Tong for fifty years. Chui Sai Peng, during the presidency of his father, was 24th in the hierarchy of the Tung Sin Tong; in 2011 he is Vice-President and number four of the higher board. Ex-President Chui Tak Kei, late Vice-President Rocky Chui (Cui Le Qi); and two directors,

Ho (He Han Zhi) and Lam Cheong Sai (Lin Chong Shi) have passed away.

Kiang Wu

The Kiang Wu Charitable Association (*Jiang Hu Cishanhui* in Putonghua) was founded in 1871. It is at present the most ancient and venerable hospital in the MSAR. During the Qing Dynasty, the Kiang Wu Association was responsible for many Chinese Temples in Macau, including the *Baogong, Lian Feng, Lian Kai, Guandi* and *Kang Zheng Jun* temples. Kiang Wu has been in charge of the Funeral Parlour and an associate temple, from the mid-1930s to the present,

Kiang Wu Hospital, one of the three main hospitals of Macau, is run by the Charitable Association, *Jiang Hu Cishanhui*, which is Chinese in essence and linked to the history of China. *Conde São Januário* and the Macau University of Science and Technology Hospital are the other hospitals. At present, Kiang Wu – in contrast to Tung Sin Tong which is more traditional – is more oriented toward Western medicine than toward Chinese medicine.

In 1892, one of the earliest Chinese physicians to practice Western medicine in Macau was Dr Sun Yat-sen who had then just obtained his degree at the College of Medicine for Chinese, a precursor of the University of Hong Kong.[191] Dr Sun introduced Western medicine to Kiang Wu Hospital. The Kiang Wu Hospital continues to follow the political philosophy and social principles of Sun Yat-sen – in particular *minsheng zhuyi*, promoting social welfare.

In 1935 Dr O Lin (Ke Lin) opened a surgery section. The Chinese medicine section was closed between 1941 and 1970 and resumed in a secondary capacity compared to the Western medicine hospital itself. This last section is also less important than the Chinese Medicine Department at Tung Sin Tong. In 2012, at Kiang Wu, there are nine or ten dentists – most of them graduated from Jinan

University. This fact again reflects the importance of Guangdong Province in education.

In January 2012, the President of the Kiang Wu Charitable Association is Ma Man Kei who currently lives in Beijing. Dr Stanley Ho is the first Vice-President. Many members of the board are influential persons. Some directors are associated with both Kiang Wu and Tung Sin Tong. This list includes the Vice-President Hoi Sai Iun, also President of Tung Sin Tong and Lam Kam Seng (Vice-president of Tung Sin Tong). Other directors of Kiang Wu are Wu Sun Him (Hu Shun Qian), Ho Wah Tim (He Hua Tian), the President of the Legislative Assembly, Lau Cheok Va, Liu Zhuo Hua, (*see Photograph* 4), the Deputy Leonel Alves, Lei (Li Ying De), Wong Yue Kai (also President of the Red Cross of Macau) and Lu Yong Gen. The Chief Executive Fernando Chui Sai On was the director of the Kiang Peng School (established in the 1940s and belonging to the Kiang Wu association) before becoming the Secretary for Social Affairs and Culture of the MSAR between 1999 and 2009.

Kiang Wu Vice-President Peng Bi De, an overseas Chinese from Ecuador who originates from Zhongshan, passed away on 23 January 2011. His life helps us to understand the relationship between power and charity, and the Chinese tradition of rich entrepreneurs and members of the social elite sponsoring charitable associations.[192] It is also part of the cultural ethics of the Chinese elite of Macau. Acts of charity are a traditional Chinese virtue. Thai tradition may also have this quality; however, the Thai elite are motivated mainly by Buddhism and the search to acquire merit, *boon.*

The College of Nursing, one of the five institutions of the Kiang Wu Association, is currently famous for its four years of nursing training. The director is Ms Van Iat Kio and Yoki Cheong Hoi Ieng is her assistant executive administrative officer. The students of the first, second, third and four years are in classes of about fifty students each. After the handover, the college achieved complete recognition for its final nursing diploma. The importance of the Mainland is evident, not only for the Nursing College but for the whole Kiang Wu Association. Previously the third and fourth year students of this college were trained in Beijing. In 2002 it became a degree granting college, offering a Bachelor in Science in Nursing. It has also a Midwife School.

The library of this college needs to be developed – currently, it has 10,000 books in Chinese and 2,000 in English. Concerning its Committee and the structure of power, it is useful to note the name of the Executive Secretary in Macau, Ms Ung Pui Kun, and that of the President, Ma Man Kei, in Beijing. The President of the Legislative Assembly, Lau Cheok Va, is also an influential member of the Board.

We would like to thank, for their kind support of our research, the executive secretary, Ms Ung Pui Kun (Wu Pei Juan), the director of the Nursing College, Van Iat Kio; Ms Lau Van Iong, who is responsible for the Museum of Kiang Wu; Ms Qi Wei; and in particular the chief of the director's office, Dr Winnie 谢 Che Sio Ieng. Wang Ting Huai, the director of the Hospital, which is the most important institution of the Association, was not present during my research-visits to the Kiang Wu Association. In particular in early March 2011, the hospital hosted a very important conference of ORL specialists – specialists in otolaryngology or ENT (ear, nose, and throat).[193]

The Funeral Parlour (*binyiguan*), built in 1933, was restructured later. In the joint Funerary Temple, *Siqingyuan,* the spirit tablets (*shenwei)* of the deceased are arranged.

The five sections of the Association are thus the Hospital, the Nursing College, the education section – primary and secondary Schools – and the Funeral Parlour. In February 2012, Kiang Wu received MOP 52 million from the Macau Foundation (*Boletim Oficial*).

The Palliative Care Centre

Nothing is more important than life and death, so the Palliative Care Centre or *Kangning Zhongxin* (康宁中心) is of great important for the Kiang Wu Association and Hospital. It is fully financed by the Government of Macau. This Centre, which was opened in early 2000, reveals the positive continuous welfare action of the Department of Health of the MSAR. In principle, palliative medicine and pain management are integrated with the psychological aspect of patient care.

The Centre has thirty patients in twenty rooms. The majority of the rooms accommodate two patients with life-limiting illnesses. Three or four rooms are reserved for individual patients and constitute particular cases. The great importance of this Centre is shown by the fact that half of the patients are very frail and will probably not survive for many months. Around 70 per cent are treated for lung problems linked to cancer. It explains the fact that there is a majority of male patients because they are more likely to be chain-smokers. The second most common diseases among these patients are gastroenterological. It is difficult to give details about such almost incurable diseases and the author owes a debt of gratitude to the two female medical doctors in charge of this Centre who work during the day. (They do not work in this Care Centre at night, over week-ends or during holidays.) The two MDs have only eighteen days holiday a year. At night and during the absence of these two MDs, a medical doctor from Kiang Wu moves to this Centre to take care of any emergencies which may occur during these times.

In September 2012, Kiang Wu won what seems to be an absolute monopoly on funerals. This has met opposition to among a certain number of deputies at the Legislative Assembly. It is too early to give more details on this recent socio-economic change concerning a MSAR Government decision and a charitable association.

Sin Meng Association

Deputy Chan Mei Yi (Chen Mei Yi) has her own charity association, called the Sin Meng (*Ximinghui*). In 2011, Ms Chan wants to continue to improve the condition of both older people and young people. She is married to ex-Deputy David Chow; the couple have two children.[194]

The Sin Meng Association has two thousand members. The association has two levels of power and follows the classical structure of the Macau formula.

The upper board includes President Chan, four vice-presidents – Vincent Wu (Hu Yong Shun) is a very active vice-president and administers the association with the assistance of a permanent secretary.[195] The annual meeting convenes all the members, generally immediately before or immediately after the Chinese New Year.

To promote the Sin Meng Association, on 16 February 2011, at Fishermen's Wharf, a lunch party for the Chinese New Year was held under the patronage of Deputy Chan.[196]

Since the foundation of the association in 2002, a Christmas Party every year gives affection to children from single-parent families. In December 2011, more than 250 children enjoyed what for Deputy Chan is the most important event of the year. She is particularly concerned for children, has a charitable ethic, and has confirmed that the symbolic importance of this party is not centred on the Lunar New Year, but on Christmas, which reminds her of her education in Catholic schools.

On 8 January 2012 from 2pm to around 4pm, a New Year Party for older people was held in Iao Hon Square. For the first time ever there were performances for their enjoyment and, of course, traditional gifts. This district is one the most densely populated districts in the world, and so the choice of Sin Meng to assist the people living here is excellent. This 2012 New Year Party for older people was a particular one. The Macau Foundation was a sponsor of the dancing-groups and singers. The Sin Meng Association was particularly generous this year. The older people received a big orange bag in which to put all their presents. Deputy Chan Mei Yi had a kind word with many of the three hundred or so older people and all of them passed in organised and crowded ranks in front of her. The main gifts were a magnificent Chinese calendar, rice, oil, dry sausages, dry mushrooms, biscuits and cereals. Among three Macau singers who performed at this innovative performance, the Cantonese artist, Leong (Liang Xu Yin), delighted the audience. The security was tight because many neighbours wanted to join in. Access to the central meeting place was well protected. I have noticed that sometimes, during this period of the year, gifts attract non-registered older people and even mobs of adults, and consequently, disturbances may happen among the mass of people.

To conclude, all the associations included in this chapter play a social, cultural, economic and political role. They also play a key role in strengthening the relationship between the MSAR and Mainland China. Concerning Chinese identity, these associations constitute cultural models to understand better the MSAR and its mosaic society.

Social and Economic Prospects

Kiang Wu is a 'significant' association founded in 1871. It is not an association founded upon doing things 'over the past one or two years', as clearly mentioned in a report by a scholar (whose name is unknown to myself) on an early version of the present work. To show the importance of associations in Macau, it is enough to say that Kiang Wu Hospital today is run by the Charitable Association *Jiang Hu Cishanhui,* which is Chinese in essence and linked to the long history of Macau and China. The Museum of Kiang Wu (which unfortunately is not classified by the Department of Tourism of the MSAR) is open every Saturday and constitutes in itself a demonstration of the importance of associations, based on the lives of the most famous Chinese of Macau such as Ma Man Kei, the

President of Kiang Wu Association and Vice-President of the Kiang Wu Association, Dr Stanley Ho. Elsewhere, the role of Chinese associations in general is crucial. Denying the importance of associations in Macau is to refuse to acknowledge the key role of the most ancient charitable associations and Chinese hospitals of the MSAR.

The Kiang Wu demonstrates how an association works in the MSAR and what an association means for Chinese of Macau. However, the Kiang Wu association does not provide the sense of close identity given by *tongxianghui* (同乡会) – associations of persons originating from the same province, town or village. The identity of the Chinese of Macau is evident in this work. So, the associations in Macau are essential institutions proving the existence of the particular identity of Chinese of Macau.

The fundamental relationship between Macau and Guangdong Province is entering a new phase with the development of Hengqin Island and this will necessarily emphasise the role of the associations. Fujian Province is the second in importance as regards the close relationship and identity between the MSAR and other provinces of the Mainland.

Welfare will continue to be a key issue.

Associations of a religious nature also exist in the MSAR. The Basic Law provides a tolerant basis for all religious associations and offers to Macau's society 'freedom of religious belief', and freedom to preach and to conduct and participate in religious activities.

CHAPTER FIVE

RELIGION, TRADITIONS AND FESTIVALS

This chapter is based on previous fieldwork in the Macau Special Administrative Region of China (MSAR), and on more recent research conducted between 2010 and 2012. Photographic documentation permits the tracing back of research findings and allows close examination. Classical anthropological research based on observation, such as my survey in 2010 and early 2011, is the basis of this chapter. However, digital photographic studies may assist qualitative analysis.[197] Visual sociology is a new tool in the new world of visual communication. Some religious phenomena are analyzed in this chapter as simple traditional customs, based on photographic research.

The Basic Law, a constitutional document, remains the main legal reference for Macau because it is the unique constitutional document fully accepted by the Central Government of China and Portugal.[198]Unfortunately, the complete Portuguese Law of Macau is not yet perfectly translated into Chinese. Article 25 of the Basic Law gives to residents equal rights 'irrespective of their religion'. Article 34 confers freedom (*ziyou* 自由) of religious belief. Religious associations and organisations are, however, required to be registered with the MSAR Government. One of the most important components of the Basic Law is Article 128 that accords religious freedom which shall not 'contravene the laws of the Region'.

The term 'religion' is difficult to translate into Chinese, and this opens the way for the assimilation of religion and culture. Marcel Granet prefers to use the term 'religious sentiment' rather than any other. [199] In his view, it seems, the Chinese are lacking in 'religious sentiment' but do have rules and practices 'to obtain a particular advantage'.[200] For

Granet, Confucianism is the 'official religion', but this study of Macau is in the twenty-first century, not the time of Granet. Consequently, the definition *Zongjiao* (宗教) is the term normally used for religion, meaning 'the teaching of the ancestors'. [201] 'Teaching' is traditionally crucial in China. Between 1552 and 1773, in particular, the (Confucian) rites were considered essential. This partly explains the success of the Jesuits in China. They insisted on the compatibility of the Chinese 'Rites for the Veneration of the Ancestors', centred on *Qingmingjie* (清明节, 'The Pure Brightness Festival'), with the Catholic faith.

In November 2011 in Luxemburg, the Secretary-General of the Council of Europe, Thorbjorn Jagland, former Prime Minister of Norway and chairman of the Nobel Committee, defended the importance of religion, as a positive force for social cohesion. [202]

Almost all religions are represented in the Administrative Region of Macau, which constitutes a multi-ethnic and multi-cultural society. For example, Islam in Macau has a very long history. However, Hao Zhidong has mentioned that the 'Chinese of Macau' are 'only marginally influenced by religion'. [203] Is this correct? Out of two hundred and twenty-five households surveyed in January and February 2011, one hundred and fifty-five interviewees declared they had no religion.

Social Integration and Religious Freedom in the MSAR
My research was centred on the turn of the Christian and Lunar years, a key period for the understanding of religion in Macau. The question of belief is, of course, very personal. In response to my questionnaires, a large number of respondents between twenty and thirty years of age (123 out of 225 interviewees) reported having 'no religion'. This apparent atheism or lack of religious feeling may simply indicate that young people are less interested in religion than persons of older generations. At first glance, as mentioned by Hao, Chinese people seem to be atheists; but

whether one has a religious belief or not is difficult to verify. It is unfortunately not possible to give a clear answer to this complex question in this book.

Sinicization is the acculturation process by which the whole of society is transformed and united within the same cultural 'melting pot' during a specific period of time. (I define it differently in my book *Islam in China* (2004) because the Chinese of Macau are not a national minority of China, but part of the same Han society.) Most of the young people who responded to my questionnaires were apparently atheists and influenced by this type of acculturation. Other examples follow, in particular, the growing importance of Putonghua.

Despite excellent social integration with the Mainland, there are still differences between the MSAR and the Province of Guangdong. The use of the Cantonese dialect and traditional Chinese characters by many Chinese of Macau – in particular by Catholics and Christians – is remarkable. So, Cantonese – and Portuguese which is less important for Chinese people – are essential languages for the practice of religion in the MSAR.

Buddhism has had an impact in Macau. Buddhist vegetarian restaurants – including Raymond Un's Vegetarian Farm, just in front of the main Guanyin temple – are part of Macau's cultural heritage. Chinese religion is often considered as a syncretism of Buddhism and Daoism. Around five per cent of the interviewees in my survey said they were Buddhist, although less than one per cent of them claimed to be Daoist. Eleven per cent were Catholics – this percentage is much higher than the 6.7 per cent found by Hao.[204] In the 1990s, in Pui Ching, a Christian school, the annual survey of the percentage of Chinese students responding 'Christian' was above fifty per cent. However, a very small number of them said that they attended church.

In my survey, a mere ten out of 225 respondents, or 4.6 per cent, replied that they were 'Christian' (meaning 'Protestant'), or that they belonged to the Christian Church (*jidujiao* 基督教). Nevertheless, it is evident that both Catholic and Protestant schools are important in the MSAR. It is worth noting that, in Hong Kong, Christianity – both Catholic and Protestant – has been growing in popularity, mostly among young people, for quite a while, and this is now also the case on the Mainland as well.

The 11 per cent of respondents who said they were Catholics is significant and may relate to the fact that, before the handover in 1999, Portuguese citizenship was given to young people born in Macau in the 1980s who asked for Portuguese citizenship, although these Chinese people did not speak Portuguese. Some of them may go to church, in particular at Christmas time, without being Catholic, as a part of their Macau cultural identity. The main difference between the Chinese of Macau and the Macanese is still that all the Macanese are Catholic, although only a very tiny minority of Chinese in the enclave is Catholic. In East Timor, however, an important number of Timorese Hakka Chinese is Catholic.

Lun's work on the Hakka of Northern Guangdong, which constitutes eighty per cent of the local population there, confirms the importance of research on identity and the sociology of religion.[205] The relationship between identity and religion should be investigated in a serious and scientific manner. To finalise this question of the relationship between religion and culture, let us look at Luhmann's work, which suggests that the mass media has built a picture of 'culture' that is adopted by populations as a whole in modern societies.[206] This may explain the recent, increasing, importance of culture on the Mainland, which may have political reasons. Culture is promoted to create 'harmony' in society. This culture is modern, and the media has helped to solve the difficult question of mixing culture and religion. Religion is part of culture, but it has a spiritual component not existing in culture.

On the first night of Lunar New Year 2011, between 2 and 3 February, I discovered that the small Zhulin (*Zuklam* in Cantonese), 'Bamboo Forest' Buddhist Temple (photo

13), was closed, but, I went there again on the morning of 3 February 2011, and again on 23 January 2012. The worshippers were numerous. The Mazu ('Mazumiu' in Cantonese) Temple and the Guanyin Temple are the most popular in Macau during the New Year. Zhulin Temple in particular is central for the worship of spirit tablets, *shenwei*, one of the main foundations of the ancestor cult. Zhulin was Taiwan-oriented before the Cultural Revolution (1966-1974 in Macau). The Chinese characters here are sacred as in most of the Chinese temples, and, in 2010 and 2011, the necessary Chinese mantra in the temple were written and handed to the worshippers by a Japanese Buddhist scholar. In 2012 he was replaced by a young Chinese of Macau, Leong Hing Long. In particular at the beginning of the New Year, worshippers like, for example, to hear their own names said aloud by one of the temple staff members possessing religious training, who writes their names on paper, to be burned there in front of an altar dedicated to Guanyin and other divinities. This reinforces their own identity and promotes cultural religion which upgrades community ethics.

It seems that in 2012, Guanyin is being promoted. I do not know why, but it was a surprise for me at Mazu temple during the 2012 Lunar New Year to note that Guanyin was being honoured much more than previously.

Chinese Festivals as Identity Markers in Macau

Sampaio (1827-1875) noted the significance of Chinese festivals. [207] Festivals are indeed very important in Macau. Although 'the distinction between sacred and profane' is less appreciable in China than in the West.[208] So, it is not strange to note that an important percentage of the Chinese of Macau observe the festivals, but at the same time declare that they have 'no religion'. Granet again notes 'respect for traditions' and 'a tendency to positivism which excludes faith'.[209] The Chinese people do not have strong religious inclinations, but still they observe religious festivals. Dr Pansy Ho has stated that her father, Dr

Stanley Ho, also has 'no religion'. Responses to my questionnaires also show a certain lack of religious inclination among the Chinese of Macau. It seems then that festivals are not automatically part of religion, but are an essential component of Chinese tradition. The point to be considered about festivals in the MSAR is to explore whether or not they constitute identity markers for Chinese of Macau.

Hao Zhidong, in his recent book, thinks that religion is not fundamental for Chinese society in Macau, but explains in detail religious traditions in Macau, where the festivals confirm the crucial importance of 'Chineseness'. 'Chineseness' has already been confirmed by Cathryn Clayton, an anthropologist who taught at the University of Macau, and by my own work.[210] However, religion, as well as tradition, does confirm the identity of at least a part of the Chinese of Macau. The five per cent of interviewees, who identified themselves as Buddhists, and the larger number of Catholics and other Christians among the respondents in my survey are not negligible.

Sampaio also noted the important number of Chinese resident in the Macau Peninsula. In 2012, the population is still increasing. Additionally, the development of tourism in China now brings many tourists – they are called 'gamers' (or more commonly 'visitors' to protect the good image of Macau). But they stay for only two days at New Year and often for an even shorter time during other periods of the year. These Mainlanders may possibly visit Chinese temples, but the unique mosque of Macau is never included in package tours, even for the Muslims of Xinjiang (Uyghurs), Xian, or Yunnan (Hui).

This mosque is unique because it is located in an area with a history of more than five hundred years, as demonstrated by the old Portuguese name of the street, 'Moros' meaning 'Arabs'. It is interesting that 'Gongbei' (拱北) is the name of the Zhuhai-Macau border, but it is also an Arabic word, meaning 'old sacred tomb'. The reader has to understand that in Gansu Province and Xinjiang there are hundreds of such old and sacred Muslim tombs with the same Arabic name which has been adopted into Chinese as the loan-word, 'gongbei'. There is religious tolerance but a visit to a mosque is not 'touristic'. Consequently, the numerous Chinese Muslim tourists are given no time to see the Mosque of Macau, although it is located in a historical spot, in a street with a Portuguese name, 'Moros', an ancient name for the Arabs, as already mentioned.

Chinese New Year

The Chinese New Year Festival remains the essential Chinese event of the year. Family is very important for the Chinese of Macau and gatherings during the Chinese New Year are central. (*See Photograph* 2, 'A family of four generations'.) We may say that this festival constitutes an identity marker for the Chinese of Macau. The New Year starts before the first day of the first moon of the lunar calendar. Many family meetings occur on the eve of the New Year (22 January 2012), or one day before, at a festive dinner called *Tyunnin faan* (团年饭) in Cantonese (a lunch is also possible). For almost all Chinese, and in particular for a Buddhist informant aged eighty-two, who stressed the key role of this 'rite of passage', this meal is the most important. It is a pillar for maintaining their traditions.

The term 'rite of passage' suits this Chinese Lunar New Year ritual meal. It is fundamental, according to my perception, to the study of different Chinese people, including, of course, the Chinese of Macau. This *Tyunnin faan* is also, 'A rite of passage' concerning a particular recurrent human behavioural trait and includes traditional rituals. The first to use this sociological concept was the French anthropologist, Arnold van Gennep (1909). His book, *The Rites of Passage,* is essential for an understanding of the recurrence of traditions and festivals.

Is this 'rite of passage' of the Chinese of Macau similarly important for other Chinese people? I will not deny the importance of this ritual dinner for all Chinese, but the Chinese of Macau are flexible, and, for family reasons, many of them have their own way of following this tradition. The Chinese of Macau, unlike Mainlanders, are not particularly attracted by the Lunar New Year's eve television programmes which often constitute a 'must' in China, thanks to their high quality.

As an example to show the 'flexible' character of this festival in Macau, in 2012 a very 'traditional' mother of ten children agreed for the first time to have this particular dinner two days before Lunar New Year's eve on 20 January, and not on the 21, 22 or 23 January which would have been 'the most common'. At seventy-four, she cannot cook at home any more – and also her family of four generations is very large – so she decided that the whole family should go to a restaurant. But as the restaurants had all been booked long in advance, the night of 20 January was the only possibility. Other Chinese families in Beijing or New York or Dili, Timor, would probably not agree to be so flexible.

In Macau, Cantonese cuisine is the most common. Cantonese cuisine is another marker of the identity of Chinese of Macau.[211]

The Chinese New Year is the most important festival for the majority of my informants. Generally, at around 8pm on the eve of the first day of the Chinese New Year, 2 February 2011, Chinese family members met at their father's home. In Macau, most of the time, married daughters visit the parents of their husbands. If the father has passed away, as is the case for family Number One in my survey, the mother becomes the central character. The tenth and last son in this family is the preferred child. The mother decides and rules; the youngest son organises this very particular dinner of the New Year and the observance of all the Chinese festivals for this family.

In Appendix 3, among the three Chinese interviewees who do not celebrate the Chinese New Year, only one person – a man of sixty-nine, born in Zhongshan and a

Macau resident for more than fifty years – did not meet any family member during the Chinese New Year.

In addition to the family meetings on the eve of the New Year, the first day of the New Year as well as the following days are important and follow the Chinese calendar *nongli* 农历. The programme for each family differs, and more families today travel outside Macau. Other families prefer to stay by themselves and do not go out, saying that the city is too crowded and noisy at this time.

In the nineteenth century, Sampaio noticed that very few Chinese of Macau worked during this festive period, and this has been generally true in Macau up to the present, although staff in the gaming industry may work during the Chinese New Year period. Many Mainlanders enter Macau during this period, more interested in gaming than in worshipping.

Another tradition of Macau is the fireworks industry which was developed in Macau long ago. Joseph Kessel in his novel on Macau (*Hong-Kong and Macao,* 1957, reprinted 2011) has described the centrality of fireworks, a tradition still important in Macau, a way of sending out the old year and chasing away the bad spirits when the New Year comes. Sampaio mentioned the '*Panchões em grande profusão* during the Chinese New Year'.[212] Firecrackers are part of tradition, and it is common to hear their festive detonations for about five days.

Over the major part of the twentieth century, Macau was a sort of capital for fireworks, with numerous factories on Taipa Island producing them. Nowadays, on the Mainland (and in Hong Kong too), there are strict regulations imposed on the use of fireworks, so this aspect of the New Year period may be more festive in the MSAR. In 2012, being further from the centre of population, I heard the first detonations on the morning of 21 January (one day before Lunar New Year's Eve).

On Chinese New Year's eve, at midnight on 2 February 2011, when all the Board members of 'the' temple of

Macau paid their respect to the goddess Mazu, the noise of the firecrackers was intense.

My survey confirms both the centrality of the Chinese New Year as the key festival of the year and the continuity of the tradition of setting off fireworks.

Following Chinese New Year, firecrackers are heard in some streets for eight days in the MSAR. This shows administrative differences between Macau and the Mainland confirmed by the Basic Law.

According to De Groot, the belief in ghosts is a corner-stone of China's universalistic religion.[213] This explains the persistence of the firecracker tradition. De Groot uses the term *gui* to classify evil spirits, ghosts, specters and demons.[214] Firecrackers are useful, both to chase away bad spirits and to prevent misfortune during the coming year.

On the Mainland, watching television on Chinese New Year's eve is common, and to a certain degree has replaced traditions such as the use of firecrackers. This special TV programme is watched by a majority of both middle class and working class Chinese. The elite attend national and well-advertised shows; ordinary people watch them on television.

Although less true in 2012 than in 2000, it seems correct to say that the Chinese of Macau are less frequent travelers than Hong Kong residents and many Mainlanders. In particular for the Lunar New Year – traditionally, and in particular before the handover – the Chinese of Macau do not like to travel far away.

An informant with a good job, who previously liked to travel to Thailand, at present only goes to Zhongshan, where he has bought a flat, and to Guangzhou. He travels 'en famille' mainly to Zhongshan and Guangzhou in his car (which is registered in Macau and Guangdong) and at present has no time to fly. His job and the family take all his time. He wants, in particular, to stay close to his mother (aged seventy-four in 2011). She scrupulously respects the festivals and the family 'has' to follow her will, although not feeling at all compelled to do so. This lady is a

Buddhist, but she does not see any monk or nun at present. Her home is the worship centre, not a particular temple or altar, as she does not want to walk too much.

Many shops did not open in Macau before 6 February 2011, but activity in the MSAR returned to normality after 8 February. Thus less than one week was dedicated to the New Year.

Laisi

There are many customs related to the New Year. The desire for peace, and the hope for happiness and wealth are the main themes. It is interesting to note, through the excellent reprinted work on Vietnam by Maurice Durand, that some Chinese Lunar New Year traditions are also well preserved there.[215]

For the Tet Festival in Vietnam, celebrated in 2012 on 23 January, there is still a tradition of presenting red envelope gifts, just as in Macau and Hong Kong, and equally significant. In Macau, Portuguese people offer *laisi* to Chinese people, although this Chinese tradition is not part of their own culture.

The Lunar New Year tradition of red envelopes symbolising good luck and warding off bad spirits is a Chinese tradition that has been transmitted throughout East and Southeast Asia. These envelopes are red. This is why they are called *hongbao* 红包, *laisi* in Cantonese, *angpao* in Minnan, *Li Xi* in Vietnamese and *Sae Bae Don* in Korean. On 3 February 2011, from morning to evening, almost all the staff working in my residence expected to receive *laisi*. In this building, the tradition is very well preserved. However, some residents of the building do not give *laisi* to all the staff, but only to those they consider particularly diligent and hard working. Unexpectedly, the wife of one of the staff also collected these gifts. (Her husband works as a night guard and in fact returned home to sleep at 11am that particular day.) On 23 January 2012, in the new building where I live (and where the percentage of residents from the Mainland is higher), the collection of *laisi* is not systematically organised by the staff, although this type of tradition is always welcomed.

Qingmingjie

*'Qingming*jie', together with the Chinese New Year celebrations, contributes to reinforce the idea of a particular identity.

As first published in 1922, Marcel Granet notes of the Chinese, that, 'There is no other defined religion except the Ancestor belief'.[216] It is difficult to confirm a specific Macau cultural trait, but at least this festival *Qingming* is part of the key 'Chineseness' of the Chinese of Macau and a Chinese way to celebrate a crucial rite of passage in the MSAR.

'Religious ritual involves spirits of the dead in one form or another', wrote Robert P. Weller as published in 2007.[217] More crucial and family-related than Chinese New Year celebrations, *Qingmingjie* is the second rite of passage of the Chinese of Macau (as confirmed by the responses to my questionnaires).

As in all human societies, death and funerals play a key role in Chinese societies, and this is true also in the MSAR. Their importance is shown in the photograph, the 'Funeral March', taken in 1998 by Franck Regourd.[218] After the New Year rites, the essential ancestor cult, centred on *Qingmingjie,* is one of the most important rites of passage in Macau. The 'Pure Brightness' Festival is celebrated on the fifteenth day from the Spring Equinox. It generally occurs in April (5 April in 2012) and is also refered to as 'Sweeping the Graves'.

Some respondents in my survey put *Qingmingjie* ahead of the Chinese New Year in importance. However, they do not fail to celebrate what is called *Tyunnin faan* in Cantonese. As previously seen, the yearly family banquet is fundamental to define the identity of the Chinese of Macau.

For two high-ranking Chinese Catholic families of the MSAR, *Qingmingjie* is more important than Christmas and much more important than the Chinese New Year. For them, *Qingmingjie* is the only festival uniting brothers, sisters, nephews, nieces and grandchildren. These are their only important family gatherings because the family is separated, some living in the MSAR, some on the Mainland and some in Hong Kong.

Respect for ancestors is rooted in early human beliefs. For prehistoric man, respect for ancestors was a religious phenomenon and an essential element of group identity. But, in China, it is not considered a 'religion'. When Chinese of Macau say 'we have no religion', they may still respect the 'Pure Brightness' Festival of *Qingmingjie*. Together with their families, the Chinese of Macau often go either to the cemetery where their parents are buried, or to the temple where the *shenwei* ('spirit tablets') of their deceased parents are located, and many perform rites and ceremonies for them.

Case Number 117 in my survey is the story of an extraordinary migration from Hengshan, Guangdong Province, in 1951. A boy of ten and his younger sister came with their parents to Macau and all were converted to Catholicism, a rather unique case. An association named Fatima helped them during their first years in post-World War II Macau – a very hard time – so the church became a sort of home for them. The oldest son, sixty-seven years old when he responded to my questionnaire, is an active leader who spiritually looks after eight younger brothers and sisters. The father has passed away, so the mother, ninety-one years old in 2012, is *de facto* the frail pillar of the family; all the children and grandchildren gather around her in particular for Christmas. The exception is a younger brother who attends Christmas in Hong Kong with his in-laws, wife, daughter and son, but this nuclear family leaves Hong Kong and comes to Macau to visit the mother and grandmother for Chinese New Year, although, for them, it is not the main festival. For the majority of the

Chinese of Macau, *Qingmingjie* is the second most important festival. The third most important festival is the Winter Solstice.

Winter Solstice Festival
The Winter Solstice Festival (which fell on 22 December in 2010), is more important in South China – especially among the Cantonese – than it is among the northern Chinese. However, in Macau, many shops are open during the Winter Solstice. In 2010, I joined the family of one of my informants for the Winter Solstice; indeed, since 1995 I have participated in many festivals with them. In 2010 we had a nice banquet, as usual, but not at their home, because the informant's wife does not cook, and his mother cannot work as hard as she did previously in her life, taking care of six sons and four daughters, although at present she often sees her thirteen grandchildren. Not every family has such a special lunch for the Winter Solstice, although in Hong Kong many families hold banquets in restaurants to celebrate this festival.[219] One family in Macau reported that the family banquet was held on Sunday, 26 December 2010, because one sister was not able to come on the 22nd, and in this way the tradition was preserved.

A Christian Chinese friend of mine, who lives in Macau, never has special banquets for Chinese festivals, including the Winter Solstice Festival. He may be invited to dinner at Christmas, but not always. The reason is not his Christian belief, but the key role of his Taiwanese Hakka wife, who shows little interest in Chinese festivals and observances. Festivals are not important for them, but nevertheless the family is very united. This family has two children. The daughter – a medical doctor – has 'no religion', and lives in Taiwan. The son is a PhD student in computer science and also lives in Taiwan. But although this family has no special lunch or dinner for Chinese festivals, the son or the daughter come to Macau during holidays centred on Chinese festivals. Their tradition is to stay at home as a family and have a normal lunch or dinner for the New Year or another festival. They do not refuse invitations during the New Year, but for them it is an ordinary invitation.

The Mazu Temple: The Decline of an Icon

The Mazu Temple ('Mazumiu', in Cantonese) is the local symbol of the MSAR, and was chosen to illustrate the MOP10 note that was launched in January 2012 for the Year of the Dragon. (*See Photograph 5.*) On 7 October 2012, a rare ceremony, in which the board members of the temple participated, was held in front of the Mazu Temple attended by several dignitaries, including: João Manuel Costa Antunes, Director of the MSAR Government Tourism Office; Manuel Carvalho, the General Consul of Portugal; Choi Cheong Meng, a representative of the finances of the MSAR; Cheong Cheok Kio, architect and Director of the Cultural Heritage Department at the Cultural Institute of Macau; and a high-ranking Daoist monk of Macau. After 11am a lively procession with many traditionally dressed actors and big drums marched from Mazu Temple toward the Municipality of Macau.

Macau Mazu Temple is the most ancient Mazu Temple after the Meizhou Temple which is located near Putian, in Fujian Province.

However, there is an apparently diminishing interest in Macau's iconic Mazu goddess: the new banknote promotes the 2012 dragon on its two faces, but the gate of the temple appears only once. Furthermore the 'Templo de A-Ma' is large on the 2008 MOP10 note, but in 2012 it is smaller, under the shadow of the powerful Bank of China.

In front of Mazu Temple, at around 11am on 23 January 2012, to celebrate the Chinese New Year, a long dragon of some 238 meters was deployed by around two hundred male members of the Chong Sam Tai Yok Wui Association. (*See Photograph 6.*) Leong Heng Teng, Member of the MSAR Executive Council, is one of its main leaders.

However, a pilgrimage to this main temple of Macau is essential at Chinese New Year. On 2 February 2011, at 11:40pm, I met a family of informants at the Mazu Temple on the eve of the Chinese New Year. – The parents want their two children to understand what Chinese culture and religion are, so the tradition of going to the Mazu Temple for the New Year continues, although it is less important than it was before the handover in December 1999. – For the 2012 Lunar New Year, the family went during the day to Mazu Temple, not at night as usual. The Chinese of Macau – and tourists also – give preference to this temple, the Mazu Temple.

The four hundred years old Mazu Temple is a jewel of the MSAR and a major piece of ancient Chinese traditional religious architecture. For the majority of the visitors to this place of pilgrimage, religion does not play an important role. Those who took part in my survey who declared they have 'no religion' might nevertheless visit this place of worship during a Chinese festival.

Mazu is Macau's iconic goddess and could, in principle, be considered an antithesis to the gaming industry. This famous Mazu Temple promotes culture. Gaming, on the other hand, may be considered less ethical in principle than a temple.

At present, it seems that popular religion is not on the agenda of most Chinese of Macau. There was a large crowd of worshippers before 1am on 23 January 2012, but it was limited to the vicinity of the temple. They did not jostle in long files in the avenue, to reach the Mazu Temple, as they did in 1995-1999. Probably, the number of Fukienese worshippers of Mazu has diminished in Macau. This is denied by the board of the Mazu Temple which claims it is their present good management which successfully channeled the multitude of people, avoiding the jostling of former years.

The title 'Queen of Heaven', *Tianhou,* is given to Mazu. She is the 87th generation after Bigan, commonly considered the god of Wealth. Is it logical to call Mazu the goddess of Macau? – It is interesting to note that, in a painting in a chapel on Coloane Island, the Virgin Mary is also represented as *Tianhou*. Before the handover of Macau this painting was located in the nave of the church, but now it hangs in a small side-chapel. Mazu is originally from Fujian but she is also very popular in Macau and among the Hokkien people.[220]

Elsewhere – a Hokkien tradition – the Mazu Festival in the city of Peikang, Taiwan, is popular on a grand scale. To attend the Mazu festival, which occurs between the Lantern Festival (the fifteenth day of the first lunar month) and the birthday of Mazu (the twenty-third day of the third lunar month), around one million visitors come to this small city. Most of them belong to 'incense-offering-groups' (*jinxiang tuan*). These groups proudly bear images of Mazu and some even bring a portable brazier from their own home temple. Young men even practice self-mutilation, cutting their arms, demonstrating their courage.

In Macau the Mid-Autumn Festival is also important and the display of lanterns is in fact more central than during the Lantern Festival itself.

Jochim notes that these groups are constituted at the home temple and include devout as well as curious pilgrims. Daoist priests beg silently amidst 'incessant explosions of firecrackers'. Pilgrims repeatedly kneel and prostrate themselves in the direction of the Mazu temple, where bells ring and drums sound. A key requirement of the rites associated with this pilgrimage is that images and flags of the pilgrims pass over the large brazier at the temple's sacred portal. Taking some 'ashes and flaming spirit money' from Peikang's main brazier and transferring them to the small groups' braziers brought from the home temple is recommended. The days just preceding Mazu's birthday are the most popular and auspicious. At night, this Taiwanese goddess's birthday is marked in Peikang by an annual parade through darkness, similar to Macau's Mazu parade on the evening, night and morning of the first day of the Lunar New Year.[221]

On the eve of the Chinese New Year in Macau, it is abundantly clear that Mazu is the most important Chinese goddess; her temple receives more visitors than any other temple. Before midnight on the eve of every Lunar New Year – and this was particularly true before the year 2000 – many Chinese families march in pilgrimage towards the temple, the symbolic Centre of Chinese religion in Macau.

During the period 1995-2000, I followed the crowds of worshippers along the Inner Harbour for five consecutive New Year celebrations. Many of the worshippers carried huge helices and long candlesticks. I do not say that this did not occur in 2011 and 2012, but fewer people paid homage to Mazu. For the New Year, many Chinese of Macau go to Guangdong Province, while others go further, to Beijing or Taiwan, or even to warmer places in Southeast Asia.

Before 2000, I was usually obliged to queue for about an hour before entering the Mazu Temple, but on 2 February 2011, on the eve of Chinese New Year I passed through the main entrance gate after waiting for only fifteen minutes. The board members say that entering the temple at 9pm, earlier than in 2000, made a difference. Nevertheless, I moved with difficulty to the administrative centre of this temple, near the main altar of Mazu, hoping to meet the board. It was not easy to approach this altar. At 11:45pm, finally, I arrived in the room of the main statue of Mazu. (*See Photograph 14.*) I asked if I could enter the most inaccessible part, where the board of trustees meets. O Man Peng and his brother, whom I had met one year previously, kindly let me follow them, their sister and older brother, who is president of the board. A few minutes later, they took their places in front of the main altar of the goddess Mazu. Firecrackers exploded, and many people there covered their ears. At midnight sharp, that evening in 2011, all bowed and paid their respects to the goddess; it was the most important event of the year at the Mazu Temple.

In 2012 I met members of the board at a book launch one month before the eve of Chinese New Year, 22 January; so it was easier for me to join them at the Mazu Temple at the celebration. However, the scenario was very different from 2011. My acquaintances, the president of the board and his younger brother, were outside, when, at midnight sharp, the firecrackers marked the crucial time. The board had decided not to bow and pay their respects to the goddess at midnight.

However, the tradition of worship continues, and it is interesting to quote an educated informant who explained that he had 'no religion': 'Worshipping does not [necessarily] mean having a religion'. In December 2011 the elite and one tenth of the population marched from the Statue of Guanyin in NAPE (National Association of Power Engineers) area to the Mazu Temple during the annual charity event, 'Walk for Millions'. In connection with this walk, the Mazu Temple is less symbolic; being treated as an ordinary destination landmark.

In contrast with the more traditional period 1995-1999, where religious feeling was more evident, visitors to the Temple of Mazu were not so numerous on the morning of the first day of Chinese New Year in each of 2011 and 2012. Mainland tourists however were there, curious to observe Macau 'culture'. Such tourists usually stay longer in the enclave for the Lunar New Year – perhaps for two days instead of one. They come from all parts of China. In 2011, I spoke to a family from Shandong Province, and all of them were really interested to know the cultural significance of the goddess Mazu.

The obvious cultural link between Macau's Mazu Temple and Mazu Temples in Fujian and Taiwan is demonstrated by the active popularity of the religious cult of Mazu not only among Hokkien people in general, but also, particularly between 1995 and 2000 and previously, among Chinese of Macau. Furthermore, the Hokkien pronounciation of Mazu is 'Mazo(k)'. Some Chinese of Macau may say 'Makok' meaning 'Mazo(k)' Temple, pronouncing it in the Hokkien way. In Putonghua the term 'pavilion' or *ge* (pronounced *'kok'* in Cantonese) appears exceptionally on a gate under the name 'Mazu Ge'. All those Chinese who know enough Cantonese understand that *Makok Miu* or *Mazu Miu* is the Temple of Mazu in Macau. There is also an assimilation of names between this temple and the district 'Makok' or Barra around the temple which may refer to the goddess itself.[222] Despite the diminishing local popular religion centred on the temple, the goddess Mazu remains unique, protects Macau and continues to give an identity to Macau; her assimilation to the 'Queen of Heaven' (*Tianhou*) is another indication of the respect with which she is regarded.

In particular in 2009, official visits of the board members of Macau Mazu Temple to Fujian Province and Taiwan are important and well recorded. On 6 December 2009, the board visited the oldest temple of Mazu in Taiwan, a hundred kilometers from Taipei (as it is called in Taiwan; 'Taibei' in Putonghua), and this visit reinforced the cultural link between Macau and Taiwan. That same year the board also visited the Mazu Temple in Xiamen.[223] The photographic records of these visits to the ancient temples in Taiwan and Fujian Province are well displayed, vertically, at the board's headquarters inside the most sacred temple of Macau, close to the most venerated altar of Mazu in the MSAR. All this demonstrates the reality of Hokkien/Minnan culture, its strong link with Macau and also the importance of those Fukienese people who became permanent residents of Macau.

It is also useful to define the future of the district where the iconic temple of Mazu is located. In December 1940, to improve communications, a good road was opened along the Inner Harbour to reach the main Mazu Temple more directly.[224] In 2011, a renovation around the temple was planned. Just before the Chinese New Year, discussions took place about renovating the district surrounding the temple. According to the survey of this area of Macau, seventy per cent of residents and shopkeepers around the temple accepted the preservation and decoration of the streets in this district but did not want a reconstruction in the style of Qingzhou-Ilha Verde.[225]

Although Qingzhou-Ilha Verde urban planning may become a model for the whole MSAR, it seems that consultation with the people will avoid the problems encountered in Qingzhou. In 2011, the residents of Barra-Mazu district were reluctant to accept any destruction of the buildings in which they were living. The renovation is pending, awaiting the construction of the urban light train (LTR), which is planned to be in service by 2015-2016. – The demolition of the wooden barracks in this district in 1940, and incidents associated with the renovation of Qingzhou in 2010 have not been forgotten. – Planned renovation like this is currently a key question for the Chinese of Macau.

There is another old temple of A-Ma ('Mother') – another name for Mazu – on Coloane Island. It was first established in 1677, and rebuilt in the 2000s. The construction permit was given by former Macau Chief Executive Edmund Ho. The Mazu Foundation of Macau (*Aomen Zhonghua Mazu Jijinhui*) owns this huge temple and its renovation has strengthened the religious attraction of A-Ma. This A-Ma Temple in Coloane is also commonly visited for the Chinese New Year, but it is far away from city Centre.

Why do so many Chinese in Macau kowtow to Mazu? In fact, the Mazu Temple in Macau Peninsula has retained its preeminence.

Other Temples and Altars

In the Mazu (A-Ma) Temple at Coloane there is an interesting altar for a Chinese god, *Taisui,* the Master of the Year (similar to the Roman god, Jupiter), and his sixty representations, one for each of the sixty years of the Chinese cycle. A similar altar exists in Zuklam (Zhulin) Temple on the Peninsula. I have visited all of them during Lunar New Year.

Another main place for worship is the Guanyin Temple, not far from Horta e Costa Avenue. It is the second most visited temple in the Peninsula. According to Sampaio the anniversary day of Guanyin falls on the nineteenth of the ninth lunar month. Mazu Temple and the main Guanyin Temple are the two most popular temples in Macau.

On Lunar New Year, 3 February 2011, I headed toward Macau's two Guanyin temples. The second Guanyin Temple – older but smaller than the first – is on the same avenue as the first Guanyim Temple, close to the Red Market, a landmark in this district. It was the beginning of my visit to seven temples in the Peninsula of Macau. During that day, the two Guanyin temples also had many visitors and worshippers.

Concerning other temples, the old Shishan (Nezha) Temple on Rua das Verdades had few worshippers on the first day of the Chinese New Year in 2012. (Nezha is the Taoist ('Daoist' in Putonghua) 'Marshal of the Central Altar'.) On 28 October 2012, I met the Honourable Ng Peng Chi, the president of the main association, the Macau Taoist Association.

The Nuwa Temple, located on the road to the Ruins of St Paul's ('Tai San Pa'), is dedicated to the goddess creator, Nuwa. Few worshippers came in on the first day of the Chinese New Year in 2012. However, a Chinese fast food stall just outside had customers.[226]

At the *Guandi* Temple near the city Centre at Almeida Ribeiro ('*Sunmalo'* in Cantonese) and Rua dos Mercadores, at 11:30am on this Chinese New Year Day, only one Hong Kong family of three (father, mother and daughter) popped in. Two women and two men of the Temple's staff were taking their lunch at the time. Next door, at the headquarters of the Association of the Drunken Dragon, two men were friendly and chatted with me, but, in *Guandi* Temple, the female staff, too busy, did not answer my questions. The Drunken Dragon is a lively cultural event in Macau centred on *Guandi* Temple. It has its roots in Guandong Province, but Macau keeps this tradition alive.

To understand the importance of religion in the MSAR, it is useful to consider *Menkou Tudi Caishen* ('the Door, Land and Wealth god'), represented by the most common type of altar in Macau. The cult is part of the popular religion of Macau; it is still a very common Chinese god in the MSAR. Paul Mus, a specialist in the study of Southeast Asia and Vietnam, has commented on popular religion, linking it to society *shehui* 社会.[227] For him, the importance of this local god relies on its relationship with the land *tu* 土 and the territory 土地.

It is obviously crucial to study the link between the land and the identity of the Chinese of Macau. Cantonese opera actors, for example, sincerely believe in the importance of this local or earth god. This god is the 'patron spirit of the community' and represents the 'moral and social structure of the community', derived from Chinese philosophy.[228] A land god is essential in defining the community's identity. This god symbolises the earth and confers its social and moral structure to the community. The Fok Tak Ancestral Hall, near Rua do Campo, is a famous memorial temple. The Chinese of Macau, as well as Cantonese opera performers (*see Photograph* 8), need such a reference to confirm their identity and the earth is part of their identity. We are 'Sons of the Soil' say the Macanese; they are Catholics but do respect Chinese traditions.

The 'god *tudi*' gives good luck to the family. In early 2011, among the five flats on the same floor as the flat where I lived then, there were two altars to this god, who is particularly worshipped during the Chinese New Year. In all the streets of the Peninsula, Taipa and Coloane, it is easy to find hundreds of altars dedicated to this local god of the earth. This god is mainly worshipped to promote prosperity and wealth, and is commonly venerated in shops, buildings or residences.

The pluri-ethnic region of Macau, China, is not comparable to Yunnan Province. Minorities are not comparable to the Han majority of Macau, but Susan McCarthy's work – about the religious identity of the Bai and Dai – is useful for a comparative study. McCarthy's studies in 1995 and early 1996, showed a desire to get rid of statues and shrines of the god of Wealth in Beijing restaurants.[229] These shrines had become popular among restaurant and shop owners because they were seen as a quick route to prosperity. Others complained of this lack of education and modernity in a 'cosmopolitan city'. In the MSAR these gods are not systematically targeted, but are less numerous than in 2000.

Compared to the Mainland and even to Hong Kong, there is still a high density of *Guandi* altars in MSAR homes and shops. *Guandi* is venerated not only by many Chinese of Macau but also by policemen and triads because of his righteousness. However, it is possible to notice a decline of this tradition in Macau. Nevertheless, the tradition of worshipping *Guandi* for good luck remains noticeable in families and also in restaurants, small enterprises and shops.

In Taipa and Coloane, old banyan trees (*Rongshu*, or *Ficus Religiosus* in Latin) continue to be worshipped. Sacred trees are old and powerful. [230] A spirit dwells in these trees. It is difficult to know if this spirit personifies the tree, or if it comes from elsewhere and does not stay long in the tree. However, if I remember well the period 1995-2000, it seems that in 2012 there are fewer altars and local gods in the streets than before.

Prospects

The Tourist Department eagerly wants to promote cultural tourism, so, in 2010, the Traditional Chinese Lantern Festival became fashionable in the MSAR. The MSAR Government must have been satisfied with the impact this had on the promotion of tourism, for João Manuel Costa Autunes, the Director of the MSAR Government Tourism Office, was awarded a Medal of Merit on 28 January 2011.

In 2011, to promote the Lantern Festival, professor of architecture in Shanghai, Carlos Marreiros (*see Chapter Four*, '*Other Associations*'), also a member of the Electoral

Committee for the designation of the Chief Executive, organised an exhibition relating to traditional Chinese lanterns at the Albergue Art Gallery. The successor of the Leal Senado, the Civic and Municipal Affairs Bureau (IACM), has, unfortunately, less financial autonomy than before the handover, but it managed to put emphasis on this Lantern Festival. This festive period was used to promote the expected arrival of a couple of young pandas before the 2011 anniversary of the handover, 19 December.

In 2010, paper panda ornaments and paper lanterns representing these animals made their appearance for the first time in the MSAR during the Lantern Festival and again at Christmas. The MSAR was actively involved in promoting these two pandas. – Pandas are a component of China's global diplomacy. – Albano Martins, president of the association ANIMA, wanted legal protection for these Pandas in the MSAR, but also on the Mainland.[231] The Christmas promotion of these talismanic animals in 2010 symbolised the harmonious relationship of Macau and the Mainland. However, compared to 2010 and most of 2011, the publicity in Macau for pandas Hoi Hoi and Sam Sam is less noticeable in 2012. In particular, during the 2011 Christmas period, only Santa Claus was displayed in the streets.

It seems that *Qingmingjie* plays a more important role in Macau than in Mainland China. This is confirmed by eighty-one per cent of my respondents. Western sociologists of religion, Azria and Hervieu-Leger, acknowledged an 'unexpected' religious resurgence in 1970.[232] Before the 1980s it was difficult to mention any important development of religious activities on the Mainland. However, Azria and Hervieu-Leger are quite right in what they say about popular religion. Interestingly they mention the importance of new discoveries, not investigated earlier, confirming ancient common popular belief among merchants, a part of the nobility and the 'political elite', who share a main common interest and culture about religion.

In Macau, a high-ranked Christian religious leader confirmed that the only festival uniting his brothers, his only living sister, and his nephews and nieces, is *Qingmingjie*. They have no other important family meetings because some of the family live in the MSAR, some on the Mainland and some in Hong Kong. So, except for the Festival for the Ancestors, this family, finds it impossible to organise special banquets for other festivals such as the Chinese New Year. However, to dine as a family on the eve of the Chinese New Year – *Tyunnin faan* – remains essential for 222 (99 per cent) of the 225 respondents in my sociological survey. (In 2011, it could be replaced by a family festive lunch on the first day of the Chinese New Year.) The family worshipping of the ancestors is essential for 150 interviewees, but the Lunar New Year (过年) remains the main festival in the MSAR.

In an age when it is not possible to ignore globalisation, the group identity of the Chinese of Macau demonstrates in particular the importance of the Chinese New Year. It is also remarkable among all the Chinese on the Mainland and among overseas Chinese all over the world. It is also more universal because the Lunar New Year, borrowed from China, is also the key Vietnamese Tet Festival and Korean Seollal New Year celebration. As in Macau and all China, the Korean New Year and the Vietnamese *Tet* are also a time for family reunions, visits to temples, family banquets and the giving of lucky money to children and the elderly. Around 70 per cent of the Chinese of Macau have no religion. However, the Chinese New Year tradition is part of the globalisation process, indicating how Chinese traditions are 'globalised'. Except for celebrations of the Lunar New Year, religion in East Asia 'is felt as an unnecessary distraction from the more important goal: modernisation and economic growth'.[233]

However, even by his book title alone, Minkov notes that there are still cultural differences in a globalising world: local viewpoints continue to be very important in the twenty-first century. On 20 December 1999, Macau returned to China. This tremendous social change has been even more significant for the Macau SAR than for the Hong Kong SAR. According to my observations between 1995 and 2011, it seems that the increase of religious practice on the Mainland has been greater than any similar increase in the MSAR. Religion in Macau is affected by two different sociological factors. The most important is the growing importance of the Mainland in Macau, and the second is the importance of the gaming industry, which dents the philosophy, religion and ethics of society. Since 1995, the social change and nationalist impact on Macau has been marked by the gradual but inevitable dethroning of its goddess Mazu. The annual Chinese New Year night parade through darkness toward Macau's Mazu Temple has become a paler religious rite compared with the previous mobilisation of an astonishing number of Chinese of Macau to worship their goddess. However, the goddess Mazu of Macau – despite the diminishing popular religion – continues to be a particularly symbolic image for Macau. She is more popular in Macau than in Hong Kong or in Peikang (Taiwan), although she is nevertheless very popular in Hong Kong. The social change demonstrated in the religious field is comparable to the impact brought about by the large number of Mainland visitors entering the Macau SAR. In 2011, Mainlanders were the majority (some 58 per cent) of the twenty-eight million visitor-entries into the MSAR, as confirmed by official statistics. – Festivals evidently are favourable to the development of tourism.

Chinese festivals in Macau continue to give an identity to the Chinese of Macau. It seems paradoxical that a certain number of the Chinese of Macau celebrate Christmas as a local tradition in Macau, even if they are not Christians, but this particularity also contributes to 'particularize' Macau identity. However, to think that religion and tradition are the only key markers of the identity of the Chinese of Macau in general is out of the question. The handover of Macau to Mainland China in 1999 and the increasing influence of Beijing in education and other spheres compel the downgrading of questions such as those concerning religion; nevertheless religion cannot be denied. The Portuguese language and Catholicism are important components of the Portuguese colonial heritage, promoting culture in the MSAR. It is enough to note the dedication of the Chinese of Macau to the memory of one of Macau's benefactors, Luis Ruiz SJ, Luyi – Luis Ruiz Rodrigues Suarez – who spent sixty years of his long life (1913-2011) in Macau, helping poor Chinese families and others. Rarely, have the Catholic Chinese of Macau and others demonstrated so much affection. This was particularly noticeable in his old age and after his death at the age of ninety-eight. In 1995 the Government of Hunan invited him to establish a centre for HIV patients. For his funeral, at the Cathedral of Macau, the attendance was very high. The author personally attended and can compare it with the funeral of others, higher in the Catholic hierarchy, such as that of late Bishop Emeritus Lam Ka Tseung.

To conclude, the sociology of religion is a dynamic branch of sociology which permits us to recognise the uniqueness of Macau and confirms the Chineseness of the Chinese of Macau.[234] As Robert Weller has pointed out, 'the family remains the most fundamental unit. One worships at home or in the temple by burning incense as a minimal offering'. Popular religion is common in Taiwan but seems to be diminishing in the Macau SAR.[235]

CHAPTER SIX

CONCLUSION

Can we say that 'Chinese of Macau' constitutes the only identity in the MSAR? Certainly not – there are many other identities in Macau, including those of the resident Burmese, Chinese, Europeans, Filipinos, Indians, Indonesians, Japanese, Nepali, Portuguese, Thais, Timorese, Vietnamese, and others. Even among the Chinese of Macau there is a complexity of subgroups; but the Chineseness of all of them 'is reproduced in the intimacies of daily life'.[236]

The significant number of those, speaking for their household, who replied to the question, 'Are you 'Oumunjan' (Macau person), 'Oumundak Zunggwokjan' (Chinese of Macau) or 'Zunggwokjan' (Chinese)?', with the words, "We are Chinese', proves something very important. Out of the 225 interviewees who responded to my questionnaires, the large majority clearly affirmed their Chineseness. The percentage of 'Chinese' and 'Chinese of Macau' is superior to the simple identity, 'Macau'. So, on the basis of one hundred households surveyed (a more 'balanced' group in terms of age than the group of 225 who responded as individuals), 65 per cent asserted their 'Chineseness' (see Appendix 2, based on my Excel file). In his chapter on the Basic Law, Tong Io Cheng has demonstrated the importance of the Basic Law for the identity of the Chinese of Macau. At present, even for Chinese people, it is not easy to become a permanent resident in the MSAR. Except for the visitors coming for one or two days only, it is less easy to stay in the MSAR, compared to the past. For different reasons, some non-residents are even obliged to report daily (except for week-ends and holidays) to the immigration department if they wish to continue to stay in Macau. In comparison with the

1990s, the Basic Law protects, even more than in the past, the way of life of the Chinese of Macau. At present, it is extremely difficult for non-Chinese – except for Portuguese – to become a permanent resident. Does this difficulty really protect the Chinese of Macau?

Language constitutes a fundamental core of overall identity. In Macau the *de facto* situation in 2000 was the pre-eminence given to the simple term 'Chinese language', which seemed, for the Chinese of Macau, to mean 'Cantonese'. [237]

Some Chinese may have forgotten that Chinese *and* Portuguese are the official languages of the MSAR. The Chinese of Macau are affected by the forces of both globalisation and 'Mainland-isation', and we understand the importance of Putonghua and Sinicization. [238] It seems that Cantonese is slowly losing its dominance, but it is still the identity-language of Macau. Already in neighbouring Hong Kong, Putonghua and English are gaining a larger audience than previously.

Traditional written Chinese characters continue to dominate in the MSAR, and it remains to be seen in what manner, in 2049, Macau will finally begin to use simplified characters, already used on the Mainland and in Singapore.

The modernity of Singapore will be recognised one day in Macau and Hong Kong as bearing a relationship with this step forward. However, in 2011, we have to recognise that the supremacy of traditional Chinese characters is a part of Macau's 'way of life', as well developed in Chapter Two.

The Macau SAR has its own Basic Law. However, in 1995, Article 19 of the Law on Education on the Mainland insists on the common Chinese written language and on the supremacy of the national language, Putonghua. Consequently we believe also in the importance of the Chinese phonetic alphabet, *pinyin*; and consider that it will be imposed slowly, even in Macau.

Portuguese has been spoken in Macau for almost five hundred years, but – challenged by English – has lost its former leading international position. English is currently the language of communication between Chinese and non-Chinese in the MSAR, not in exactly the same way as in Hong Kong; but the Chinese of Macau are making progress in English. In the MSAR, however, it is more difficult than it is in Hong Kong to find Chinese above the age of forty who are proficient in English.

The Government of the MSAR has always placed great importance on cultural affairs. In 2010 and 2011, for instance, significant changes were put into effect. The Secretary for Social Affairs and Culture, Cheong U, is the head of the Committee of Cultural Industries (or 'Cultural Industry Committee', CIC), which also includes the president of the Civic and Municipal Affairs Bureau (IACM), the heads of the Macau Polytechnic Institute, and other institutes.

The main programme of Secretary Cheong is a commitment to build a 'city of culture', an idea that was often put forward during Portuguese times. Such a project is ambitious and necessary, and will give a good image to Macau. In January 2011, the President of the Cultural Institute of Macau, Ung Vai Meng, said that, since the opening of the Mandarin's House had attracted more than 100,000 visitors, Macau has shown progress in the field of culture. The question of creativity and follow-up are important issues. For Macau, it is useful to note that Augustin Girard (1926-2009) forecast the necessarily increasing role of public authorities and the development of new audio-visual products in order to modernise cultural institutions and safeguard local culture.[239] In fact an harmonious alliance of Confucianism and tolerance continues to prevail, despite the drastic change in the culture, economy and society of the MSAR since the year 2000. Confucian (work) dynamism 'correlates positively with economic growth'.[240]

In the field of culture also, there are examples of new cultural development; for example, Macau is encouraging local film culture. In April and May 2011, the fifth consecutive annual International Film and Video Festival was held in Macau, organised by the Macau Cultural Centre. Fernando Eloy thinks that the creation of a department and an institute specialising in cinema is necessary in Macau.[241] Also highlighting the support for developments in film and video, The Macau Foundation has recently generously invested in a successful film called 'The Youth of Xinghai'.

Another idea being promoted is the creation of an Academy for Creative and Cultural Industries. It remains to be seen if the MSAR Government accepts such propositions.

Elsewhere, the President of the Macau Foundation, Dr Wu Zhiliang, asked the CIC to increase contributions to local associations, arguing that they are essential for both local culture and the links with Guangdong and Fujian provinces.[242]

MSAR Associations create links with the Mainland

In 1867, Sampaio recognised in advance the key role of Chinese commercial associations in Macau.[243] Guangdong and Fujian Provinces are the most important in creating a link with the Mainland. Associations also help to develop the service economy which is lacking in the MSAR. Associations can actively and positively boost society, as an essential part of the binomial expression 'society and economy', promoted by this work, as basic to cultural and economic development.

What Deng Xiaoping said in 1961 – 'Rise up and develop well Hainan Island, what one wills one can do' – could be applied to the MSAR.[244]

Forty-five per cent of the two hundred and twenty-five Chinese of Macau who answered the questionnaires used in my survey were members of at least one association – usually one related to their place of origin, which is a fundamental identification for them.

The MSAR is still far behind Hong Kong, concerning harmony and development, despite great progress over the last ten years. The point is not to give money to the citizens of Macau, although this was done in both Macau and Hong Kong in 2011. Vong Iek Soi, the current Secretary of the Returned Overseas Chinese Association, has mentioned some negative effects of the annual distribution of funds to the people. This former chief editor of the *Va Kio* daily paper thinks that such a distribution of cash in the MSAR may have a negative effect on creativity. It is, nevertheless, evident that we must not exclude older people, the poorest and all those who are really in need, such as the sons and daughters of not-so-rich families who request consideration.

There are, of course, similar practices elsewhere. In the former Portuguese territory of East Timor, now an independent state, there is an understandable tendency to assist the people, so as to win their votes in elections. In 2012, it is evident that, to create dynamic economic development, the main priority for each of Macau SAR and East Timor remains the restructuring of education

Education is a priority

In Macau, dramatic changes occurred in several recent points of history: after World War II, during the Cultural Revolution, following the handover of the former Portuguese colony to China and during the period 2000-2010. In 2011, the next great change is the planned transfer of the University of Macau to Hengqin Island, which will accelerate the general development of education in the MSAR. However, although the Province of Guangdong is playing a key role, even more important is the role of the Mainland, which is essential for the MSAR.

To develop society and the economy, education and health are two priorities for the Chinese of Macau (photo 16). The Sin Meng Association's Survey points out the importance of education policy, with health institutions as second in importance.[245] It is certain that the happiness or 'subjective well-being' of Macau is quite high and things are changing in the MSAR.

It is not easy. The relocation of the University of Macau to Hengqin Island is a challenge not only for Tertiary Education Services (GAES) but for many sectors of the MSAR Government. In 2013, an important part of the faculties of the main university of Macau will have to move to Hengqin Island (photo 10 of the main entrance of the University of Macau in 2012). The countdown has already started.

Lao Chi Ngai of Hong Kong's Association of Economic Sciences has called for a necessary increased investment in education and vocational training.[246] The Sin Meng Association found that 79.6 per cent (2010) and 78.7 per cent (2011) considered seriously the problems of young people.[247] Culture and education are essential to try to solve these problems and upgrade local identity.

In comparison with Hong Kong, young people in Macau are traditionally not interested in questions of policy relating to the future of society. In 2011, some limited social movements occurred in Macau before the Chinese New Year. However, the Chinese of Macau are much less interested in the so-called 'democratisation of society' than are the 'Hongkongers'. It seems that in the MSAR, there is a tendency among those with higher levels of education to emphasise their Macau identity. Overall, 109 out of my 225 interviewees put 'Macau' ahead of the other two identities suggested ('Chinese of Macau' and 'Chinese'). The identity of the younger generation is more a 'Macau' identity than simply a 'Chinese' identity.

Young people and new legislation for the development of primary and secondary education are each essential.[248] Both primary and secondary education sectors, headed by the Director, Sou Chio Fai, have praised the extension of free education in the MSAR to fifteen years of schooling, as voted in 2007.[249] It will be useful to place the responsibility for schools and colleges at different levels, but it is not easy to implement this complex type of collective and individual responsibility. Ms Ho Teng Iat is sure that, after the handover, more women in Macau have access to tertiary education. Although Macau still needs to upgrade its education, a comparison with the situation twenty years ago shows a stark difference. In comparison with the situation in the southeast-asian Portuguese-speaking land of East Timor, Macau can be proud of its achievements, and Macau, with its use of English and Putonghua, will have powerful international languages.

Is Globalisation really a good opportunity for Macau?

As I pointed out in the conclusion of my *Macao 2000,* the Basic Law continues to be 'an essential legal, political and diplomatic marker, but it also represents a complex social and economic synthesis of uncertainties and bright expectations'. Following the handover, and just after the beginning of the twenty-first century, the essential importance of China and the Hong Kong SAR was mentioned, but also raised were the question of identity and the need to develop a competitive spirit in Macau – so necessary to succeed in a new era, the coming century of globalisation. Unfortunately, the use and reputation of the MSAR as a '24-hour holiday tourism destination' has become too common.

For Li Peilin, Director of the Institute of Sociology of the Academy of Social Sciences of China, the market economy in China is a factor and the reforms are a debatable subject; it is also true of the MSAR. [250] Both the Mainland and Macau are in constant transformation. In 1981, 75 per cent of the the five million 'tourists' who entered Macau were Hong Kong residents. Nowadays Mainlanders are the most numerous visitors, more than 50 per cent of the total; visitors from Hong Kong are now fewer than 30 per cent. In 1996 Macau welcomed eight million visitors. This number of visitor arrivals is not impressive compared to the twenty-five million 'tourists' who entered the MSAR in 2010. [251] More visited in 2011.

In 2011, Mainlanders were the majority (some 58 per cent) of the twenty-eight million visitor-entries in Macau, as confirmed by official statistics. These figures show that it is necessary to encourage mutual aid and co-operation among the leaders of the administrative region and also from among the people themselves to cope with this mass of tourism.

The main reason for this socio-economic development is the gaming industry. In the current period of world crisis, it is certain that the wise warning of Ieong Tou Hong, Director of APEM, about the risks involved in the fact that Macau has a single industry, must be seriously considered. Nevertheless, it is a fact that gaming was financially successful in 2011.

This is why in June 2011 a Macau business delegation went to Singapore and East Timor, led by ex-Chief Executive of the MSAR, Ho Hau Wah, currently Vice-President of the People's Political Consultative Conference of China. On 9 June 2011, Ho met the Prime Minister of Singapore, Lee Hsien Loong. Mr Ho also visited, in Singapore, Resorts World on Sentosa Island.

Ho Hau Wah's visit underlines the long-lasting importance and value of the Portuguese link in each of Macau and East Timor.[252] Portuguese is an official language in both East Timor and the MSAR. One of the purposes of this book – to underline the importance of the joint study of economy and society – is again confirmed by this.

A second key point is the influence of Greater China, in Macau and Southeast Asia, as demonstrated during this visit by the role of the Chinese Ambassador in Singapore, Wei Wei, and also by that of the Chinese Ambassador in East Timor, Fu Yancong.

East Timor research is a new economic interest for the MSAR, but globalisation is a key problem for the Chinese of Macau. Everybody is becoming more and more concerned by faraway news and globalisation is becoming more and more of an issue. With the current paramount importance of globalisation, local questions have, it seems, become less crucial. After even a brief study of the price of bread, and of inflation in general, in the MSAR, the global question of cereals and food security become evident even in relation to Macau.

Why is globalisation crucial for the Chinese of Macau? These *Oumunjan* (Macau persons) are rather 'family-centric' but their Chineseness is confirmed in my survey. The Chinese of Macau and Mainlanders have a long history, so they are well prepared to resist all sorts of coercion. In the MSAR and also in the Hong Kong SAR, young people tend to consider themselves localized; however, their identity seems more flexible in Macau than in Hong Kong. 'Hongkongers' are more proud of their origin. Yet again, the Chinese of Macau do not like to travel too much. But the Macanese and all other Chinese – Mainlanders and Overseas Chinese, in particular in Southeast Asia – are certainly more 'globalised' today than they were in the 1960s and much more 'global' than the Chinese of Macau. In the 1960s, it was difficult for the Chinese of Macau to find a job in Macau, so many of them did not travel. They had no money to do so, no education to find solutions, and even no will to go abroad.

The Chief Executive, elected on 19 December 2009, Fernando Chui Sai On, will undoubtedly seek to develop new models of public and private cultural intervention. In 2011, Macau is in competition with Las Vegas and indirectly also with Singapore. Globalisation is 'truly a myth', but it is, nevertheless, a powerful discourse.[253] However, let us hope that globalisation does not really mean the homogenisation of our world. The small autonomous region, Macau, is a kaleidoscope of sub-groups and minorities. One of the main theses of this book is the joint study of economy and society.

Like mobile phones and the web, McDonald's is part of a global social phenomenon, globalisation. In a remote suburb in the northwest of the MSAR, at the corner of Bracial Sul Street in Patane, a McDonald's restaurant is open twenty-four hours a day, as it is elsewhere on Horta e Costa Avenue. Other McDonald's will also stay open day and night in New York City. The links with the BRIC group of countries (Brazil, Russia, India and China) particularly Brazil, and China-India relations, are certainly economically more important for the MSAR.[254]

Recently the field of education in the MSAR is demonstrating the importance of the Mainland, but it is also a tributary in its capacity to follow the evolution of the world and its current 'globality'. Laura Chan, a member of a team in Hong Kong that grants scholarships, affirms that Hong Kong's future relies upon the ability of educated people to 'understand the wider global world'.[255] The same is true of Macau. However, the proliferation of casinos in Macau – part of this globalisation – is an interesting problem to study and re-study, as discussed above.

In the coming years, if the current international economic crisis continues, Macau will certainly suffer more than during the years 2008 and 2009, as it will be impossible to maintain the incredible flow of 'gamers' and tourists entering the MSAR. We cannot say that the Chinese of Macau who have relatively good jobs in the casino industry will be exempt from the perturbations of the 'globalised' world. Society is linked to the economy. Concerning a possible new financial crisis, Chen Zhiwu of Yale University considers that, following the last Wall Street global crisis in 2008 and 2009, there are uncertainties.[256] The sociologist Luhmann does not seem to believe that changing structures to avoid crises is possible. 'Success in re-stylising crisis is by changing structures but such a possibility does not seem likely'.[257] Mass media suggest via 'culture' and 'ethics' and the picture remains built up by the media themselves.[258] Mass Media are important and may help or not help in case of a new crisis. The huge transformation of China and its globalisation are not risk-free for China itself. As for the consequences of a hypothetical new financial and economic crisis, Macau has a long and positive history of rebounding from commercial downturns.[259]

The Macau SAR is not as big as the Hong Kong SAR, so the Cantonese language must be protected to keep the identity of Macau alive. It may be subject to discussion, but sinicization, centred on Beijing, brings unity, modernisation and progress, but also some constraints for the Chinese of Macau, who now have to use more English and Putonghua. It is easier in Macau to host a greater percentage of newcomers from the Mainland than in Hong Kong. – Hongkongers are more able to protect their rights than the Chinese of Macau. – Some fifty per cent of that part of the population of Macau, formerly from the Mainland, became resident in the MSAR only over the last twenty years.

It would be utopian to try to promote Macau too strongly, as its current territory of only 29.7 square kilometers obviously limits its possibilities.[260] However, Jiji Tu, director of the Hello-Jobs Company, believes that Macau's market 'has not yet reached its maturity stage in recruiting talent online'.[261]

The improvement of electoral governance in 2009, a relatively clean legislative election under 'Beijing political will', proves the importance of Mainland China.[262] It shows also relative progress. After interviewing her in December 2011, the author imagines that Dr Pansy Ho certainly understands well the question of what Macau and the Chinese of Macau can really achieve. 'East and West' is a *leitmotiv* in Macau. The question of rethinking the 'East' and the 'West', from c. 1550 up to the present time, is a key question in the MSAR, and this question needs to be constantly re-asked and re-formulated. However, the identity of 'the East' *(Dongfang),* remains the Beijing Government's way of referring to this particular region of the world, which includes the MSAR.

Ritually, in December 2011, and maybe for the first time officially, President Hu Jintao and his future successor, Xi Jinping, together met Macau Chief Executive Chui Sai On and asked him to diversify the economy of Macau.[263] So, in early February 2012, the leading Macau entrepreneur, ex-Deputy and Consul of Cape Verde, David Chow, courageously went to Benin to meet its President Boni and to study the possibilities of co-operation and investment in the country. Dr Thomas Boni Yayi is the new President of the African Union, representing fifty-four countries. The diversification of the economy of Macau was a task already on the agenda of Governor Rocha Vieira in the 1990s, but it was almost impossible to accomplish.

The second request of the Chinese administration in Beijing to the Macau SAR – the improvement of the quality of life of Macau residents – is easier to fulfil, but requires a new type of creativity. In December 2011, a programme was established to link Macau and Tianjin, so, in coming years, the creative city of Tianjin will play a key role. This follows the direction for the improvement of 'Macau's way of life', promoted by the Basic Law and by this book. On 21 December 2011, in a TDM (Teledifusão de Macau, Macau TV) debate, organised by Gilberto Lopes and Deputies Tong Io Cheng, José Coutinho and Leonel Alves, it was clear that nobody is asking for universal suffrage. An increase in the direct representativeness of the political process is however a possibility.

Before the Christmas festive period in 2011, various personalities told the *Macau Times* what their wishes were. The deputies José Coutinho and Ng Kok Cheong asked for a better quality of life for Macau residents. Another lawmaker, Kwan Tsui Hang, supported Regional Development, already proposed for the Pearl River Delta by the Chief Executive, and by Dr Pansy Ho during the recent interview she gave me. Henry Lei Chun Kwok of the University of Macau wanted to know the needs of low-income class families. Teresa Vong of the University of

Macau proposed mainly Joy. Paul Pun Chi Meng of Caritas wished Joy, Peace and Love to everybody.

Because of the rapid social and economic changes in the MSAR, it remains important to study and restudy the uniqueness of the Chinese of Macau and to try to find new ways to preserve their local Cantonese culture, traditions and way of life. Creativity remains a key element in the development of culture in Macau. The Chinese of Macau are an essential part of local culture and society.

In 2012, the world is enmeshed in a long, financial, economic and social crisis. – This time it is different of course, but it looks like the periods 1914-1918 and 1940-1945. During those periods, Macau managed to survive better than the rest of the world. Now also it is ready to do its best. A gaming monopoly does not constitute a problem in a time of crisis. People who do not know what to do, may have the temptation to gamble. The Macau SAR and the Chinese of Macau, with their historically excellent survival spirit, are well prepared for this time of world uncertainty.

TABLE ONE

The percentage of Chinese of Macau from Guangdong and Fujian Provinces among the 137 Chinese of Macau who gave their place of origin in response to the questionnaire dated 2011

Origin	Number	Percentage
Cantonese from Zhongshan, Shiqi, Zhuhai, Shunde (Shuntak) and Panyu	78	55
Cantonese from Xinhui, Jiangmen, Nanhai, Toumen and Heshan	32	24
Cantonese from Taishan, Foshan and Guangzhou	17	13
Fukienese (Minnan, Fuzhou, Mindong, Minbei and other)	10	8
TOTAL	137	100

Note

Although there were 225 respondents to my questionnaire, it is not possible to improve Table One. I was able to monitor only the questionnaires administered by the sociology students at the University of Macau and, of course, the questionnaires directly supervised by myself.

TABLE TWO

Responses by generation of 100 interviewees from 100 selected households, extracted from the data for 225 households, to the question, 'Are you 'Oumunjan' (Macau person), 'Oumundak Zunggwokjan' (Chinese of Macau) or 'Zunggwokjan' (Chinese)?'

	'Macau person'	'Chinese of Macau'	'Chinese'
Age 30 or below	19	23	6
Age 31 to 59	13	13	7
Age 60 or above	6	10	6
per cent overall	38	46	19

TABLE THREE

Origin of the Chinese of Macau based on responses to the questionnaires administered during Jean Berlie's research

Zongshan: 39 families
Shunde: 12
Panyu: 7
Taishan: 3 families
Foshan: 8
Guangzhou: 6
Zhuhai: 18 families
Xinhui: 6
Jiangmen: 11
Nanhai: 3
Toumen: 5
Heshan: 2
Huizhou: 1
Sanxiang: 1
Siping: 1
Shiqi: 2

Fujian (Minnan)
Jinjiang: 1 family
Nanan: 4
Huian: 1
Quanzhou: 1
Xiamen: 2

<u>Fuzhou and other provinces of China</u>
Fuzhou: 1 family
Anhui: 2
Hubei (Wuhan): 1
Hunan: 2
Jiangsu: 1
Jiangxi: 1
Yunnan: 1

The table shows the importance of Zhongshan and the Minnan speakers among the Chinese originally from Fujian Province.

This table is useful, but the survey is not complete. The 225 households investigated were not all studied carefully enough. I was not able to check personally the accuracy of the responses in some cases.

Results for 100 Respondents
selected from among 225 Respondents

	Code		
1	MF	males	58
		females	42
2	Mb	Macau born	54
3	Mar	Married	44
4	M	Macau person (identity)	38
5	ChM	Chinese of Macau (identity)	46
6	Ch	Chinese (identity)	19
7	U	University education	37
8	Jb	Elite job	4
9	C	Cantonese speaker	100
10	H	Hokkien or Minnan speaker	16
11	Int	International link	14
12	*Hu*	Total of persons in 100 households (3.57 persons per household)	357
13	As	Member of an association	43
14	Och	Often on the Mainland	27
15	HK	Hong Kong family link	41
16	SEA	Southeast Asia family link	12
17	Cj	Lunar New Year celebrated in family	97
18	Qmj	*Qingmingjie* celebrated in family	81
19	Dj	Winter solstice celebrated in family	30
20	Xm	Christmas is a family festival	7
21	R	Religion worshippers (0='no religion')	29

APPENDIX

Questionnaire administered to 225 respondents
(Residents of Macau over 20 years old)

澳门的中国人（在澳门生活满**20**年）的调查
被访问者：　　先生/女士　　　（姓名、联系电话）

Who are you? (Chinese of Macau, Chinese-*Zhonghuo ren*...). Explain why.
请问您的身份？（澳门人？澳门的中国人？中国人？）为什么？

Where were you born? Link with your family (China and all over the world...).
您出生何地？母语讲哪种地方方言？与家族的联系（国内外联系，请说出具体的市/县）

Your Job.
您从事何种职业（尽量具体说明）？

Composition of your household (family, friend, grandparents, parents, children and grandchildren).
您的家庭成员（祖父母、双亲、儿女、孙子孙女）

Education (university, professional school, secondary school, primary school...).
您所受的教育（大学、中学、职业中学、小学）

How many times per year you go to inland China (visit of family Guangdong, Fujian...).
Do you belong to an association (charity association, health association, *tongxianghui*...).

您每年回内地多少次（看望在广东或福建等地的亲戚）？

您曾参与哪些社团组织（基层组织、慈善机构、同乡会、体育会、文娱组织、教会组织等）

Relationship with Hong Kong (work, family, friends, classmates...).

您与香港的联系（工作、家庭、朋友、同学等等）

Relationship with Southeast Asia.

您与东南亚的关系（请说出具体的市）

Chinese festivals (in Macau, in inland China...). Chinese New Year, *Qingmingjie*, others...

您怎样过中国节庆（在澳门、在中国内地）：春节、清明节、其它

Which religion (or no religion) are you belonging to ? How many times per year you go to temple? or church ?

您信仰哪种宗教？每年去多少次庙宇或者教堂

访问者：姓名　　　　　联系电话

2011年　月　日

ABBREVIATIONS

APEM: Association for the Promotion of the Economy of Macau

ARB: *Aomen Ribao* (Macau Daily News, in Chinese)

CIC: Cultural Industry Committee

DSEC: Documentation and Information Centre of the Statistics and Census Service

DSSOPT: *Direcção dos Servicos de Solos, Obras Públicas e Transportes* (Land, Public Works and Transport Bureau)

EFEO: Ecole Française d'Extrême-Orient

GAES: *Gabinete de Apoio do Ensino Superior* (Tertiary Education Services)

HKD: Hong Kong Dollar

HKSAR: Hong Kong Special Administrative Region

IACM: Civic and Municipal Affairs Bureau

IMM: International Institute of Macau

JTM: *Jornal Tribuna de Macau*

MSAR: Macau Special Administrative Region

MDT: *Macau Daily Times*

MOP: *Meio Official de Pagamento,* the currrency of Macau

MSAR: Macau Special Administrative Region

PRC: People's Republic of China

RMB: *Renminbi,* the currency of Mainland China

SCMP: *South China Morning Post* (HKSAR)

UMFLL: *Universidade Técnica de Lisboa Lei e Legislação* (Department of Law and Legislation of the Technological University of Lisbon)

REFERENCES

ALMEIDA, Fatima and R. Carvalho. 'Ilha Verde Without Families', in JTM (in Portuguese), 4 January 2011, p. 3.

AMARO, Ana Maria. *Jogos, Brinquedos e Outras Diversões Populares de Macau* ('Games, Toys and other Popular Entertainments'). Macau: Imprensa Nacional, 1972.

– *Jogos, Brinquedos e Outras Diversões Populares de Macau* ('Games, Toys and other Popular Entertainments') – 2a parte, 1 Vol. Author's Publication, Lisbon, 2011 .

ANDERSON, Benedict R. O'Gorman. *Imagined Communities. Reflections on the Origin and Spread of Nationalism.* London: Verso, 1991 (1st pub. 1983).

AZRIA, Regine and Danièle Hervieu-Leger, *Dictionnaire des Faits Religieux* (Dictionary of Religious Facts), Paris: PUF, 2010. See within the paragraph on Chinese religions, pp. 1075-1083.

BARTH, Fredrik. *Ethnic Groups and Boundaries. The Social Organization of Culture Difference.* Oslo: Universitetsforlaget, 1969 (reprint 1998).

BATALHA, Gracieta N. 'Language of Macao. Past and Present', in Luis Sa Cunha (ed.), *The Macanese Anthropology History Ethnology, Review of Culture* No. 20, 1994, pp. 131-156.

BEALS, Alan R. *Culture in Process* (3rd ed.). New York: Holt, Rinehart and Winston Inc., 1979.

BERLIE, Jean. 'East Timorese Identity', in *Magazine. President of East Timor.* N° 3, 2010.

– *Sinisation.* Paris: Trédaniel, 1998.

BERLIE, Jean A. 'Sinicization and the Pandas' (in Portuguese), in JTM, 21 January 2011, p. 17.

– 'East Timor: A Dependent State Expert in Mass Communication', in *Asian Journal of Social Science* 38-6, 2010, pp. 949-957.

– *Islam in China. Hui and Uyghurs between Modernization and Sinicization.* Bangkok: White Lotus, 2004.

– 'Macau's Overview at the Turn of the Century' in *The American Asian Review* XVIII-4, Winter 2000, pp. 25-68.

BERLIE, Jean A. (ed.). *Macao 2000.* Oxford/New York : Oxford University Press, 1999.

BERNARDINI, Jean E. (University of Alberta). *Linguistic Nationalism. The Case of Southern Min.* Philadelphia:

University of Pennsylvania, Department of Oriental Studies, 1991.

BOURDIEU, Pierre. *Esquisse d'une Théorie de la Pratique.* Paris: Seuil, 2000, pp. 217-432.

– *The Weight of the World. Social Suffering in Contemporary Society.* Cambridge UK: Polity, 1999.

– 'Le Mythe de la Mondialisation...' (Globalisation), in *Contre-Feux* (Back-Fire), Paris: Liber, 1998, pp. 34-50.

BOUTHOUL, Gaston. *Traité de Sociologie. 2e Partie Sociologie Dynamique.* Paris: Payot, 1954.

– *Sociologie de la Politique.* Paris: Presses Universitaires de France, 1965.

BRAGA, Jack M. *Macau a Short Handbook.* Macau: Information and Tourism Department, 1970 (1st ed. 1963).

BRANNER, David Prager. *Problems in the Chinese Dialectology. The Classification of Min and Hakka.* Berlin: Mouton de Gruyter, 2000.

Bric in Macau. Edited by Gary Ngai and Ivo Carneiro da Sousa. Macau: SaintJosephAcademic Press, 2011.

CHAO, Paul. *Chinese Kinship.* London: Kegan Paul, 1983.

Chaozhou Association: *Chengli 25 Zhounian Yinxihui Qingteji Zhuankan* (Book for the 25th Anniversary Celebration of the Establishment of the Association 1985-2010) Macau: Chaozhou Association, 2010.

CHEN Zhiwu. *The Logic of Finance.* 2009. Conference on 18 October 2010 at Hong Kong University.

CHENG, P. W. M. 'Chinese Settlements on Taipa and Coloane Island in the Qing Dynasty: From Village to Market Town', in R. D. Cremer (ed.), *Macau City of Commerce and Culture. Continuity and Change,* 2nd Edition, Hong Kong: API Press, 1991 (1st ed. 1987), pp. 51-60.

CHOI, C. C. 'Settlement of Chinese Families in Macau', in R. D. Cremer (ed.), *Macau City of Commerce and Culture. Continuity and Change. 2nd Edition,* Hong Kong: API Press, 1991 (1st ed. 1987), pp. 61-80.

CIORAN, Emil. *Aveux et Anathèmes.* Paris: Gallimard, 1987.

CIPRIANI, R. and E. C. Del Re, 'Visual Sociology and Religion', in *Annual Review of the Sociology of Religion,* n. 1, 2010, pp. 403-420.

(The) *Consular* 1/1, Hong Kong and Macau, December 2010.

CLAYTON, Cathryn H. *Sovereignty at the Edge: Macau and the Question of Chineseness.* London: The Harvard University Asia Center, 2009.

CREMER, R. D. (ed.) *Macau City of Commerce and Culture. Continuity and Change.* 2nd Edition, Hong Kong: API Press, 1991 (1st ed. 1987).

Demographic Statistics 2009. Macau: DSEC, 2010.

DEUTSCHER, Guy. *Through the Language Glass.* London: Heinemann, 2010.

Dictionary of Taiwanese Hokkien-Mandarin 台湾语常用词辞典. Online, Taiwan: Ministry of Education, last correction 2011.

DUMONT, Louis. *Homo Hierarchicus.* Paris: Gallimard, 1966.

DURAND, Maurice. *Imagerie Populaire Vietnamienne.* Paris : EFEO, 2011.

DURKHEIM, Emile. *Les Règles de la Méthode Sociologique.* Paris: PUF, 1947.

ENTZINGER, Han. 'Open Borders and Welfare State', in Antonie Pécoud and Paul de Guchteneire (ed.), *Migration without Borders,* Chinese translation by Wu Yun, Yilin Press, 2010.

EVANS, Grant and Maria Tam (eds.). *Hong Kong. The Anthropology of a Chinese Metropolis.* Richmond Surrey: Curzon, 1997.

FERNANDES, Moisés Silva, 'Macao in Sino-Portuguese Relations 1949-1955', in *Portuguese Studies Review,* 16 (1), 2008, pp. 153-170.

FITCH, Kristine L. 'Culture and Personal Relationships', in Sandi W. Smith and Steven R. Wilson (eds.), *New Directions in Interpersonal Communication Research,* London: Sage, 2009, pp. 245-263.

– *Speaking Relationally: Culture, Communication, and Interpersonal Connection,* NY: Guilford Press, 1998.

FOK, K. C. 'The Ming Debate on How to Accommodate the Portuguese and the Emergence of the Macao Formula', in *Revista de Cultura* 13-14, 1994, pp. 328-344.

FORTE, Francesco. 'City Design, Creativity, Sustainability', in Luigi Fusco Girard et al. (eds.), *Sustainable City and Creativity: Promoting Creative Urban Initiatives,* Surrey, England: Ashgate, 2011, pp. 289-321.

FRANCHINI, Philippe. *Métis.* Paris: Jacques Bertoin, 1993.

GEERTZ, Clifford (1926-2006). *The Interpretation of Cultures.* New York: Basic Books, 1973 (reprint 1993).

GENNEP, Arnold van. *The Rites of Passage.* London: Routledge, 2004 (1st French ed. 1909).

GODELIER, Maurice. 'Baruya and Australian Kinship', *Lecture,* Paris: EHESS, 15 November 2010.

– *Communauté, Société, Culture.* Paris: CNRS, 2009.

– *Métamorphoses de la Parenté.* Paris: Fayard, 2004.

GRANET, Marcel. *La Pensée Chinoise.* Paris: Albin Michel, 1999 (1st ed. 1934).

– *La Civilisation Chinoise.* Paris: Albin Michel, 1988 (1st. ed. 1929).

– *La Religion des Chinois.* Paris: Albin Michel, 2010 (1st ed. 1922). (English translation: *The Religion of the Chinese People.* Harpercollins, 1977, introduction by Maurice Freedman).

GROOT, Jan J. M. de. *The Religious System of China, Its Ancient Forms, Evolution, History and Present Aspect, Manners, Customs and Social Institutions Connected Therewith.* Leiden: E. J. Brill, 1910.

– *The Religious System of China.* 6 vols. Taipei: Literature House, reprint 1964.

GULDIN, Gregory Eliyu. 'Hong Kong Ethnicity of Folk Models and Change', in Grant Evans and Maria Tam (eds.), *Hong Kong. The Anthropology of a Chinese Metropolis,* Richmond Surrey: Curzon, 1997, pp. 25-50.

GUNN, Geoffrey. *Encountering Macau: A Portuguese City-State on the Periphery of China, 1557-1999.* Boulder Colorado: Westview Press, 1996.

HAO Zhidong. *Macau History and Society.* Hong Kong: Hong Kong University Press, 2011.

Happiness Survey: 'Happiness Index Study on Macau Residents 2010', *Association of Economic Sciences* (chairman Joey Lao Chi Ngai), Hong Kong. *Macau Daily Times* (MDT), 20 January 2011, 41 pp. See also 'Survey of Residents' … *Macau Happiness Index 2011,* 2012.

Identity: 'Ethnicity not a Stable Identity: Experts', in *Republica,* Kathmandu, 25 April 2011, p. 2.

IEONG Wan Chong, *Anotações a Lei Básica da RAEM,* translation Vivian Tan et al., Associação de Divulgação da Lei Básica de Macau, 2005.

JIANG Jiancheng. 'Aomen Yunongye' (Macau's Fishing and Agriculture), in *Aomen*, Zhuhai: Zhuhai Chubanshe, 1999, pp. 191-194.

JOCHIM, Christian. *Chinese Religions. A Cultural Perspective.* New Jersey: Prentice Hall, 1986.

KAUFMANN, Jean-Claude. *L'Invention de Soi. Une Théorie de l'Identité.* Paris: Hachette/Colin, 2004.

KROEBER, Alfred L. *Anthropology.* New York, 1948.

KUAN K. H. 'An Observation on the Effect of Chinese and Portuguese Legal Document from the Perspective of Interpretation', in *Cuadernos de Ciência Jurídica*, No. 2, Lisbon: UMFLL, 2006.

LAM Fat Iam (ed.). *Qingji Xinqiaofang* (Oral History of Macau). Macau: Oral History Association of Macau, 2008.

LEBRAS, Hervé and Emmanuel TODD. *L'Invention de la France. Atlas Anthropologique et Politique.* Paris: Gallimard, 2012.

LEVI-STRAUSS, Claude. *Nature, Culture and Society* (in French). Paris: Flammarion, 2008.

– *Anthropologie Structurale.* Paris: Plon, 1974 (1st ed. 1958).

LI Fulin. *Aomen Sigeban Shiji* (Four Centuries and a Half on Macau). Macau: Aomen Songshanhui, 1995.

LI Peilin. 'Thirty Years of Reform and Changes of Social Policies', in Li Qiang (ed.), *Thirty Years of Reforms and Social Changes in China.* Leiden: Brill, 2010, pp. 453-491.

LIMA, Fernando and E. C. Torres. *Macau entre Dois Mundos.* Lisbon: Fundação Jorge Alves, 2004.

LO Shui-Hing, Sonny. 'Consultative Governance, Legitimacy Problem and Democracy Deficiency in Macau Consultative Style', in *Yiguo Liangzhi Yanjiu* Review on line of the Macau Polytechnic University, 2011, pp. 90-97 (www.ipm.edu.mo/Cweb/Cenpds/2systems_content11_1.htm/).

– *Political Change in Macao.* London/New York: Routledge, 2008.

– *Political Development in Macau.* Hong Kong: The Chinese University Press, 1995.

LONGMAN Dictionary of Contemporary English. London/China: Longman, 1995.

LUHMANN, Niklas, *The Reality of Mass Media,* Tr. by Kathleen Cross, Cambridge, UK: Polity Press, 2007.

LUN Tam Wai, 'Religions in Northern Guangdong' in John Lagerwey (ed.), *Religion and Chinese Society. Taoism and Local Religion in Modern China,* vol. 2, Hong Kong: HK Chinese University Press/EFEO, 2004, pp. 817-836.

MA Man Kei (Ma Wanqi) (ed.). *Jiang Hu Yiyuan Cishanhui Chuangban 130 Zhounian Jinian Tekan* ('Special Souvenir Issue for the past 130 years Commemoration Anniversary of the Charitable Association and Hospital Jiang Hu'), Macau: Jiang Hu Hospital and Association, 2001.

MA, Mary. 'Students, the World…', in *The Standard,* Hong Kong, 1 December 2010, p. 4. <editor@thestandard.com.hk>

'(2011) Macau Happiness Index' (*Aomen Kuaile Zhishu 2011),* Macau: Ximinghui (Sin Meng Charitable Association of Deputy Chan Mei Yi), 2011.

McCARTHY, Susan. 'God of Wealth, Temples of Prosperity: Party-State Participation in the Minority Cultural Revival', in *China an International Journal* 2-1, Singapore: NUS, March 2004, pp. 28-52.

McGIVERING, Jill. *Macao Remembers.* Hong Kong/New York: Oxford University Press, 1999.

MEAD, George H. *Essays on Social Psychology.* Transaction Books, 2001.

   – *The Individual and Social Self. Chicago University Press,* 1982.

   – *Mind, Self and Society. Chicago University Press,* 1934.

MINKOV, Michael. *Cultural Differences in a Globalising World.* Bingley, UK: Emerald, 2011.

MOODY, Andrew. 'Macau English: Status, Functions and Forms', in *English Today* 95, September 2008, Cambridge UP, U.K., pp. 1-15.

MORAIS SIMOES, José. 'Amanha Celebrase Aniversario do Deus da Terra' (Tomorrow is the Anniversary of the god of Earth), JTM, 5 March 2011, p. 5.

MORGAN, D. H. J. *Social Theory and the Family.* London: Routledge & Kegan Paul, 1975.

MUCCHIELLI, Alex. *L'Identité.* Paris: Puf, 2007.

MUS, Paul. 'Les Religions d'Indochine', in *Indochine,* 1931. Reprint in Aefek.free.fr/iso_album/mus.pdf (2007, opened 17 June 2011).

   – *Viet-Nam. Sociologie d'une Guerre.* Paris: Seuil, 1952.

(A) Museum in an Historical Site (sic). *The Monte Fortress of St. Paul.* Macau : Museu de Macau, 1999.

MYRDAL, Gunnar. *Beyond the Welfare State: Economic Planning and its International Implications.* New Haven: Yale University Press, 1960.

New Gen 57, Macau, December 2010 (in Chinese).

NGAI Gary. 'Macau Communities: Past, Present and Future', in Ieda Siqueira Wiarda and Lucy M. Cohen (eds.), *Macau. Cultural Dialogue Towards a New Millennium. Proceedings of a Symposium,* USA: Xilibris, 2004, pp. 101-132.

– 'Localisation Means Sinicization', in *Ponto Final* (in Portuguese), 25 September 1998, pp. 6-8.

NOACK, Georg. *Local Traditions, Global Modernities: Dress, Identity and the Creation of Public Self-Images in Contemporary Urban Myanmar.* Berlin: Regiospectra, 2011.

PIRES, B.V., 'Origin and Early History of Macau', in R. D. Cremer (ed.), *Macau City of Commerce and Culture. Continuity and Change,* 2nd Ed., Hong Kong: API Press, 1991, pp. 7-22. See also: www.library.gov.mo/macreturn/DATA/PP197/PP197007.HTM.

PLOPPER, C. H. *Chinese Religion through the Proverb.* Shanghai, 1926, p. 123.

'Panda Pair' by Amy Nip, *South China Morning Post,* 20 March 2011, p. 4.

Pandas: www. macaupanda.org,mo.

PORTER, Jonathan. 'A Question of Sovereignty', in *China Perspectives* 26, December 1999, pp. 8-17.

– *Macau the Imaginary City. Culture and Society, 1557 to the Present.* Boulder, Colorado: Westview Press, 1996.

PUGA, Rogerio Miguel. 'The Establishment of the English East India Company in the Pearl River Delta and Macao's Importance for the Old China Trade', in the Workshop *China Trade 1760-1860,* Macau Ricci Institute, 2-3 March 2011, not published.

RANGEL, Alexandra Sofia. *Filhos da Terra. A Comunidade Macaense, Ontem e Hoje.* Macau: IIM, 2012.

RIESENBERG, Peter. *Citizenship in the Western Tradition: Plato to Rousseau,* Chinese translation by T. H. Guo, Jilin Press, 2009.

ROCCA, Jean-Louis. *Une Sociologie de la Chine.* Paris: La Découverte, 2010.

ROZA, Francisco Antonio da. 'Journeys' (Story of a Life lived in Macau and Shanghai in the 1950s), in a forthcoming book by Pacheco J. da Silva (ed.), *The Portuguese Community in Shanghai,* Macau: IMM, c. 2012.

SA CUNHA, Luis. 'A Project of Identity: Macau, in the World Unit', in *Macau on the Threshold of the Third Millennium.* Conference 14-15 December 2001, Macau: Ricci Institute, 2003, pp. 291-300.

SAMPAIO, Manuel de Castro. *Os Chins de Macau.* Hong Kong: Typ. De Noronha e Filhos, 1867.

SCHNEIDER, David M. *A Critique of the Study of Kinship.* Ann Arbor: The University of Michigan Press, 1984.

SILVA, Renelde Justo Bernardo da. *A Identidade Macaense/The Macanese Identity.* Macau: IMM, 2001.

SINN, Elizabeth. *Power and Charity. A Chinese Merchant Elite in Colonial Hong Kong.* Hong Kong University Press, 2003 (1st ed. 1989).

SKINNER, G. William (ed.). *The Study of Chinese Society. Essays by Maurice Freedman.* Stanford UP, 1979.

Statistics available in 2011:

<<http://www.dsec.gov.mo/Statistic/Social/EnvironmentStatistics/EnvironmentStatistic 2009Y.aspx>>

Survey of Residents's Happiness in 2010 (in Chinese): *Aomen Jumin Kuaile Zhishudiaocha 2010.* Macau: Sin Meng Association, 2011.

TEIXEIRA, Manuel. *Toponímia de Macau. Ruas com Nomes Genéricos* (Toponymy of Macau...). Vol. 1. Macau: Imprensa Nacional, 1979 (Reprint Instituto Cultural de Macau, 1997) .

TONG Io Cheng. 'Between Harmony and Turbulence', in *Juridikum* nr 3/2010, Vienna, pp. 287-299.

TONG Io Cheng and Wu Yanni, 'Legal Transplants and the on-going Formation of Macau Legal Culture', in *ISAIDAT Law Review,* Vol. I, Issue 2, 2010, pp. 619-675.

Tong Shan Tang Yibaishi Zhounian Jiniannian 1892-2002 ('Tung Sin Tong Association 110 Years Anniversary Book 1892-2002'). Macau: Tung Sin Tong, 2002.

Tourism Indicators. Macau: DSEC, December 2010.

Tung Sin Tong Annual Fund Raising Campaign, Macau: Tung Sin Tong, Winter 2010.

UNESCO. *Cultural Industries. A Challenge for the Future of Culture.* Paris: Unesco, 1982.

VANDERMEERSCH, Léon. Book Review: 'G. W. Skinner, The Study of the Chinese Society. Essays by Maurice Freedman', *L'Homme* 21, 1981, pp. 128-129.

WADE, Geoff. 'Southeast Asia in the 15th Century', in G. Wade and L. Sun (eds.), *Southeast Asia in the Fifteenth Century. The China Factor.* Hong Kong University Press, 2010, pp. 3-43.

WALLERSTEIN, Immanuel. 'Culture as the Ideological Battleground of the Modern World-system', in David Oswell (ed.), *Cultural Theory, Volume III. Environment and Global Humanity,* 2010, pp. 221-251.

WAN Yuh-Yao. 'Analytic Perspectives on Changing Culture: The Case of Taiwan', Ph. D. Thesis, University of Oregon, USA, 1993.

WANG, Gungwu. *The Chineseness of China: Selected Essays.* Hong Kong: Oxford University Press, 1991.

WANG Jimin and Wu Liande. *History of Chinese Medicine.* Tiensin Press, 1932 (reprint 1973).

WELLER, Robert P. 'Identity and Social Change in Taiwanese Religion', in Murray A. Rubinstein (ed.), *Taiwan a New History,* New York: M.E. Sharpe, 2007, pp. 339-365.

Wenweipo.com: 'Five Year Plan for Hong Kong and Macau', 6 March 2011.

WEST, Jackie, Zhao Minghua et al. (eds.). *Women of China. Economic and Social Transformation.* New York: St. Martins Press, 1999.

Whorunshk: www.scmp.com/whorunshk

Wikipedia.org (see Hokkien and Min Nan) 4 December 2010.

WITTGENSTEIN, Ludwig. *Uber Gewissheit* (On Certitude). Edited by Gertrude E.M. Anscombe and Georg H. van Wright, Oxford : Basil Blackwell, 1969.

WONG, Ka-yee Carrie. 'A Investigation into Chinese Kinship Terms in Hong Kong Society'. Thesis. Hong Kong University, 2000.

WOON, W. L. 'Chinese Dialects in Macau', in R. D. CREMER, (ed.) *Macau City of Commerce and Culture. Continuity and Change. 2nd Edition,* Hong Kong: API Press, 1991, pp. 117-127.

WU Zhiliang et al. (eds.). *Aomen Baike Quanshu* ('Enciclopédia de Macau'). Fundação Macau, 2005 (1st ed. 1999).

XIAO Weiyun, 'Conferência Sobre a Lei Básica de Macau' ('Conference on Macau's Basic Law'). Macau: Associação Promotora da Lei Básica de Macau, 2005.

YANG, David Da-hua. 'Civil Society as an Analysis Lens for Contemporary China', in *China an International Journal* 2-1, Singapore: NUS, March 2004, pp. 1-27.

YAO, Esther S. Lee. *Chinese Women. Past and Present.* Mesquite, Texas: Ide House, 1983.

Yearbook of Statistics 2009. Macau: DSEC, 2010.

YIN Guangren and Zhang Ruili. *Aomen Jilue Jiaozhu* (The Annals of Macau). Macau: Aomen Wenhuasi (Cultural Institute).

YU, Eilo Wing-Yat. 'Electoral Fraud and Governance: The 2009 Legislative Direct Election in Macao', in *The Journal of Comparative Asian Development,* London: Routledge, 20 June 2011, pp. 90-128.

www.informaworld.com/smpp/ title-content=t91360733

ZHANG Wenqin. *Aomen yu Zhonghua Lishi Wenhua* (Macau and the Chinese History and Culture), Macau Foundation, 1995.

NOTES

[1] See Chapter One, 'Identity of the Chinese of Macau'.

[2] See Chapter Two, 'Basic Law and the Chinese of Macau'.

[3] See Appendix for the questionnaire and Table Three for data based on the answers for 100 select households.

[4] *Longman Dictionary of Contemporary English.* London / China: Longman, 1995.

[5] Louis Augustin-Jean, 'Macanese Identity and Food', in J. A. Berlie (ed.), *Macao 2000,* Oxford/New York: Oxford University Press, 1999, pp. 105.

[6] Twenty years of residence is the number of years to become a 'Chinese of Macau', a particular designation used in the questionnaire. (See Appendix 1.) Similarly in Article 46 of the Basic Law, twenty years of residence in Macau is the minimum required for the Chief Executive.

[7] MOP (patacas, the currency of the MSAR), 7,000 per year (around 700 Euros).

[8] *Hojemacau,* 21 December 2011, p. 31.

[9] Putonghua (Mandarin Chinese) is transliterated in *pinyin* and Cantonese in Jyutping (the transliteration developed and promoted by the Linguistic Society of Hong Kong, beginning in 1993). Please note that there may be some mistakes in the romanisation in this book. The family names in particular are complex to transcribe. It should be noted, also, that the romanisation of Cantonese names in Macau and Hong Kong may sometimes differ.

[10] Hao Zhidong, *Macau History and Society,* Hong Kong University Press, 2011, p. 207.

[11] Alex Mucchielli, *L'Identité* (Identity), Paris: PUF, 2007, p. 5. For 'diversity' see Lebras and Todd, 2012, pp. 9, 11, 25. The concept of 'way of life' is also essential, see Chapter Two of this book.

[12] *Jornal Tribuna de Macau* (JTM), 28 November 2011, p. 7.

[13] Francisco Antonio da Roza, 'Journeys' (Story of a Life lived in Macau and Shanghai in the 1950s), in a forthcoming book by Pacheco J. da Silva, 'The Portuguese Community in Shanghai', Macau: IMM, c. 2012.

[14] Roza, c. 2012, pp. 15-17.

[15] *A Museum in an Historical Site ...* Macau Museum, 1999, pp. 9-10.

[16] Hao, 2011, p. 198.

[17] The Goanese Association is very active in Macau. The majority of its members are Catholic and Hindu. On Saturday 10 December 2011, the Association named 'Nucleo de Animação Cultural de *Goa,*

Damão e Diu' met in Coloane for the Christmas party. The President is Sharoz D. Pernencar and the board has five members.

[18] Interview with Gary Ngai, 17 February 2011.

[19] Hao, 2011, pp.206-207.

[20] *Suara Timor Lorosae,* 2 April 2012.

[21] Cathryn H. Clayton, *Sovereignty at the Edge: Macau and the Question of Chineseness,* London: Harvard University, 2009, pp. 9, 264; Clifford Geertz, *The Interpretation of Cultures,* New York: Basic Books, 1973.

[22] Wang Gungwu, *The Chineseness of China,* Hong Kong: Oxford University Press, 1991.

[23] Li Fulin, *Aomen Siban Shiji* (Macau: Four Centuries and a Half of Macau's History), Macau, 1995, p. 17; C. C. Choi, 'Settlements on Chinese Families', in R. D. Cremer (ed.), *Macau City of Commerce and Culture. Continuity and Change.* Hong Kong: API Press, 1991, pp. 61-63, 77.

[24] Paul Spooner, interviews with the author in February 2011.

[25] *French-Chinese Dictionary,* Hong Kong: Commercial Press, 1983.

[26] Emil Cioran, *Aveux et Anathemes* ('Confessions and Anathema'), Paris: Gallimard, 1987, p. 21.

[27] Author's research.

[28] See Table Three.

[29] J. A. Berlie (ed.), *Macao 2000,* Oxford/New York: Oxford University Press, 1999.

[30] *Macau's Demographic Statistics*, Macau: DSEJ, 2009, p. 6.

[31] *Yearbook of Statistics,* 2009, p. 77.

[32] *Tourism Indicators* No. 5, Macau: DSEC (Department of Statistics), May 2011, pp. 1-2.

[33] Note that three households selected two answers instead of one. So the total Macau+Chinese of Macau+Chinese is 103 households and not 100 as it should be.

[34] JTM, 28 November 11, pp. 1-3.

[35] Benedict R. O'Gorman Anderson. *Imagined Communities. Reflections on the Origin and Spread of Nationalism.* London: Verso, 1991 (1st pub. 1983), p. 134.

[36] Clayton, 2009, pp. 274-5.

[37] Gregory E. Guldin, 'Hong Kong Ethnicity of Folk Models and Change', in Grant Evans and Maria Tam (eds.), *Hong Kong. The Anthropology of a Chinese Metropolis,* Richmond Surrey: Curzon, 1997, p. 38.

[38] See Appendix 2.

[39] Guldin, 1997, p. 50.

[40] Georg Noack, *Local Traditions, Global Modernities: Dress, Identity and the Creation of Public Self-Images in Contemporary Urban Myanmar.* Berlin: Regiospectra, 2011.

[41] I owe a debt of gratitude to Jill McGivering for the quotations from her book, *Macao Remembers.* Hong Kong/New York: Oxford University Press, 1999.

[42] Interviews are important. The author was based in Macau between 1995 and December 1999; and between 2000 and April 2012, in Hong Kong, East Timor, Southeast Asia, China and Macau. Most of the author's research in 2011 and 2012 was done in Macau.

[43] The former Chief Executive, Edmund Ho, is the chairman of the Council for the Basic Law. The former President of the Legislative Assembly, Susana Chou Kei Jan, is the vice-chairman of this body.

[44] Lam Fat Iam, *Aomen Qingji Xinqiaofang* (Macau: Oral History), Macau Oral History Association, 2008, p. 136.

[45] Interview of Mr Leong Heng Teng with the author on 19 March 2011.

[46] *Aomen Ribao* (ARB), 4 December 2010, p. A10.

[47] J. A. Berlie, ' Society and Economy', in J. A. Berlie (ed.), *Macao 2000,* 1999, p. 36.

[48] Jill McGivering, *Macao Remembers.* Hong Kong/New York: Oxford University Press, 1999, pp.10-19.

[49] Author's interviews in 2011 and research. See also Fernando Lima and E. C. Torres. *Macau entre Dois Mundos.* Lisbon: Fundação Jorge Alves, 2004, pp. 63-70.

[50] *Ponto Final,* 21 March 2011, p. 6.

[51] Comendador Ho Yun (1906-1983) is the father of the former Chief Executive of Macau, Edmund Ho. Ho Yin was also the diplomatic representative of the PRC in Macau for many years.

[52] Author's research and Jill McGivering 1999, pp. 57-61.

[53] Jill McGivering, 1999.

[54] We do not know clearly who or how many Chinese and Portuguese or British legislators in charge of the preparation of the Basic Law discovered the important concept 'way of life' to define the society of a Special Administrative Region.

[55] About the history of the name 'Macau' and its Chinese equivalent, see Jin Guo Ping, 'On the Origin of Macau', in C.L. Ng (ed.), *A New Compilation of Macau History,* Macau Foundation, 2008, pp. 45-78.

[56] B. V. Pires, 'Origin and Early History of Macau', in R. D. Cremer (ed.), *Macau City of Commerce and Culture. Continuity and*

Change, 2nd Ed., Hong Kong: API Press, 1991, pp. 7-22. See in particular p. 9.

[57] Han Entzinger, 'Open Borders and Welfare State', in Antonie Pécoud and Paul de Guchteneire (ed.), *Migration without Borders,* Chinese translation by Wu Yun, Jilin Press, 2010, p. 119.

[58] Xiao Weiyun, Conferênçia Sobre a Lei Básica de Macau ('Conference on Macau's Basic Law'), Associação Promotora da Lei Básica de Macau, 2005, p. 55.

[59] Similar attempts to define Macau can be found in R. D. Cremer (ed.), *Macau City of Commerce and Culture. Continuity and Change.* Hong Kong: API Press, 1991, in which specialists in different sectors are invited to address the case of Macau.

[60] Tong Io Cheng and Wu Yanni, 'Legal Transplants and the on-going Formation of Macau Legal Culture', in *ISAIDAT Law Review,* Vol. I, Issue 2, 2010, pp.651-652.

[61] For a brief account of the Macau gambling monopoly, see Geoffrey C. Gunn, *Encountering Macau – A Portuguese City-State on the Periphery of China, 1557-1999,* 2005, pp. 87-89.

[62] Gunnar Myrdal, *Beyond the Welfare State: Economic Planning and its International Implications.* New Haven: Yale University Press, 1960; Han Entzinger, 'Open Borders and Welfare State', in Antonie Pécoud and Paul de Guchteneire (ed.), *Migration without Borders,* Chinese translation by Wu Yun, Yilin Press, 2010, p. 117.

[63] Peter Riesenberg, *Citizenship in the Western Tradition: Plato to Rousseau,* Chinese translation by T.H.Guo, Jilin Press, 2009, p.105.

[64] Xiao Weiyun, 2005, p. 67.

[65] Similar expressions can also be seen in Ieong Wan Chong, *Anotações à Lei Básica da RAEM,* translated by Vivian Tan et al., Associação de Divulgação da Lei Básica de Macau, 2005, p. 45.

[66] K. H. Kuan, 'An Observation on the Effect of Chinese and Portuguese Legal Document from the Perspective of Interpretation', in *Cuadernos de Ciência Jurídica,* No. 2, 2006, Lisbon: UMFLL, p. 165.

[67] Jorge Neto Valente, 'The Opening Speech', *Abertura do Ano Judicial 2009,* 21 October 2009.

[68] G. L. Xie, 'Legal Transplant, Legal Culture and Legal Development – Criticising the Current Situation of Macau Law', in Conference of Macau Legal Reform and Legal Construction, held 19-20 March, Macau University of Science and Technology, pp. 49-52.

[69] Tong Io Cheng and Wu Yanni, 'Legal Transplants and the on-going Formation of Macau Legal Culture', in *ISAIDAT Law Review,*

Vol. I, Issue 2, 2010, p. 674.

[70] Xiao Weiyun, 2005, p. 59.

[71] Tong Io Cheng and Wu Yanni, 'Legal Transplants and the ongoing Formation of Macau Legal Culture', in *ISAIDAT Law Review,* Vol. I, Issue 2, 2010, p. 670.

[72] David Yang Da-hua, "Civil Society as an Analysis Lens for Contemporary China", in *China an International Journal* 2-1, Singapore: NUS, March 2004, pp. 1-2.

[73] Jiang Jiancheng. "Aomen Yunongye" (Macau's Fishing and Agriculture), in *Aomen,* Zhuhai: Zhuhai Chubanshe, 1999, pp. 191-194.

[74] ARB, 23 February 2011, p. C12.

[75] JTM, 19 January 2012, pp. 8-9.

[76] Leo Semaskho, 2005, <www.peacefromharmony.spb.ru/eng/> 25 March 2012.

[77] Jean-Louis Rocca, *Une Sociologie de la Chine.* Paris: La Découverte, 2010, pp. 51-67.

[78] Immanuel Wallerstein, "Culture as the Ideological Battleground of the Modern World-system", in David Oswell (ed.), *Cultural Theory,* Volume III. *Environment and Global Humanity,* 2010, p. 236.

[79] Marcel Granet, *La Religion des Chinois, La Religion des Chinois.* Paris: Albin Michel, 2010, p. 171.

[80] MDT , 2 February 2011, p. 3.

[81] Leo Semaskho, 2005, <www.peacefromharmony.spb.ru/eng/> 25 March 2012.

[82] Jean-Louis Rocca, *Une Sociologie de la Chine.* Paris: La Découverte, 2010, pp. 51-67.

[83] Immanuel Wallerstein, "Culture as the Ideological Battleground of the Modern World-system", in David Oswell (ed.), *Cultural Theory,* Volume III. *Environment and Global Humanity,* 2010, p. 236.

[84] Professor Xiong Yuegen of Peking University notes during his power-point presentation at the Conference "The Re-emerging China...", The Hong Kong Institute of Education, 12 January 2012, that regarding social policy in China 'civil society within the strong Party-state' is immature.

[85] *Workers*, 16 January 2011.

[86] MDT, 23 March 2011, p. 2.

[87] *macaudailynewstimes.com.mo,* 28.10.2009.

[88] J. A. Berlie et al. "Conclusion and Prospects", in J. A. Berlie (ed.), *Macao 2000,* 1999, p. 208.

[89] *Va Kio,* 5 January 2011.

[90] *Tourism indicators* No. 12, Macau: DSEC, December 2011 and JTM, 24 November 2011, p. 7.

[91] *Tourism indicators*, No. 12, Macau: DSEC, December 2011.

[92] ARB, 14 December 2010, p. A10; ARB, 29 December 2010, p. A 10 and 2 January 2010, p. C1.

[93] *Employment Survey no 4*, Macau: DSEC, April-June 2011.

[94] MDT, 5 January 2011, p. 3.

[95] *Novos Aterros Para Diversificar* (New Possibilities on Diversification), *Hojemacau* 5 December 2011, p. 7.

[96] *Employment Survey 2011*, Macau: DSEC, 2012, pp. 5, 11, 17, 35.

[97] *Macau Business Magazine,* January 2012, pp. 26-27.

[98] *Macao in Figures,* 2011, DSEC, p. 14.

[99] *Seng Pou,* 14 January 2011, p. 4.

[100] *Seng Pou,* 15 January 2011, p. 1.

[101] *Tourist Price Index* No. 4, 4th Quarter 2011, Macau: DSEC, p.11.

[102] *Va Kio,* 2. February 2011, p. 1-1; ARB, 2 February 2011, p. A1.

[103] MDT, 2 March 2011.

[104] *The Standard,* 23 December 2010, p. 7.

[105] *Aomen Ribao,* 23 January 2011, p. A11.

[106] MDT, 22 January 2011, p. 3 and *Monthly Bulletin of Statistics,* Macau: DSEC, February 2012, p. 33.

[107] Fatima Almeida and R. Carvalho. "Ilha Verde Without Families", in JTM (in Portuguese), 4 January 2011, p. 3.

[108] ARB, 2 October 2011, p. C5; *Jornal do Cidadão,* 2. January 2011.

[109] ARB, 5 January 2011, p. B7.

[110] MDT, 14 January 2011, p. 3.

[111] ARB, 1 February 2011, p. B5.

[112] MDT, 28 January 2011, p. 2.

[113] *Va Kio,* 11 February 2011, and Sonny Lo Shui-Hing. "Consultative Governance, Legitimacy Problem and Democracy Deficiency in Macau Consultative Style", in *Yiguo Liangzhi Yanjiu* (Recherche on 'One Country Two Systems'). Review on line of the Macau Polytechnic University, 2011, pp. 90-97 (www.ipm.edu.mo/Cweb/Cenpds/2systems_content11_1.htm/).

[114] *Va Kio,* 8 February 2011, p. 2-3.

[115] ARB, 18 February 2011, p. A7.

[116] ARB, 21 February 2011, p. A1.

[117] ARB, 4 December 2010, p. A10.

[118] ARB, 6 March 2011.

[119] Francesco Forte, "City Design, Creativity, Sustainability", in

Luigi Fusco Girard et al. (eds.), *Sustainable City and Creativity: Promoting Creative Urban Initiatives,* Surrey, England: Ashgate, 2011, no specific page.

[120] Rogerio Miguel Puga, "The Establishment of the English East India Company in the Pearl River Delta and Macao's Importance for the Old China Trade", in the Workshop *China Trade 1760-1860,* Macau Ricci Institute, 2-3 March 2011, p. 4.

[121] ARB, 10 December 2010, p. E6.

[122] MDT, 19 December 2011, p. 6.

[123] ARB, 20 February 2011, p. A6.

[124] *Consular,* 2010, p. 5.

[125] MSAR statistics, *Gaming Sector Survey*, Macau: DSEC, 2010, p. 8.

[126] ARB, 8 January 2011, p. D6.

[127] MDT, 4 January 2010, p. 3.

[128] MDT, 2 March 2011. p. 3.

[129] JTM, 21 January 2011, p. 2.

[130] ARB, 25 January 2011.

[131] MDT, 25 January 2011, p. 5.

[132] *Va Kio,* 29 January 2011, p. 6; JTM, 29 January 2011, p. 3; Whorunshk: www.scmp.com/whorunshk, 2011.

[133] MDT, 29 January 2011. p. 2.

[134] ARB, 1 February 2011, p. A1. The Hong Kong Sanatorium Hospital was established in 1922. Located in Happy Valley, its Guy Hugh Chan Refractive Surgery Center is one of the most famous Departments of Opthamology in Hong Kong.

[135] MDT, 1 February 2011, p. 3.

[136] Cremer, 1987, p. 161.

[137] Cremer, 1987, p. 164.

[138] *Macao in Figures 2011,* p. 17.

[139] *Hoje Macau* 2 March 2011, p. 6.

[140] WhorunsHK, 2011. In fact there is a long story behind 'sleazy', an interpreted adjective.
According to Dr Pansy Ho, during a business meeting it was in fact mentioned, but there is no negative meaning for Macau at all.

[141] *Macau Times,* 18 January 2012, p. 2.

[142] MDT, 28 November 2011, p. 3.

[143] ARB, 21 December 2010, p. C5.

[144] David Yang, 2004, p. 3.

[145] K. C. Fok, 'The Ming Debate on How to Accommodate the Portuguese and the Emergence of the Macao Formula', in *Revista de Cultura* 13-14, 1994, p. 343.

[146] *Macau Today,* 16 February 2011, p. 1.

[147] *Va Kio,* 30 December 2010, p. 2-2.

[148] Most developed world countries have accepted the chronological age of 65 years as a definition of 'elderly' or older person, but like many westernized concepts, this does not adapt well to the situation in Asia. While this definition is somewhat arbitrary, it is many times associated with the age at which one can begin to receive pension benefits. At the moment, there is no United Nations standard numerical criterion, but the UN agreed cutoff is 60+ years to refer to the older population. See http://www.who.int/healthinfo/survey/ageingdefnolder/en/index.html (2 October 2012).

[149] *Va Kio,* 19 December 2010, p. 2-3.

[150] *Va Kio,* 19 December 2010, p. 2-3.

[151] ARB, 17 February 2011, p. B10.

[152] ARB, 21 January 2011, p. B5.

[153] ARB, 19 February 2011, p. B6.

[154] ARB, 20 February 2011, p. B8.

[155] ARB, 2 March 2011, p. B6.

[156] ARB, 15 February 2011, p. A6.

[157] ARB, 20 February 2011, p. B8.

[158] ARB, 5 January 2011, p. B6.

[159] ARB, 7 March 2011, p. C8.

[160] *Va Kio,* 13 February 2011, p. 2-2.

[161] ARB, 20 December 2010, p. B5.

[162] ARB 11 December 2010, p. B5.

[163] The Rotary Club Guia was founded in 1993 by J. B. Leão. See his life story above.

[164] ARB, 21 January 2011, p. B8. For the history of the Rotary Club in Macau see <www.rotaryfirst100.org/global/countries/macau/index.htm>

[165] ARB, 16 January 2011, p. A6.

[166] ARB, 3 February 2011, p. B9.

[167] ARB, 3 February 2011, p. B9.

[168] ARB, 13 February 2011, p. A7.

[169] ARB 17 February 2011, p. B10.

[170] ARB, 31 January 2011, p. B7.

[171] ARB, 24 January 2011, p. E3.

[172] Esther S. Lee Yao. *Chinese Women. Past and Present.* Mesquite, Texas: Ide House, 1983, p. 167.

[173] Jackie West and Zhao Minghua et al. (eds.), *Women of China. Economic and Social Transformation.* New York: St. Martin's Press, 1999, pp. xii, 41.

[174] *Macao in Figures 2011*, p. 6. The number of divorces on the Mainland is increasing dramatically. In the MSAR, the number of divorces is also growing steadily, per 1,000 persons, 1.2 in 2008, 1.4 in 2009 and 1.6 in 2010. The actual figure of divorces registered n 2010, was 889.

[175] ARB, 1 February 2011, p. B6.

[176] ARB, 31 January 2011, p. C5.

[177] ARB, 3 February 2011, p. B9.

[178] Based on interviews by the author on 23 February 2011, and 15 December 2011.

[179] Li Fulin, *Aomen Sigeban Shiji* (Four Centuries and a Half of Macau's History). Macau: Aomen Songshanhui, 1995, p. 171.

[180] See photo 9.

[181] *Va Kio,* 2 February 2011, p. 2-2.

[182] *Ponto Final,* 4 February 2011, and ARB, 22 December 2010, p. A3.

[183] Elizabeth Sinn, *Power and Charity. A Chinese Merchant Elite in Colonial Hong Kong.* Hong Kong University Press, 2003 (1st ed. 1989), Chapter Four: 'Management, Organization, and Development 1869-1894', pp. 50-81.

[184] Wang Jimin and Wu Liande. *History of Chinese Medicine.* Tiensin Press, 1932.

[185] ARB, 20 February 2011, p. A6.

[186] *Va Kio,* 11 December 2010, p. 2.

[187] *Va Kio,* 11 December 2010, p. 2 (*sic*).

[188] ARB, 17 and 18 January 2011; Seng Pou, 20 December 2011, p. 1.

[189] ARB, 19 February 2011, p. B 10.

[190] Dr Lam Kam Seng is Vice-President of the Industrial Association of Macau and member of the board of the University of Macau. He received the Mérito Industrial e Commercial (Industrial and Commercial Merit) in 2001.

[191] Jack M. Braga, *Macau a Short Handbook.* Macau: Information and Tourism Department, 1970 (1st ed. 1963), p. 43.

[192] Sinn, 2003.

[193] ARB, 4 March 2011, p. E1.

[194] Interviews with Deputy Chan Mei Yi in November 2010, 17 March 2011 and December 2011.

[195] *Va Kio,* 22 March 2011, p. 2-2.

[196] ARB, 17 February 2011, p. B10.

[197] Robert Cipriani and Emanuela Del Re, papers presented on 2 July 2011 at the 31st ISSR Conference (Sociology of Religion), Aix-en-Provence. See Cipriani R. and E. C. Del Re, 2010.

[198] Jorge Menezes Oliveira quoted by Paulo Cardinal, 'Fragmentos em Torno da Constituçâo Processual Penal de Macau-Do Principio da Continuidade ao Principio da Dignidade Humana', in *Studia Iuridica* 100-III, 2010, p. 760.

[199] Granet, *La Religion des Chinois,* 2010, p. 19.

[200] Granet, *La Religion des Chinois,* 2010, p. 228.

[201] Granet, *La Religion des Chinois,* 2010, p. 15.

[202] www.coe.int/t/secretarygeneral/sg/archives_en.asp

[203] Hao Zhidong, *Macau History and Society,* Hong Kong: Hong Kong University Press, 2011, p. 122.

[204] Hao, 2011. p. 122.

[205] Lun Tam Wai, 'Religions in Northern Guangdong', in John Lagerwey (ed.), *Religion and Chinese Society. Taoism and Local Religion in Modern China,* Vol. 2, Hong Kong and Paris: Chinese University of Hong Kong Press/EFEO, 2004, pp. 817-836.

[206] Niklas Luhmann (1927-1998), *The Reality of Mass Media,* Tr. by Kathleen Cross, Cambridge, UK: Polity Press, 2007, pp. 85-87, 122.

[207] Manuel de Castro Sampaio, *Os Chins de Macau* (The Chinese of Macau), Hong Kong: Typ. De Noronha e Filhos, 1867, pp. 92-107.

[208] Granet, *La Religion des Chinois,* 2010, p. 227.

[209] Granet, *La Religion des Chinois*, 2010.

[210] Hao Zhidong, 2011 and Clayton, 2009.

[211] Boiled lettuce (*shengcai*) is a traditional dish for celebrating the Chinese New Year in the MSAR and South China.

[212] Sampaio, 1867.

[213] Jan J. M. de Groot, *The Religious System of China.* Vol. 6. Taipei: Literature House, reprint 1964, pp. 929-931.

[214] See Poo Moo-Chou, 'The Concept of Ghost in Ancient Chinese Religion', in John Lagerwey (ed.), *Religion and Chinese Society. Ancient and Medieval China,* Vol.1, Hong Kong: Chinese University of Hong Kong Press/EFEO, 2004, pp. 173-192.

[215] On 9 June 2011, at the Asiatic Society of Paris (founded in 1822), Philippe Papin presented the reprinted book of Maurice Durand entitled *L'Imagerie Populaire Vietnamese* (Vietnamese Popular Imagery). It was published in 2011 in Paris by the EFEO. This superb book in colour, for the first time, shows the surprising lost tradition of cards for the Lunar New Year in Vietnam (*Tet* in

Vietnamese). This Chinese tradition of the Lunar New Year continues to be fundamental in China, and in particular Macau and Vietnam. Vietnam has kept a part of this Chinese *savoir faire,* but not the New Year cards. Fortunately these Chinese cards traditionally red-coloured are still on fashion and often modernised even in Macau in 2011. Many of my informants in the MSAR, even youth, participate actively in these vivid customs.

[216] Granet, *La Religion des Chinois,* 2010, p. 226.

[217] Robert P. Weller, 'Identity and Social Change in Taiwanese Religion', in Murray A. Rubinstein (ed.), *Taiwan a New History,* New York: M.E. Sharpe, 2007, p. 341.

[218] JTM, 17 January 2010.

[219] *The Standard,* 23 December 2010, p. 7.

[220] Hokkien people from southeastern Fujian (East of Guangdong Province) are numerous in Taiwan. Around sixteen million or 70 per cent of the total population of Taiwan are Hokkien Chinese. These Hokkien speak Minnan, the dominant dialect in southeastern Fujian.

[221] Christian Jochim, *Chinese Religions. A Cultural Perspective.* New Jersey: Prentice Hall, 1986, pp. 152-156.

[222] I have indirectly consulted 林玉风(assistant professor Lam Yok Fong of the University of Macau and one of the editors of 澳門百科全書), she agrees with the viewpoint that the term *Makok Miu* is actually a redundant term since *Miu* and *Kok* both mean 'temple' and people use it just to distinguish the temple and the Makok district.

[223] In 2012, the board of Macau Mazu Temple promoted Putian Temple, by displaying vertically their visit there in 2009, in its private show room. Putian is the birthplace of the goddess and has also the most ancient temple of Mazu in Meizhou Island, on the shore of Putian.

[224] Manuel Teixeira, *Toponomia de Macau. Ruas com Nomes Genericos* (Toponymy of Macau...), Vol. 1, 1979, p. 172.

[225] ARB *(Aomen Ribao),* 31 January 2011, p. A2.

[226] The goddess creator, Nuwa, helped to solve a quarrel between the Water Spirit *(Gong Gong* 共工) and the Fire Spirit *(Zhuanxu).* This quarrel may mean 'extreme calamity' which is coined in a Chinese proverb *(shuishen huore).* Nuwa is portrayed as a serpent and Gong Gong as a black dragon, against the established order, who is responsible for the great floods.

[227] Paul Mus, 'Marxisme et Traditionalisme', in P. Mus, *Viet-Nam Sociologie d'une Guerre* (Sociology of a War), Paris: Seuil, 1952,

pp. 248-256.
[228] Paul Mus, 1952, p. 253.
[229] Susan McCarthy, 'God of Wealth, Temples of Prosperity: Party-State Participation in the Minority Cultural Revival', in *China an International Journal* 2-1, Singapore: NUS, March 2004, pp. 28-29.
[230] In Dili, East Timor, many centenarian banyans were cut down in 2011 and 2012. The reason of this ecological catastrophe is not known.
[231] *Hojemacau*, 1.12.2011, pp. 1, 12.
[232] Regine Azria and Danièle Hervieu-Leger, *Dictionnaire des Faits Religieux* ('Dictionary of Religious Facts'), Paris : PUF, 2010, p.1082. See the article on Chinese religions, pp. 1075-1083.
[233] Michael Minkov, *Cultural Differences in a Globalising World.* Bingley, UK: Emerald, 2011, p. 232.
[234] Early July 2011, concerning a dynamic branch, visual sociology, the question of religion and Macau was mentioned during the last Conference of the International Sociologists of Religion in Aix-en-Provence.
[235] Robert Weller, 2007, p. 341.
[236] Clayton, 2009, p. 303.
[237] Basic Law I-9.
http://www.mfa.gov.cn/eng/wjb/zzjg/tyfls/tyfl/2626/t15467.htm (open 12 June 2011)
[238] Hao, 2011, p. 198.
[239] Unesco: *Cultural Industries. A Challenge for the Future of Culture.* Paris: Unesco, 1982.
[240] Minkov, 2011, p. 69.
[241] Interview of Fernando Eloy with the *Jornal Tribuna de Macau,* 1 August 2011, pp. 8-9.
[242] MDT, 30 December 2010, p. 7.
[243] Sampaio, 1867, chap. XII.
[244] *Dahui Zai Aomen* ('Grand Meeting in Macau'), Hainan: Hainan Baoping (5th International Federation of Hainanese Association and Macau Hainan Provincial Association), c. 1992, p. 13.
[245] *Happiness Survey,* 2011, p. 28. Some laymen and scholars express doubts about the measurability of happiness. The World Health Organization, however, shows that societies with less happy people tend to have more health problem (Minkov, 2011, p. 80).
[246] MDT, 20 January 2011.
[247] *Happiness Survey*, 2011, p. 28.
[248] JTM, 4 January 2011, p. 13.
[249] *Ponto Final,* 22 February 2011, p. 6.

[250] Li Peilin, 'Thirty Years of Reform and Changes of Social Policies' in Li Qiang (ed.), *Thirty Years of Reforms and Social Changes in China.* Leiden: Brill, 2010, pp. 477-478.

[251] *Tourism Indicators* No 6, Macau: DSEC, 2011, p. 1.

[252] A business delegation of the MSAR led by the former Chief Executive, Ho Hau Wah met the President José Ramos-Horta, the PM Xanana Gusmão and the President of the National Parliament Fernando La Sama de Araujo. Many ministers and Timorese businessmen and V.I.P. ladies met the Macau's representatives, in particular the Minister of Economy and Development, José Gonçalves, Julio Alfaro (president of the television, TL), Oscar Lima (vice-president of TL), Eduardo Morais dos Santos (Group Sagres), Joaquim Perdigão (Hotel Timor), Jackson Lay (Tourism), Américo Leong Monteiro (Tourism), Jorge Serrano (Tourism and Infrastructures), José Rocha (Tourism), Milena Abrantes (Tourism), Tony Jape (Trade and Tourism), Lita Foo Hau Kiun (Trade), Claricia Lay (Trade), Ted Lay (Tourism), Fernando Lay (Tourism), Ketelin Gonçalves (Businesswoman), Lourenço Oliveira, Ricardo New, Faustino da Costa, Nina Rangel, Zenilda Gusmão (PM's Daughter), Julia and Angela Fernandes.

[253] Pierre Bourdieu, 'Le Mythe de la Mondialisation... (Globalisation)', in *Contre-Feux* (Back-Fire), Paris: Liber, 1998, pp. 39, 46.

[254] *Bric in Macau,* Edited by Gary Ngai and Ivo Carneiro da Sousa., Macau: SaintJosephAcademic Press, 2011.

[255] Mary Ma, 'Students, the World...', *The Standard,* Hong Kong, 1 December 2010, p. 4. <editor@thestandard.com.hk>

[256] Chen Zhiwu, *The Logic of Finance,* 2009. Conference on 18 October 2010 at Hong Kong University.

[257] Niklas Luhmann, *The Reality of Mass Media,* Tr. by Kathleen Cross, Cambridge, UK: Polity Press, 2007, pp. 3-4.

[258] Luhmann, 2007, pp. 7-9.

[259] Berlie, 1999, p. 67.

[260] *DSEC – Environmental Statistics 2010.* www.dsec.gov.mo, 16 May 2011.

[261] http://calvinayrwayre.com/2011/07/13/casino/macau-needs-more-workers/ July 15 2011.

[262] Eilo Yu Wing-Yat, 'Electoral Fraud and Governance: The 2009 Legislative Direct Election in Macao', in *The Journal of Comparative Asian Development,* London: Routledge, 20 June 2011, p. 125.

[263] *Va Kio,* 27 December 2011, p. 1.

A Family of four generations starting 60 years ago in Macau. Chinese New Year Dinner in 2012. *Photo by Jean Berlie.*

Chinese of Macau – A mononuclear family from Zhongshan. *Photo by Jean Berlie.*

I

120th Anniversary of Tung Sin Tong – Chief Executive Fernando Chui and ex-Chief Executive Edmund Ho, 8 August 2012.
Photo by Jean Berlie.

The Legislative Assembly of the MSAR presided over by Lau Cheok Va.
Photo by Jean Berlie.

II

MOP10 Banknote launched at Lunar New Year 2012 for the Year of the Dragon. *Photo by Jean Berlie.*

Dragon at Mazu Temple, 23 January 2012 – Supported by 200 men from Chong Sam Tai Yok Association. *Photo by Jean Berlie.*

III

The Fujian Association Meeting North of Macau Peninsula, 27 January 2011. *Photo by Jean Berlie.*

Cantonese Opera, 2011. Pun and Guorong Chinese Opera in Macau, Fok Tak Ancestral Hall. *Photo by Jean Berlie.*

IV

Ho Tin Enterprise in Areia Preta. *Photo by Jean Berlie.*

The University of Macau Main Entrance, 23 May 2012.
Photo by Jean Berlie.

V

Interview with Ho Teng Iat, President of the Women's General Association of Macau, 5 December 2011. *Photo by Lo Pou Leng.*

Rotary Club of Macau Central, May 2012. *Photo by Jean Berlie.*

VI

Manager of Bamboo Forest Chuk Lam Buddhist Temple.
Photo by Jean Berlie.

Mazu Temple, on the First Day of the Chinese New Year 2011.
Photo by Jean Berlie.

VII

Twelfth Anniversary of the Return of Macau to China, 20 December 2011. *Photo by Jean Berlie.*

The future of Macau. *Photo by Jean Berlie.*

VIII

Index

ABOUT PROVERSE HONG KONG

Proverse Hong Kong is based in Hong Kong with long-term and expanding regional and international connections.

Proverse has published novels, novellas, fictionalized autobiography, non-fiction (including autobiography, biography, history, memoirs, sport, travel narratives), single-author poetry collections, children's, teens / young adult and academic books. Other interests include diaries, and academic works in the humanities, social sciences, cultural studies, linguistics and education. Some Proverse books have accompanying audio texts. Some are translated into Chinese.

Proverse welcomes authors who have a story to tell, wisdom, perceptions or information to convey, a person they want to memorialize, a neglect they want to remedy, a record they want to correct, a strong interest that they want to share, skills they want to teach, and who consciously seek to make a contribution to society in an informative, interesting and well-written way. Proverse works with texts by non-native-speaker writers of English as well as by native English-speaking writers.

The name, "Proverse", combines the words "prose" and "verse" and is pronounced accordingly.

THE PROVERSE PRIZE

The Proverse Prize, an annual international competition for an unpublished book-length work of fiction, non-fiction, or poetry, was established in January 2008. It is open to all who are at least eighteen on the date they sign the entry form. Unusually for a competition of this nature, there is no restriction based on nationality, residence or citizenship.

The objectives of the Proverse Prize are: to encourage excellence and / or excellence and usefulness in publishable written work in the English Language, which can, in varying degrees, "delight and instruct". Entries are invited from anywhere in the world. Semi-finalists to date include writers born or resident in Andorra, Australia, Canada, Germany, Hong Kong, New Zealand, Nigeria, Singapore, South Africa, Taiwan, The Bahamas, the Peoples'

Republic of China, the United Arab Emirates, the United Kingdom, the USA.

FOUNDERS: Verner Bickley and Gillian Bickley. To celebrate their lifelong love of words in all their forms as readers, writers, editors, academics, performers, and publishers.
HONORARY LEGAL ADVISOR: Mr Raymond T. L. Tse.
HONORARY ACCOUNTANT: Mr Neville Chow.
HONORARY JUDGES: Anonymous.
HONORARY ADVISORS: Bahamian poet Marion Bethel; UK translator, Margaret Clarke; UK linguist & lexicographer David Crystal; Canadian poet and academic, Jonathan Hart; Swedish linguist Björn Jernudd; Hong Kong University Librarian, Peter Sidorko; Singapore poet Edwin Thumboo; Czech novelist & poet Olga Walló.
HONORARY UK AGENT AND DISTRIBUTOR: Christine Penney
HONORARY ADMINISTRATORS: Proverse Hong Kong.

PROVERSE PRIZE WINNERS WHOSE BOOKS HAVE ALREADY BEEN PUBLISHED BY PROVERSE HONG KONG

Laura Solomon, Rebecca Jane Tomasis, Gillian Jones, David Diskin, Peter Gregoire, Sophronia Liu, Birgit Linder, James McCarthy, Celia Claase, Philip Chatting.

Summary Terms and Conditions
(for indication only & subject to revision)

The information below is for guidance only. Please refer to the year-specific Proverse Prize Entry Form & Terms & Conditions, which are uploaded in April each year onto the Proverse Hong Kong website:
<www.proversepublishing.com>.

The free Proverse E-Newsletter includes ongoing information about the Proverse Prize. To be put on the E-Newsletter mailing-list, email: info@proversepublishing.com with your request.

The Prize
1) Publication by Proverse Hong Kong, with
2) Cash prize of HKD10,000 (HKD7.80 = approx. US$1.00)

Supplementary publication grants may be made to selected other entrants for publication by Proverse Hong Kong.

Depending on the quality of the work in any year, the prize may be shared by at most two entrants or withheld, as recommended by the judges.

In 2015, the entry fee was: HKD220.00 OR GBP32.00.

Writers are eligible, who are at least eighteen on the date they sign The Proverse Prize entry documents. There is no nationality or residence restriction.

Each submitted work must be an unpublished publishable single-author work of non-fiction, fiction or poetry, the original work of the entrant, and submitted in the English language. School textbooks and plays are ineligible.

Translated work: If the work entered is a translation from a language other than English, both the original work and the translation should be previously unpublished. The submitted work will not be judged as a translation but as an original work.

Extent of the Manuscript: within the range of what is usual for the genre of the work submitted. However, it is advisable that novellas be in the range 30,000 to 45,000 words); other fiction (e.g. novels, short-story collections) and non-fiction (e.g. autobiographies, biographies, diaries, letters, memoirs, essay collections, etc.) should be in the range, 75,000 to 100,000 words. Poetry collections should be in the range, 5,000 to 25,000 words. Other word-counts and mixed-genre submissions are not ruled out.

Writers may choose, if they wish, to obtain the services of an Editor in presenting their work, and should acknowledge this help and the nature and extent of this help in the Entry Form.

KEY DATES FOR THE PROVERSE PRIZE IN ANY YEAR
(subject to confirmation and/or change)

Receipt of Entry Fees / Entry Documents	[Variable but no later than] 14 April to 31 May of the year of entry
Receipt of entered manuscripts	1 May to 30 June of the year of entry
Announcement of semi-finalists	July-September of the year of entry
Announcement of finalists	October-December of the year of entry
Announcement of winner/ max two winners (sharing the cash prize)	December of the year of entry to April of the year that follows the year of entry
Cash Award made	At the same time as publication of the work(s) adjudged the winner / joint-winners of the Proverse Prize
Publication of winning work(s)	In or after November of the year that follows the year of entry

NON-FICTION (INCLUDING BIOGRAPHY)
Published by Proverse Hong Kong

The Chinese of Macau a decade after the handover, by Jean Berlie. HK & UK, November 2012. Pbk. c.248pp. with 8pp. colour illustrations. ISBN-13: 978-988-8167-37-1.

The complete court cases of Magistrate Frederick Stewart as reported in The China Mail, July 1881 to March 1882. Edited with commentary and chapters by Gillian Bickley. Essay by Dr Ian Grant. HK & UK, 2008. Preface by The Hon. Mr Justice Bokhary PJ, Court of Final Appeal. CD. 761pp. inc. notes. Supported by the Council of the Lord Wilson Heritage Trust.
ISBN-13: 978-988-17724-1-1

The development of education in Hong Kong, 1841-1897: as revealed by the early Education Reports of the Hong Kong Government, 1848-1896. Ed. Gillian Bickley. HK & UK, 2002. Hbk. 633pp., inc. bibliography. Supported by the Council of the Lord Wilson Heritage Trust.
ISBN-10: 962-85570-1-7; ISBN-13: 978-962-85570-1-1.

The diplomat of Kashgar: A Very Special Agent. The Life of Sir George Macartney, 18 January 1867 to 19 May 1945, by James McCarthy. HK & UK, 2014. ISBN 13: 978-988-8227-62-4.

Forward to Beijing! a guide to the Summer Olympics, by Verner Bickley. HK & UK, 2008. Message by Timothy Fok. Preface by The Hon. Dr Arnaldo de Oliveira Sales. With an essay, "A big idea" by Chris Wardlaw. Pbk. 260pp. with 16 b/w photographs.
ISBN-13: 978-988-99668-3-6.

The Golden Needle: the biography of Frederick Stewart (1836-1889), by Gillian Bickley. David C. Lam Institute for East-West Studies, Hong Kong Baptist University. HK & UK, 1997. Foreword by Lady Saltoun. Introduction by Sir David Wilson (now Lord Wilson). Pbk. 308pp., inc. bibliography, archival photographs. ISBN-1: 962-8027-08-5; ISBN-13 978-962-8027-08-8.
The Golden Needle: the biography of Frederick Stewart (1836-1889). Full audio version on 14 CDs. Read by Verner Bickley. ISBN: CD-962-8027-08-5;ISRC: HK-D94-00-00001-40.

Also, Teachers' and students' guide to the book and audio book, 'The Golden Needle: the biography of Frederick Stewart (1836-1889)'. Proverse Hong Kong Study Guides.
E-book. ISBN-10: 962-85570-9-2; ISBN-13: 978-962-85570-9-7.
24Reader e-book edition (2010), ISBN-13: 978-988-19320-5-1.

A magistrate's court in nineteenth century Hong Kong: Court in Time. Contributing Editor, Gillian Bickley. Contributors: Garry Tallentire, Geoffrey Roper, Timothy Hamlett, Christopher Coghlan, Verner Bickley. Preface by Sir T. L. Yang. 1st edn. HK & UK, 2005. Pbk. 531pp. inc. bibliography, notes, archival illustrations. ISBN-10: 962-85570-4-1; ISBN-13: 978-962-85570-4-2.

A magistrate's court in nineteenth century Hong Kong, with additional discussion of "The Opium Ordinance": Court in Time. 2nd edn. HK & UK, 2009. Pbk. 536pp. inc. bibliography, notes, archival illustrations. ISBN-13: 978-988-17724-5-9.

Searching for Frederick and adventures along the way, by Verner Bickley. Hong Kong, 2001. Pbk. 420pp. Supported by the Hong Kong Arts Development Council. ISBN-10: 962-8783-20-3; ISBN-13: 978-962-8783-20-5.

The Stewarts of Bourtreebush, by Gillian Bickley. Aberdeen, UK, Centre for Scottish Studies, University of Aberdeen, 2003. Pbk. 153pp. Extensive documentation of the Scottish family of Frederick Stewart, founder of Hong Kong Government Education. ISBN-10: 0-906265-34-7; ISBN-13: 978-0-906265-34-5.

AUTOBIOGRAPHY, MEMOIRS, LETTERS, DIARIES, TRAVEL
Published by Proverse Hong Kong

Chocolate's brown study in the bag, by Rupert Kwan Yun Chan. HK & UK, March 2011. Pbk. 112pp. + 16 colour pp. illustrations. Proverse Prize Finalist (2009).
ISBN: 978-988-19932-1-2.

Gin's tonic: ocean voyage, inner journey, by Virginia MacRobert. HK & UK, 2010. Preface by Ed Vaughan. Pbk. 600pp., inc. index, illustrations: colour photographs, author portrait. Supported by Hong Kong Arts Development Council.
ISBN-13: 978-988-17724-3-5.

In time of war, by Richard Collingwood-Selby. HK & UK, 2013. ISBN-13: 978-988-8167-36-4. Supported by Lord Wilson Heritage Trust.

A personal journey through sketching: the sketcher's art, by Errol Patrick Hugh. HK & UK, 2009. Introduction by Li Shiqiao. Hbk. 96pp. inc. 100+ original sketches and photographs by the author &

author's portrait. 300mm x 215mm x 14mm. w. CD-ROM.
ISBN-13: 978-988-18479-1-1.

Semper fi! The story of a vietnam era marine, by Orville Leverne
Clubb. HK & UK, 2012. Pbk. 216pp. + 6pp photographs,
sketch-map, inc. glossary.
ISBN-13: 978-988-19933-4-2.

Steps to Paradise and Beyond: Hawaii to China, Saudi Arabia, Hong
Kong and Elsewhere, by Verner Bickley. HK & UK, 2013. Pbk.
480pp. + photographs, facsimiles.
Preface by Charles E. Morrison, President, East-West Center,
Hawaii. Supported by Hong Kong Arts Development Council.
ISBN 13: 978-988-8167-40-1

Wannabe backpackers: the Latin American & Kenyan journey of
five spoiled teenagers, by Gerald Yeung. HK & UK, 2009. Pbk.
164pp. inc. several b/w pix.
ISBN 978-988-17724-2-8.

NON-FICTION – CHINESE LANGUAGE

The Golden Needle: the biography of Frederick Stewart (1836-1889):
Selections 《香港開埠時的雙語教育——史劍城和母語教學》by Gillian
Bickley. Translated by Hong-Lok Kwok. 2010. E-book. ISBN-13:
978-988-18905-4-2.

GENRES

Proverse publishes novels, novellas, short story collections and
poetry collections; non-fiction including autobiography, biography,
children's illustrated books, educational books, Hong Kong
educational and legal history, memoirs, teenage / young adult
books, and travel. Other genres may be added.

FIND OUT MORE ABOUT OUR AUTHORS AND BOOKS

Visit our website
http://www.proversepublishing.com

Visit our distributor's website
<www.chineseupress.com>

Follow us on Twitter
Follow news and conversation: <twitter.com/Proversebooks>
OR
Copy and paste the following to your browser window and follow the instructions: https://twitter.com/#!/ProverseBooks

'Like us' on Facebook: www.facebook.com/ProversePress

Request our E-Newsletter
Send your request to info@proversepublishing.com.

Availability
Most titles are available in Hong Kong and world-wide
from our Hong Kong based Distributor,
The Chinese University Press of Hong Kong,
The Chinese University of Hong Kong, Shatin, NT,
Hong Kong SAR, China. Web: chineseupress.com

All titles are available from Proverse Hong Kong
and the Proverse Hong Kong UK-based Distributor.

We have stock-holding retailers in Hong Kong,
Singapore (Select Books),
Canada (Elizabeth Campbell Books),
Principality of Andorra (Llibreria La Puça, La Llibreria).

Orders can be made from bookshops in the UK and elsewhere.

Ebooks
Most of our titles are available also as Ebooks.